International Comparisons in
Mathematics Education

D0190398

Studies in Mathematics Education Series

Series Editor: Paul Ernest, University of Exeter, UK

Studies in Mathematics Education Series: 11

International Comparisons in Mathematics Education

Edited by

Gabriele Kaiser, Eduardo Luna and
Ian Huntley

UK   Falmer Press, 1 Gunpowder Square, London, EC4A 3DE
USA Falmer Press, 325 Chestnut Street, 8th Floor, Philadelphia, PA 19106

© G. Kaiser, E. Luna and I. Huntley 1999

All rights reserved. No part of this publication may be reproduced, stored in a retrieval system, or transmitted in any form or by any means, electronic, mechanical, photocopying, recording or otherwise, without permission in writing from the publisher.

First published in 1999

A catalogue record for this book is available from the British Library

ISBN 0 7507 0903 0   cased
ISBN 0 7507 0902 2   paper

Library of Congress Cataloging-in-Publication Data are available on request

Jacket design by Caroline Archer

Typeset in 10/12 pt Bembo by
Graphicraft Limited, Hong Kong

Printed in Great Britain by Biddles Ltd., Guildford and King's Lynn on paper which has a specified pH value on final paper manufacture of not less than 7.5 and is therefore 'acid free'.

Every effort has been made to contact copyright holders for their permission to reprint material in this book. The publishers would be grateful to hear from any copyright holder who is not here acknowledged and will undertake to rectify any errors or omissions in future editions of this book.

Contents

Contents

Series Editor's Preface

Mathematics education is established world-wide as a major area of study, with numerous dedicated journals and conferences serving ever-growing national and international communities of scholars. As it develops, research in mathematics education is becoming more theoretically orientated. Although originally rooted in mathematics and psychology, vigorous new perspectives are pervading it from disciplines and fields as diverse as philosophy, logic, sociology, anthropology, history, women's studies, cognitive science, semiotics, hermeneutics, post-structuralism and post-modernism. These new research perspectives are providing fresh lenses through which teachers and researchers can view the theory and practice of mathematics teaching and learning.

The series Studies in Mathematics Education aims to encourage the development and dissemination of theoretical perspectives in mathematics education as well as their critical scrutiny. It is a series of research contributions to the field based on disciplined perspectives that link theory with practice. The series is founded on the philosophy that theory is the practitioner's most powerful tool in understanding and changing practice. Whether the practice concerns the teaching and learning of mathematics, teacher education, or educational research, the series offers new perspectives to help clarify issues, pose and solve problems and stimulate debate. It aims to have a major impact on the development of mathematics education as a field of study in the third millennium.

One of the central issues which has caught the attention of mathematics education researchers, politicians and policy makers, as well as the public, is that of international comparisons of mathematical attainment. Selected results of international comparison projects such as the IEA studies, FIMS, SIMS, and TIMSS projects have made headlines in many of the countries that took part. In several western countries including England, Scotland, USA and Norway, whose scores in some aspects of mathematics have been average or below average, there has been much criticism and public questioning of the mathematics curriculum and its teaching. Often the public, media and political critiques of schooling have been ill-founded and based on partial or misinterpreted data. On the other hand, there are no grounds for complacency in the teaching of mathematics in most countries, which can still be a deadly dull and too often misunderstood subject. Unfortunately, ideologically motivated individuals and pressure groups have exploited these confusions and misunderstandings to promote reactionary aims and agendas for mathematics teaching. Both in the USA and UK the back-to-basics movements have been fuelled by misuse of the results of international comparisons.

If it were not so important an issue, it would be amusing to review recent history and interpret many western countries' responses to international comparisons as hero worship! In the 1970s and 1980s the Americans and British were deeply concerned with Soviet successes in the arms race and decided that Soviet mathematics and science teaching must be the key to success. So we studied their methods to copy them. After all, it was only twenty years earlier that there was panic in the west following the Soviet launch of sputnik, which gave rise to a political impetus to modernize mathematics and science teaching.

Next, Germany's excellent industrial and economic performance in the 1980s led the British to try to learn what they were doing in order to emulate it. As the Japanese and Tiger economies took off in the 1990s and the Pacific Rim countries performed outstandingly in international comparisons in mathematics and science, so official missions were sent to study their teaching methods to bring their successes back to the West. In each case, as countries rose in economic or military might it was thought that their teaching approaches should be copied; plans which faded from the public consciousness as each country in turn passed its peak of success. Extrapolating from this history, I predict that in the next millennium, as China and India become world class economic powerhouses, we shall be sending missions from the West to study and emulate their teaching methods. Indeed missions from the USA to China have already begun!

If there is a moral to be drawn from this parody of history it is that international comparisons are much misunderstood and abused. The assumption that there is a direct link between economic and industrial performance and national teaching styles in mathematics is highly dubious. The further assumption that 'national teaching styles' in mathematics, if such a thing exists, can be transferred from one nation to another, is even more doubtful. Yet such assumptions underpin many of the educational policies of governments in the West.

The present volume aims to shed some more light on this murky area by putting an expert tool into the hands of those who want to understand the underlying concepts and theories as well as the results and issues. It does this in three ways. First, it clarifies the nature of what is assessed and the purpose of international comparisons. Providing a conceptual analysis and theoretical background is evidently essential for any informed understanding of international comparisons. Second, it provides an overview of the most important recent projects in this area, and their results. Uniquely, this book brings together the foremost world scholars involved in the most significant of these projects. There have been many advances in the area and the planned, taught and learned curriculum have all come under the scrutiny of these studies. Third, the book provides a critical evaluation and reflection on the international comparison projects in mathematics and their results and uses. Such critical scrutiny is an essential element which is lacking in much of what passes for informed debate on the topic.

The book sits squarely within the philosophy of the series Studies in Mathematics Education, aiming as it does to extend theoretical and critical understanding of mathematics education research and to link it firmly with practice. The book is destined to become a standard reference for scholars, researchers, teachers and students wanting a state of the art survey of work and thought in this important and sensitive area. One can only hope that its message reaches the politicians and media pundits too!

Paul Ernest
University of Exeter
1998

Introduction

The last decades have seen a growing interest in comparative studies around the world, among politicians and parents as well as educators. The recent publication of the results of the Third International Mathematics and Science Study (TIMSS) has raised this interest enormously, especially within those states which achieved results below the international average in the ranking lists.

This book deals with international comparisons in mathematics education under a broad perspective. It considers the merits of international comparative studies and the chances they offer for a better understanding of one's own educational system — both its strengths and weaknesses. This knowledge is not only of academic interest, but allows an identification of possible approaches to improved education. The book also develops a basis for the critical discussion of comparative studies in mathematics education. The limitations of such studies and the underlying assumptions and simplifications are discussed, as well as the uncritical usage of the ranking lists, to which the results of highly complex studies are often reduced. These ranking lists are often used in the public debate to plea for additional research funds or 'required' changes — producing the danger of a backlash effect. In addition, these studies are often uncritically transferred to so-called Third World countries, whose educational systems are then compared to those of highly industrialized states without considering their different socio-economical background. These issues have to be taken into account in the discussion around the unquestioned high value of international comparative studies.

The book is divided into two parts. In Part I, the most important large-scale international comparative studies in mathematics education of the last 20 years are described by contributors who have been involved in these studies. In addition, a few selected small-scale comparative studies are described. In Part II, fundamental questions concerning international comparative investigations in mathematics education are discussed.

The idea of this book arose out of the work in the topic group 'International Comparative Investigations' at the Eighth International Congress on Mathematical Education (ICME–8), which took place in Seville from 14–21 July 1996. We have been fortunate to have authors who have been involved in the different studies described in the book and who come from different educational positions or backgrounds; this has ensured a broad basis for the discussion of international comparative studies in mathematics education.

We hope that the book will provide a broad audience with the basis for a fruitful discussion on the value of international comparisons in mathematics education.

Gabriele Kaiser
Eduardo Luna
Ian Huntley
May 1998

1 International Comparisons in Mathematics Education Under the Perspective of Comparative Education

Gabriele Kaiser

. . . to study education well is to study it comparatively (Thut and Adams, 1964).

Comparing the outcomes of learning in different countries is in several respects an exercise in comparing the incomparable (Husén, 1983).

These two quotations point out the possibilities and difficulties of international comparisons — they mark the extreme ends of a scale between which comparative educators have to manoeuvre. This will be detailed below, where we refer to approaches in comparative education as the home base of international comparisons in mathematics education. First, I will describe the goals and aims of comparative education, the reasons for comparative studies, embedded in a long tradition of comparative education. Second, problems and limitations of comparative studies, especially in mathematics education, will be analysed.

I shall start with a definition of comparative education as given by Postlethwaite in *The Encyclopaedia of Comparative Education and National Systems of Education.* 'Strictly speaking, to "compare" means to examine two or more entities by putting them side by side and looking for similarities and differences between or among them. In the field of education, this can apply both to comparisons between and comparisons within systems of education' (1988:xvii). In addition, however, there are many studies that are not comparative, in the strict sense of the word, which have traditionally been classified under the heading of comparative education. Such studies do not compare, but rather describe, analyse or make proposals for a particular aspect of education in a country other than the author's own. These sorts of studies are often classified as international studies.

Comparative education has a long tradition going back to the ancient Greeks. Noah and Eckstein (1969) detected five phases of comparative education. The first phase they labelled Traveller's Tales, a term that refers to the oral reports as exemplified by Greeks and Romans, and later by Marco Polo or Alexis de Tocqueville, showing how they commented on the education of young persons they observed as they travelled in foreign parts of the world.

The second phase emerged about the beginning of the 1800s. This involved the systematic collection of data about education in different countries

— a phase of 'borrowing'. Marc Antoine Jullien was one of the first persons to think of collecting data systematically, and he was therefore called the 'father of scientific comparative education' (Brickman, 1988:5). Famous researchers visited other countries, observed how education was organized, and tried to identify the main tenets of the philosophy of education in the systems they observed. In addition, certain problems were identified, which included problems in comparing terminology, gathering valid and reliable data, and marking the feasibility of borrowing ideas from one country and implanting them in another. Sir Michael Sadler of England visited German schools in 1894–95 and, in his article 'How far can we learn anything of practical value from the study of foreign systems of education?', he denied that particular elements or methods in a foreign system of education were 'detachable details'. He states that 'It is a great mistake to think, or imply, that one kind of education suits every nation alike' (1964:312). However, he did see the sympathetic and scholarly study of the working of foreign systems resulting in the researchers being better fitted to study and understand their own system.

The third phase can be characterized by its emphasis on international cooperation, and overlap with the second phase ('phase of borrowing'). Both Jullien and Sadler can be regarded as initiators.

The fourth phase, of which Sadler can be regarded as the initiator, consisted of an attempt to identify forces influencing the development of systems of education or of specific components of an educational system. Emphasis was placed, in particular, on a more analytic understanding of the relationship between society and education. From the beginning of this century until the sixties various authors now famous in comparative education — such as Kandel, Schneider or Hans — conducted studies attempting, usually through speculation, to identify the social and political causes responsible for educational practices. They attempted to relate the variations in forces in societies to differences in their schools. This kind of work — characterized by a broad historical, social and political study of changes in, and differences between, systems of education — represented a major effort until the mid-1980s.

The fifth phase began to emerge in the post-Second World War era, and burgeoned in the 1960s and 1970s. This phase saw the use of social science methods and quantitative and qualitative data to examine the effect of various factors on educational development. The studies carried out using these methods took the form of estimating coefficients indicating the strength of effect of one variable or construct on other constructs, relative to the strength of other variables. In all social science research there are the problems of measurement error, sampling error and selecting the appropriate form of statistical analysis for disentangling the relative effects of factors postulated as influencing a particular outcome or practice. There are those who reject an empirical approach to education because 'it is attempting to quantify the unquantifiable' (Postlethwaite, 1988:xix). However, the obvious danger in not using an empirical approach is that one is left in the realm of speculations about the relative effect of variables which are inter-correlated.

According to Postlethwaite there are still two major approaches in comparative education today — the one using the empirical paradigm and the other using historical and hermeneutic approaches. However, the picture has become more complicated in that, within the social sciences, there has been an upsurge of studies using qualitative studies, accompanied by a debate on the relative merits of quantitative versus qualitative studies. Postlethwaite classifies this debate as a 'pseudo debate'

> . . . because it is not really a matter of one approach versus another since most studies require a mixture of both. Indeed, from the plethora of approaches available, the comparative educator must always select the most appropriate approach or combination of several approaches in order to answer the particular questions under investigation (1988:xix).

History shows us that comparative education serves a variety of goals. It can deepen our understanding of our own education and society, it can be of assistance to policymakers and administrators, and it can be a valuable component of teacher education programmes. These contributions can be made through work that is primarily descriptive as well as through work that seeks to be analytic or explanatory, through work that is limited to just one or a few nations, and through work that relies on non-quantitative as well as quantitative data and methods. Based on this, Postlethwaite (1988) distinguishes four major aims of comparative education.

- 'Identifying what is happening elsewhere that might help improve our own system of education' (p. xix). Postlethwaite gives several examples, such as the attempt to identify the principles involved in an innovation like mastery learning (which has had such success in the Republic of Korea) and grasping the procedures necessary to implement the mastery principle.
- 'Describing similarities and differences in educational phenomena between systems of education and interpreting why these exist' (p. xix). This comprises the analysis of similarities and differences between systems of education in goals, in structures, in the scholastic achievement of age groups and so on, which could reveal important information about the systems being compared. Studies of these types may describe not only inputs to and processes within systems but also the philosophy of systems and outcomes. The questions of why certain countries have particular philosophies, and what implications these have in terms of educational outcomes, are questions of both major academic and practical interest.
- 'Estimating the relative effects of variables (thought to be determinants) on outcomes (both within and between systems of education)' (p. xx). Within education there is a great deal of speculation about what affects what. How much evidence, for example, do the people

who teach methods at teacher-training establishments have about the effectiveness of the methods they promulgate? What about home versus school effects on outcomes? These questions and similar ones are the questions to be dealt with under this perspective.

- 'Identifying general principles concerning educational effects' (p. xx). This means that we are aiming at a possible pattern of relationship between variables within an educational system and an outcome. In practice, a model will be postulated whereby certain variables are held constant before we examine the relationship between other variables and the outcomes. The resultant relationship will often be estimated by a regression coefficient. We might detect factors which are general principles in all educational systems analysed and therefore might be accepted as general principles.

To summarize, comparative studies can have various aims. The four aims discussed above are representative of much of the body of comparative education studies.

There are numerous ways to categorize the content of comparative studies. Referring to Postlethwaite (1988), there are two different kinds of comparative studies.

- Country studies — that is, studies on one country's system of education, sometimes examining several aspects of education.
- Studies on themes within and between countries. There has been a major move since the 1960s to shift away from country system description in order to examine themes in a national or international context. Some of the major themes identified are economics of education, education planning and policy, primary and secondary schooling, teacher and teacher education, curriculum, and so on.

This classification does not include the theme of the political influences in education, although many of the authors dealing with the themes categorized above do attempt to examine the influence of political, economic and social factors on the particular education phenomenon with which they are dealing.

As mentioned at the beginning, comparative education does not only offer chances and possibilities, but implies many problems. Noah (1988) describes the major problems of comparative methods as follows:

- the costs and difficulty of assembling data from foreign sources,
- the lack of comparability of data collected,
- uncertainties with regard to the validity and reliability of data collected for domestic purposes by national authorities who were not concerned with the use of such data in cross-national comparison,
- problems associated with the construction of valid scales along which national units may be arrayed,

- ethnocentric bias in defining the topic to be investigated, establishing the bases for classifying data, drawing inferences and making policy recommendations.

In general, to surmount these problems successfully requires '. . . rather large-scale international teamwork. This is difficult to establish, complicated and burdensome to administer, and costly to operate' (Noah, 1988:10).

Eckstein (1988) argues that, since most of modern comparative education work at least up to the mid-twentieth century has been devoted to European nations, it cannot be free from the suspicion of cultural bias. Some comparative educators argue that the so-called Third World countries may not be destined to repeat the educational and socio-political history of Europe because of their special cultural traditions and current conditions. Concerning the relation of schooling and national progress in less developed nations, a debate has taken place which sees educational development as a powerful tool to overcome specified conditions, such as traditional attitudes or political and social structures, which are in the way of progress. On the other hand, a different theory holds that external factors are to blame, that the more developed nations of the world depend upon their political-economic domination of the less wealthy and powerful countries, and that educational innovations and school reforms modelled on the experience of the industrialized nations are a means of maintaining their pre-eminence.

While one major stream of comparative work concerns itself with the interaction of educational and political, social or economic systems, another focuses upon particular pedagogical factors. Comparisons of instructional methods, curriculum, teacher training and their presumed outcomes (student behaviour, especially achievement), have long been at the heart of comparative work, although the focus of attention has changed. 'The crude assumption of earlier writers that there may be one "best method" for achieving superior results and that, once discovered, it can simply be implemented is no longer given much credence' (Eckstein, 1988:9).

In addition, comparative studies are questioned under methodological perspectives. Eckstein (1988) emphasizes that the assumptions of the large comparative studies — such as the ones carried out by the International Association for the Evaluation of Educational Achievement (IEA) — are the concepts underlying statistical or empirical methods in the sciences. He characterizes this approach as a positivistic view. 'They represent the view that educational and social phenomena are results of multiple causes, that there are regularities or tentative laws of input and outcomes (cause and effect), and that these are discoverable through systematic collection and analysis of the relevant facts' (p. 9).

Noah (1988) discusses, under a wider perspective, the assumption that it is possible to generalize statements about relationships amongst variables on which this positivistic approach is based. He describes a modern tendency in comparative studies to rely upon such factors as national character or

historical background for explanation and generalization only when the introduction of additional variables yields no gain in explanatory power. Thus, the
paradigm situation — calling for the employment of comparative method —
occurs when no amount of within-system adjustment of either the independent
or dependent variables can reduce the across-nation differences in observed relationships. At this point, the names of countries are introduced to tag bundles
of otherwise unexplained variances. Noah describes this development.

> In this way, the objects and methods of comparative study have been changing
> since the early 1960s from the traditional attempt to extend and enrich as much
> as possible the connotational content of country names, to the newer attempts
> to make general 'law-like', cross-national statements, bringing in country
> names only when ability to make valid generalizations across countries fails
> (1988:12).

Kelly and Altbach (1988:13f) describe alternative approaches in comparative education, which have challenged these established research traditions in
comparative education since the 1980s. These are: (a) those that question the
nation-state or national characteristics as the major parameter defining comparative study; (b) those that question the use of input–output models and
exclusive reliance on quantification in the conduct of comparative research;
(c) those which challenge structural functionalism as the major theoretical pre-
mise undergirding scholarship; and (d) those which direct attention to new
subjects of inquiry.

The first challenge to the nation-state as the exclusive research framework either looks at the world system — regional variations, racial groups,
classes, which are not bound to the nation — or does micro-analytic research
focused on regional variation. Proponents of the analysis of regional variation
argue that educational variance often is as great, if not greater, between regions within a nation as it is between nations.

The second challenge to input–output models and total reliance on
quantification asserts that education and school practices cannot be reduced
solely on quantitative aspects — knowledge about these topics can only be generated by qualitative research methods that focus on actual, lived educational
practices and processes. A few approaches propose ethno-methodological
techniques and relate educational processes to broader theories of school/
society relations.

The third challenge questions the dominance of structural functionalism in comparative education — either how education functioned to maintain the social fabric, or how it could be made to function (in the case of the
Third World) to develop a nation-state generally along western models. New
approaches propose conflict theories, because most societies are plural societies characterized by conflict, in which dominant groups seek to legitimize
their control over the state.

The fourth challenge, the emergence of new research concerns, proposes
new ways of looking at educational institutions and their relation to society

— studies on the nature of knowledge transfer and its impact on the Third World, the kind of school knowledge, the internal workings of the school. Another important and new stream of scholarship has been gender studies.

To summarize, comparative education is characterized by a wide diversity of approaches, perspectives and orientations, and this diversity of the field seems to be one of its main strengths.

In mathematics education there have been a remarkable number of international comparative studies carried out in the last 30 years. Robitaille believes that the reason for this is as follows.

> Studies that cross national boundaries provide participating countries with a broader context within which to examine their own implicit theories, values and practices. As well, comparative studies provide an opportunity to examine a variety of teaching practices, curriculum goals and structures, school organizational patterns, and other arrangements for education that might not exist in a single jurisdiction (1994:41).

Stigler and Perry emphasize the better understanding of one's own culture by comparative studies.

> Cross cultural comparison also leads researchers and educators to a more explicit understanding of their own implicit theories about how children learn mathematics. Without comparison, we tend not to question our own traditional teaching practices and we may not even be aware of the choices we have made in constructing the educational process (1988:199).

In the following I will describe briefly the most important comparative studies in mathematics education. Most of the large-scale studies have been carried out by the International Association for the Evaluation of Educational Achievement (IEA).

The first large-scale international study was the First International Mathematics Study (FIMS), carried out 1964. Twelve countries participated in this study, in which two populations were tested — thirteen years old and students in the final school year of the secondary school. In the first population the students from Israel, Japan and Belgium received the best results, and the worst results were achieved by US students. In the second population a different picture emerged — the youngsters from Israel, Belgium and England received the best results, and the US students the worst (see Husén, 1967). Robitaille and Travers (1992:692) believe that most of the high-achieving educational systems were highly selective and they state, '. . . that retentivity accounts for the major part of the variation between the countries on all items'. Freudenthal (1975) emphasizes the important role of the curriculum, and states that valid comparative results cannot be formulated without considering curricular aspects.

The second large-scale comparative study in mathematics education was the Second International Mathematics Study (SIMS), 1980–82, whose results were published at the end of the eighties and the beginning of the nineties. Twenty countries participated in this study, which considered the same age groups as FIMS and contained a cross-sectional and a longitudinal component. Considering the curricular criticisms on FIMS, SIMS discriminated different levels of the curriculum — the intended curriculum, the implemented curriculum and the attained curriculum. In addition, a content by cognitive-behaviour grid was developed, which relates the mathematical content with cognitive dimensions such as computation and comprehension. On the level of the intended curriculum, the main results have been a significant curricular shift — geometry has lost importance in contrast to number and algebra. On the level of the implemented curriculum the study pointed out the different status of repetition in the different countries. On the level of the attained curriculum the study showed that the increase in the achievements was remarkable low in many countries. Gender differences emerged in many countries, but were not consistent and were smaller than the differences between the different countries. I will not describe the results of SIMS in detail, but refer for such a description to Chapter 2 by Travers and Weinzweig in this book. SIMS has been criticized from several perspectives, and even the organizers of SIMS admitted that, despite the wealth of items, the curricula of many participating countries had not been covered sufficiently.

The last study in this series is the Third International Mathematics and Science Study (TIMSS), which was carried out in 1995 in over 40 countries. It examined the achievement of students from three populations at five grade levels (9-year-olds, 13-year-olds, and the final year of secondary school) in a wide range of content and performance areas, and it collected contextual information from students, teachers and school principals. I will not describe results of the study but refer instead to the detailed description given by Beaton and Robitaille (Chapter 3) in this book. Considering the criticisms formulated at SIMS — the unsatisfactory coverage of the curriculum of the different countries, the focus on quantified outcomes (the quantified achievement of the students) — TIMSS established several additional studies.

- The TIMSS Videotape Study, which analysed mathematics lessons in Japan, Germany and USA (for a description see Chapter 6 by Kawanaka, Stigler and Hiebert in this book).
- The Case Study Project, which collected qualitative information on the educational systems in Japan, Germany and USA (for a description of the study see Chapter 7 by Stevenson).
- The Survey of Mathematics and Science Opportunities, a study of mathematics and science teaching in six countries (the study is described in Chapter 5 by Cogan and Schmidt).
- The Curriculum Analysis Study, which studies the curricula and textbooks in many countries (for results of parts of this study see Chapter 4 by McKnight and Valverde).

With all these additional studies and the high number of countries participating in the main study 'TIMSS is the largest and most comprehensive study of educational practice in mathematics and science ever undertaken' (Robitaille, 1994:36).

Besides these large-scale studies conducted by the IEA there have been several smaller-scale studies in mathematics education in the last few years. The Educational Testing Services (ETS) carried out, in 1988, the First International Assessment of Educational Progress (IAEP) and in 1990/91 the Second International Assessment of Educational Progress. In the first study 7 countries participated, and in the second 20 countries. Concerning the ranking of the participating countries, the study confirmed what was already known from FIMS and SIMS — the Asian students achieved top results, the US-American students achieved results near the average, and the students from South-America and Africa are at the bottom (for details see Lapointe, Mead and Askew, 1992).

Other studies compare only two or three educational systems. The so-called Michigan Studies (1979–80 and 1985–86) compared the mathematical achievements of US, Japanese and Taiwanese students, and showed significantly better achievements of the Asian compared to the US students. Classroom observations and textbook analyses pointed out that there exist remarkable differences in the teaching and learning process, organization of school, structure of the curriculum, and so on (see Stevenson and Bartsch, 1992; Stigler and Perry, 1988).

The US–Japan Cross-cultural Research on Students' Problem-solving Behaviours (carried out at the end of the eighties) compared the performance of US and Japanese students in problem-solving tasks. It showed a significant higher level of mathematical sophistication in problem solving and a higher level of technical mathematical knowledge by the Japanese compared to the US students. It made especially clear that Japanese students are able to solve a problem in more different ways than their US counterparts (for details of this study see Chapter 8 by Becker, Sawada and Shimizu).

English and German mathematics teaching was compared in the so-called Kassel–Exeter study in which, since the beginning of the nineties, classroom observations and achievement tests have been carried out. The study showed remarkable differences concerning the teaching and learning style between the two countries (for details see Chapter 9 by Kaiser).

An analysis of Chinese and US textbooks has been carried out, in which the distribution patterns of different types of application problems have been examined and which reveals that the consideration of applications in US as well as in Chinese textbooks is insufficient (a detailed description can be found in Chapter 10 by Fan).

The strengths of these small-scale studies, restricted to a few countries, can be seen in a microanalytic analysis of classroom processes, which reveals deep insight into teaching and learning processes, ways of developing mathematical knowledge, and so on. This kind of analysis, which is concentrated on a small number of countries and may even be restricted to special aspects of the mathematical learning process, does not develop generalized tenets on a broad range of countries. Generalized descriptions of the teaching and learning processes in many countries are reserved to large-scale studies such SIMS or TIMSS which lose, in contrast to small-scale studies, the possibility of microanalytic analyses. This shows the necessity for both types of studies, many of which are described in the Part I of this book.

As sketched at the beginning, international comparisons are seen as a mean for fostering insight into one's own culture, or as a chance to examine the effectiveness of the home educational system. On the other hand they are criticized due to methodological limitations, or their pedagogical value is questioned. Part II of the book is devoted to this discussion and, in the following, I will describe briefly a few of the main issues which will be treated.

The positive influences on national policy and the impact of international comparisons on school education are emphasized in Chapter 12 by Romberg using the example of US-American mathematics education. He describes the establishment of new national goals by policymakers and how comparative studies propose suggestions about possible ways to reach those goals. Referring to the example of a technologically less advanced country — the Philippines — Nebres (Chapter 13) describes international comparisons as a way to improve school mathematics. He explicitly refers to an economical frame and uses the concept of benchmarking in order to clarify the chances of international comparative studies. Defining benchmarking as the search for best practices that lead to superior performance, TIMSS and other studies provide a rich resource for the identification of areas where the search for best practices might lead to significant improvements.

A less positive perspective is taken by Howson (Chapter 11), who discusses the value of comparative studies. He questions the role of curricula and asks whether the curricula of the different countries are adequately considered. In addition, he is concerned about the value of the additional data collected referring to the attitudes of the students and so on, which are difficult to connect with the achievement data. He proposes smaller-scale studies, whose results might be easier to interpret.

Similar questions are asked in Chapter 15 by Wolfe and Chapter 16 by Keitel and Kilpatrick. Keitel and Kilpatrick question whether it is possible to cover, with one achievement test, the curricula of many different countries adequately. In addition, they raise fundamental questions on the methodological level, such as the problem of the quantification of pedagogical phenomena — the assumption of the possibility of quantifying qualitative aspects or reducing such aspects on quantified data, and the problem of the representativity of the observed data. Wolfe concentrates on the influence of the item selection on the country ranking, and describes the significant changes caused by different items selected. He proposes the restriction of comparative studies to countries which are similar — comparable concerning their educational system, their economy, their social conditions, and so on. Based on this criticism he makes a plea for regionalized studies in which only comparable countries would be compared.

A different aspect is raised by Leder, Brew and Rowley, who emphasize the gender perspective in Chapter 14. They point out that the nature of assessment contributes to apparent gender differences in mathematics performance and request more equitable forms of assessment of mathematics achievement.

These aspects reflect, on the one hand, issues discussed in the general frame of comparative education with their emphasis on the problem of the curricula and the gender debate; they are, on the other hand, particular to a discussion in mathematics education. The high relevance of curricular questions is especially relevant to the debate in mathematics education, because most of the recent (as well as the older) comparative studies concentrated on comparisons in mathematical performance.

I want to close with a short review of four critical aspects on comparative studies in mathematics which are, in my opinion, the main problems.

- On the methodological level, it is necessary to ask whether the main concepts and ideas of the methodology used, such as the approach of the probabilistic test theory, are adequate. This model delivers, on the one hand, highly general results concerning ability levels. It is, on the other hand, worth questioning whether the necessary general conditions required by the model — existence of a one-dimensional construct 'mathematical ability' or 'mathematical literacy' — are fulfilled.
- On a more subject-bound level, curricular issues have to be discussed — the dependence of the results from the test items, the adequacy of the test items concerning so many different curricula, the relation of achievement results and the opportunity to learn.
- Under a general pedagogical perspective, there is a question of the innovation potential of such studies. What can we learn from descriptions of mathematics teaching in totally different cultures, such as Germany and Japan, with very different value systems, social conditions, and so on?
- Under a political perspective, we need to ask whether the scientific community is able to control how the results of the studies are used in political debates. It is a consensus among researchers that the ranking is not the main result of such studies — but the public debate concentrates mainly on the ranking lists and bases proposals for consequences on the rank achieved. How far are the results of such studies under the control of the researchers involved, and how far can they influence the usage of the results?

Within the scientific community it is a consensus that such studies have a high pedagogical potential, but the limitations of such studies have to be considered as well. I want to close with a proposal discussed among comparative researchers in mathematics education since the Second International Mathematics Study (SIMS) — to concentrate on small-scale regionalized studies. The debate on the Third International Mathematics and Science Study (TIMSS) in the next few years will show how far we need both large-scale studies with global results on as many countries as possible and regionalized studies limited to similar countries or small-scale studies restricted to special aspects of the teaching and learning of mathematics.

References

BRICKMAN, W.W. (1988) 'History of comparative education', in POSTLETHWAITE, T.N. (ed.) *The Encyclopaedia of Comparative Education and National Systems of Education*, Oxford: Pergamon, pp. 3–7.

ECKSTEIN, M.A. (1988) 'Concepts and theories in comparative education', in POSTLETHWAITE, T.N. (ed.) *The Encyclopaedia of Comparative Education and National Systems of Education*, Oxford: Pergamon, pp. 7–10.

FREUDENTHAL, H. (1975) 'Pupils' achievements internationally compared — the IEA', *Educational Studies in Mathematics*, **6**, pp. 127–86.

HUSÉN, T. (1967) (ed.) *International Study of Achievement in Mathematics (Vol. I, II)*, Stockholm: Almqvist and Wiksell.

HUSÉN, T. (1983) 'Are Standards in US Schools Really Lagging Behind Those in Other Countries?', *Phi Delta Kappan*, pp. 455–61.

KELLY, G.P. and ALTBACH, P.G. (1988) 'Alternative approaches in comparative education', in POSTLETHWAITE, T.N. (ed.) *The Encyclopaedia of Comparative Education and National Systems of Education*, Oxford: Pergamon, pp. 13–19.

LAPOINTE, A., MEAD, N. and ASKEW, J. (1992) *Learning Mathematics. Second International Assessment of Educational Progress*, Princeton, NJ: Educational Testing Service.

NOAH, H.J. and ECKSTEIN, M.A. (1969) *Towards a Science of Comparative Education*, Toronto, Canada: Macmillan.

NOAH, H.J. (1988) 'Methods of comparative education', in POSTLETHWAITE, T.N. (ed.) *The Encyclopaedia of Comparative Education and National Systems of Education*, Oxford: Pergamon, pp. 10–13.

POSTLETHWAITE, T.N. (1988) *The Encyclopaedia of Comparative Education and National Systems of Education*, Preface, Oxford: Pergamon, pp. xvii–xxvii.

ROBITAILLE, D.F. (1994) 'TIMSS: The third international mathematics and science study', *Beiträge zum Mathematikunterricht*, Hildesheim, Germany: Franzbecker, pp. 35–42.

ROBITAILLE, D.F. and TRAVERS, K.J. (1992) 'International studies of achievement in mathematics', in GROUWS, J.S. (ed.) *Handbook of Research on Mathematics Learning and Teaching*, New York: Macmillan, pp. 687–709.

SADLER, M. (1964) 'How far can we learn anything of practical value from the study of foreign systems of education?', *Comparative Education Review*, **7**, pp. 307–14. Reprinted from *Surrey Advertiser*, December 1, 1900.

STEVENSON, H. and BARTSCH, K. (1992) 'An analysis of Japanese and American textbooks in mathematics', in LEESTMA, R. and WALBERG, H.J. (eds) *Japanese Educational Productivity*, Ann Arbor, MI: University of Michigan, Michigan Papers in Japanese Studies, pp. 103–33.

STIGLER, J.W. and PERRY, M. (1988) 'Cross cultural studies of mathematics teaching and learning: Recent finding and new directions', in GROUWS, D.A., COONEY, T.J. and JONES, D. (eds) *Perspectives on Research on Effective Mathematics Teaching*, Reston, VA: National Council of Teachers of Mathematics, pp. 194–223.

THUT, I.N. and ADAMS, D. (1964) *Educational Patterns in Contemporary Societies*, New York: McGraw-Hill.

Part I

*Recent International Comparative Studies
in Mathematics Education*

2   The Second International Mathematics Study

Kenneth J. Travers and Avrum I. Weinzweig

In 1976 the IEA undertook the Second International Mathematics Study. The objective was to produce an international portrait of mathematics education with emphasis on the mathematics classroom and significant input from the mathematics education community. The framework of the study consisted of three levels — the Intended Curriculum (that which is mandated at a national or system level), the Implemented Curriculum (that which is taught in the classroom), and the Attained Curriculum (what the students learn). Preliminary surveys of the National Coordinating Centers led to the construction of a content-behaviour grid which was used to obtain on international topography of the international curriculum and to construct the achievement tests to determine the attained curriculum. The Implemented Curriculum was determined through a series of detailed questionnaires (to determine teacher practices) as well as questions on each item (to determine opportunity to learn).

Introduction

The IEA, a consortium of centers of educational research from more than 50 countries, first undertook a survey of mathematics achievement in the mid-1960s, in what has come to be known as the First International Mathematics Study (FIMS). The choice of mathematics for this first study was more a matter of convenience than interest in mathematics achievement *per se*. The organizers believed that it would be easier to make international comparisons in mathematics than in any other area, and they felt that mathematics achievement would serve as a surrogate for school achievement. Thus, the FIMS was an experiment in International Studies that provided useful information on mathematics achievement. Subsequently, using the experience gained in FIMS, the IEA conducted a number of international studies in different areas.

After a hiatus of several years the IEA, at the urging of Roy Phillips of the New Zealand Department of Education, convened a meeting in the summer of 1976, at the University of Illinois at Champaign-Urbana, to consider whether a second study of mathematics should be undertaken. There was substantial agreement at that time that, should a second study be undertaken, the focus should be on mathematics education internationally. At a subsequent meeting in St Andrews, Scotland, the decision was made to undertake such a study, and an International Coordinating Committee was established under the Chairmanship of Kenneth Travers. The goals of this project, which came to be known as the Second International Mathematics Study (SIMS), were much more ambitious and its structure considerably different from FIMS. The overall objective was to produce an international portrait of mathematics education, with a particular emphasis on the mathematics classroom. There would be significant input and guidance at every stage from the mathematics education community. Two populations were studied by FIMS, a younger population consisting of 13-year-olds and an older population consisting of students in their last year of secondary school. This latter group presented some problems, in that in some countries this group consisted only of a small percentage of the cohort specializing in mathematics while in others it consisted of a large percentage of more general students. This made for difficulties in comparing a broad population to a much more selective group.

The Second International Mathematics Study

The curriculum in many countries is mandated at the national or system level. This is spelled out in curriculum guides and presented in the approved textbooks. Teachers are then expected to translate these guides into actual classroom instruction. There is an implicit assumption that the students will learn the material presented in the classroom. How well do the teachers translate what has been mandated? How close a match is there between what actually goes on in the classroom and what has been mandated? How much and what do the students learn? SIMS was planned as an in-depth study of the curriculum, and this required an examination of each of the components mentioned above. This led to a framework of the study on three levels — the Intended Curriculum (what has been mandated), the Implemented Curriculum (what is taught by the teachers in their own classrooms), and the Attained Curriculum (what is learned by the students). The diagram in Figure 2.1 illustrates this framework.

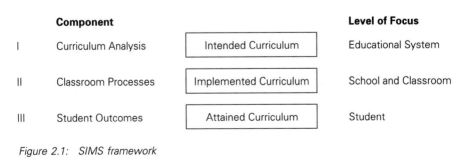

	Component		**Level of Focus**
I	Curriculum Analysis	Intended Curriculum	Educational System
II	Classroom Processes	Implemented Curriculum	School and Classroom
III	Student Outcomes	Attained Curriculum	Student

Figure 2.1: SIMS framework

The targeted populations for SIMS were roughly comparable to those for FIMS and consisted of the following two groups.

Population A: All students in the grade (year, level) where the majority have attained the age of 13:00 to 13:11 years by the middle of the school year.
Population B: All students who are in the normally accepted terminal grades of the secondary educational system and who are studying mathematics as a substantial part of their academic program.

The definition of Population B in SIMS was intended to overcome the difficulties in FIMS mentioned above. The narrower definition was intended to include only those students who are completing the requirements needed for the further study of mathematics at the post-secondary level. However, as with FIMS, the makeup of this second population still differed considerably among participating countries, and this made the interpretation of the achievement results at that level quite difficult.

The Intended Curriculum

In order to determine the Intended Curriculum a preliminary survey of the curricula in several countries was undertaken. The need to accommodate the reality that not all topics are covered with the same degree of thoroughness led to the development of a grid structure with a content dimension and a cognitive behaviour dimension. The content dimension for Population A was broken up into five strands — arithmetic, algebra, geometry, descriptive statistics and measurement — and that of Population B into nine strands — sets and relations, number systems, algebra, geometry, elementary functions and calculus, probability and statistics, finite mathematics, computer science and logic. Each of these strands was further subdivided and refined, particularly for the Population A. The cognitive behaviour dimension was partitioned into four categories based on a scheme proposed by Wilson (1971) — computation, comprehension, application and analysis. In any such classifications there are always ambiguities and disagreements as to where certain topics fit. In an effort to reduce these ambiguities and disagreements, detailed examples were provided for each cell in the grid so that the respondents could see what the International Mathematics Committee had in mind. As a further check, the respondents were asked to include examples of how they interpreted the various cells. Some respondents might regard addition and subtraction of integers as arithmetic, and others as algebra. Since our concern was primarily to determine whether this topic was included in the curriculum, countries were asked to respond according to the topic and the examples provided, regardless of whether or not they agreed with the classification. Further, they were asked to provide items that they felt fit into each of the cells. Finally, each country was asked to specify the level of importance of each cell in the grid — whether they considered that topic very important, somewhat important or not too important. These data were used to draw up a topography of the international curriculum in the form of the content-cognitive behaviour grid, with cells marked V (very important for most countries), I (Important for most countries), I_s (Important for some countries) and U (Unimportant for most countries).

The Implemented Curriculum

Extensive information was collected from teachers on how they taught mathematics to the target classes. Detailed questionnaires were provided to the teachers in order to determine their classroom practices. The response to the content-cognitive behaviour grid was used to select several topics which had the greatest potential for growth across all the countries. In order to monitor teaching methods during the school year, a detailed questionnaire was administered to the teachers. In order to make the responses as explicit as possible, the questionnaire provided, for each topic, a detailed description of a large variety of teaching methods that could be utilized in the teaching of that topic. A variety of information on teacher attitudes, beliefs and practices was also collected, including:

- goals in teaching mathematics,
- influences on teacher decision-making,
- uses of resources supporting teaching
- perceptions of the particular class sampled.

Information was also collected on the students' opportunity to learn certain topics as described below in the section on the Attained Curriculum.

The Attained Curriculum

The main instruments for determining the Attained Curriculum were the achievement tests. The topography of the international curriculum, as given by the content-cognitive behaviour grid, was used as a basis for item development, with the number of items for each cell determined according to the importance assigned to that cell. Items were collected from several sources, and many were developed specifically for this study. In addition, a number of 'anchor items' (items from the first study) were included, in order to chart any changes that occurred between the first and second study in the 11 countries that participated in both studies. All the items were reviewed by the National Committees for each country for correctness and suitability, and items were piloted several times before the final selection was made. Since the focus of the study was the classroom, in order to provide as broad coverage as possible

Table 2.1: *Breakdown of the SIMS item pool for population A*

Major strands	Number of items (Per cent)		
	Longitudinal version	Cross-sectional	Common to both versions
Arithmetic	62 (34%)	46 (24%)	46 (29%)
Algebra	32 (18%)	40 (23%)	30 (18%)
Geometry	42 (23%)	48 (27%)	39 (25%)
Measurement	26 (14%)	24 (14%)	24 (15%)
Descriptive statistics	18 (10%)	18 (10%)	18 (11%)
Total	180	176	157

Table 2.2: *Breakdown of the SIMS item pool for population B*

Major strands	Number of items (Per cent)
Sets, relations, functions	7 (5%)
Number systems	17 (13%)
Algebra	26 (19%)
Geometry	26 (19%)
Analysis	46 (34%)
Probability and statistics	7 (5%)
Other	7 (5%)
Total	136

in the achievement tests, students in population A were administered a core form and one of four rotated forms. Population B students wrote one or two of eight rotated forms constructed at that level. The structures of the item pools are given in the tables above. The breakdown of the items in the achievement tests for Population A is given in Table 2.1 and for Population B in Table 2.2.

For each item, teachers were asked if the content had been taught previously, taught that year, or not taught at all. Students were asked similar questions, and their responses were quite consistent with those of the teachers. This provided a measure of the opportunity to learn for each item in the achievement tests.

In order to make it possible for growth in mathematics achievement to be charted, the full design of SIMS was longitudinal. Pre-tests were administered at the beginning of the year and post-tests at the end. Most of the 20 participants in the study at the Population A level and the 17 at the Population B level (Table 2.3) were represented by single national probability samples. However, there were separate Flemish and French population samples for Belgium. Two provinces of Canada, Ontario and British Columbia (BC) participated separately. Scotland participated independently of England and Wales. Only eight countries participated in the longitudinal study at the Population A level and three at the Population B level. The degree of participation for each of the countries is listed in Table 2.3.

Table 2.3:   Countries participating in SIMS

Country	Cross-sectional		Longitudinal	
	Population A	Population B	Population A	Population B
Belgium (Flemish)	X	X	X	
Belgium (French)	X	X		
Canada (BC)	X	X	X	X
Canada (Ontario)	X	X	X	X
England and Wales	X	X		
Finland	X	X		
France	X		X	
Hong Kong	X	X		
Hungary	X	X		
Israel	X	X		
Japan	X	X	X	
Luxembourg	X			
Netherlands	X			
New Zealand	X	X	X	
Nigeria	X			
Scotland	X	X		
Swaziland	X			
Sweden	X	X		
Thailand	X	X	X	
United States	X	X	X	X

Some Findings

Opportunity to Learn

One of the findings on the national level is the continued wide discrepancy in the opportunity provided for students to complete secondary education to the grade 12 level or equivalent. This was true not only between developing countries and developed countries but also among developed countries. There were large between-country differences in the proportions of the age or grade cohort of secondary-school students studying Population B mathematics. In the majority of the countries participating in SIMS — including Japan, the United States and most European countries — Population B accounted for no more than 12 per cent of the age cohort. The curricula in these countries, geared as they were to the top students at that level, were probably too advanced and too difficult for a broader spectrum of the population. In Hungary, however, 50 per cent of the age cohort and in the Canadian provence of British Columbia 30 per cent of the age cohort were included in Population B. As the importance of technology increases, and as the requirement of a solid basis in mathematics encompasses more and more fields, the need for graduates well qualified in mathematics becomes even greater in order to ensure economic progress. This makes it even more important to increase the number of students enrolled in mathematics at this level. One often-expressed concern is that increasing the number of students in these courses would impact negatively on the best students, in that the courses would be watered down. The evidence indicates that, in spite of this disparity in the retention of students in the study of pre-university mathematics, the very best students in almost every country do as well as their counterparts in other countries. This would seem to indicate that the policy of retaining a high proportion of students in the study of mathematics, as in Hungary or British Columbia, does not affect the performance of the very best students. One would expect, however, that students in the more selective systems, while not doing better than the others on topics that both have studied, will have been exposed to more topics.

There has been substantial growth, in some countries, in the percentage of the cohort completing secondary school. In Belgium there was an increase from 13 to 16 per cent, and in Finland from 14 to 59 per cent, between FIMS and SIMS. In the United States, the increase from 70 to 82 per cent was not so dramatic due, in part, to the already quite high retention rate in FIMS. This 'good news' is tempered by the 'bad news' – that the proportion of students in Population B dropped drastically from 18 per cent of the age cohort in FIMS to 12 per cent in SIMS. In spite of the increased retention of students in grade 12 in the United States, the decline in the percentage of cohort enrolled in mathematics courses at the Population B level from 18 per cent of the age cohort to 12 per cent is of particular concern.

Mathematical Content

The content of the mathematics curriculum at the Population A level, in a cumulative sense, is surprisingly similar among countries. Students study many of the same topics, although not necessarily in the same order or in the same depth. Geometry is the great exception, where there seemed to be almost as many different approaches to the subject and different topics covered as there were countries participating in the study. The fact that teachers agreed that most of the items in the Population A achievement tests concerned topics which were part of the curriculum provided further evidence of the similarity in the content from one country to the next.

In most countries, the Population A curriculum in mathematics is a combination of topics from arithmetic, algebra and geometry. Indeed, from FIMS to SIMS, the importance of geometry declined while the importance of algebra and arithmetic increased, with the United States having the highest rating for arithmetic in both studies and almost the lowest in geometry. Not surprisingly, in the United States but also in Canada, the curriculum tends to include more arithmetic than anything else, with a sprinkling of algebra and geometry for some students. In the United States, only a small minority of Population A students were offered a complete course in algebra.

Unlike the situation for the Population A achievement tests, where there was strong agreement among teachers that most of the items were part of the curriculum, there was no such agreement for Population B. At this level there were large differences in content between countries. The importance of algebra and elementary functions as well as calculus increased in most countries from FIMS to SIMS, while geometry decreased in importance. In the United States, however, the change in the importance of elementary functions and calculus was very small and was lower than most countries in both studies. A significant amount of selection has also taken place by the time students reach this level, so that the Population B cohort tends to be relatively small (less than 20 per cent) with the exception of Canada (BC) with 30 per cent and Hungary with 50 per cent. The curriculum in these countries is likely to include both calculus and algebra as important strands, with less emphasis on geometry and trigonometry which are usually covered in earlier years. In Canada, where there is a high degree of student retention, the Population B curriculum consists mainly of algebra and trigonometry. This is also true in the United States, where few students take a full course in calculus. However, in Hungary teachers report both a high retention rate and a large proportion of students studying calculus. There were wide disparities in achievement levels among countries when the entire Population B cohort is included. Thus, in algebra, Hungary with the highest retention rate of 50 per cent, and Canada (BC) with a retention rate of 30 per cent, had a much lower overall achievement score than Japan with an average retention rate of roughly 12 per cent or Israel with the smallest retention rate of 6 per cent. This disparity shifted when comparisons were restricted to the best 5 per cent of students, where the achievement score for Hungary and Canada (BC) was much higher than Japan and even higher in comparison to Israel. The disparity further diminished when only the top 1 per cent of the students were compared, where the achievement scores of Hungary and Canada (BC) were comparable to those of Japan, albeit lower than Israel.

Student and Teacher Beliefs

Most students at the Population A and Population B level indicated the belief that mathematics is important, and they wanted to do well since they believed that a knowledge of mathematics would be important to them in their careers. While their opinions about mathematics were not overly negative, they were not overly enthusiastic either. It is interesting to note that Japanese students who performed very well on the achievement tests were much more likely than students elsewhere to feel that mathematics was difficult and not enjoyable. Japanese teachers also felt the same way about the teaching of mathematics, unlike the teachers in Canada and the United States who tended to find teaching mathematics easier and more enjoyable.

Difficulty

Population A students found the achievement test items fairly difficult on the whole, with the mean percentage correct across countries for all items being 47 per cent. On items involving computations with whole numbers and other straightforward applications of basic concepts, the performance was generally good. Performance fell off sharply on items calling for higher-order thinking skills. Performance levels on items involving rational numbers, whether expressed as common or decimal fractions, were generally poor.

Teacher Practices

The responses to the questionnaire on teaching practices showed many similarities across countries with 'chalk and talk' the most common approach, with whole class instruction and a heavy reliance on the textbook. Differentiated instruction or assignments are rarely given. Teaching on the 8th grade level entails an enormous amount of review, especially in the United States and Canada. North American teachers seem to assume that their students have not mastered much of the Population A curriculum at an earlier grade. Teachers in Japan, Belgium and France, on the other hand, assume that students have learned a great deal of this content in earlier grades and have mastered it, so there was no need to review or reteach this material. Teachers indicated that they tend to use more abstract teaching practices with topics that are being reviewed.

Use of Calculators

The results indicate that Population A teachers do not expect or encourage students to use calculators, nor did they seem to be in widespread use at the time of the study. We suspect that this situation has now changed.

Class Size

Class size varied considerably from one country to another, from 19 to 43 students per class at the Population A level and from 14 to 43 students per class at the Population B level. Surprisingly, countries where performance levels were the highest reported some of the largest class sizes. Hong Kong, for example, had the largest class sizes. Moreover, the students in these classes were among the youngest of those that participated in the study and their teachers were less than fully qualified to teach mathematics. Yet their performance was exceptional, perhaps indicating the relevance of factors such as motivation and the importance of doing well in mathematics in the view of the parents and the society. In the United States and Canada, class size and student-teacher ratios were larger than for most of the other industrialized countries. Moreover, North American teachers reported teaching more hours per week. All in all, the teachers in North America seem to have comparatively heavier work loads.

Tracking

Tracking of students for mathematics classes is practiced in every country at some level. This is particularly prevalent at the Population A level in Canada (BC) and the United States, where over 70 per cent of the teachers practiced grouping students by ability level. At the other extreme, 70 per cent of the French teachers of Population A, and all the teachers in Japan and Hungary, reported that students were not placed into different classes or programmes at that level; these students, particularly those from France and Japan, did very well on the achievement tests. Nevertheless, even in systems where tracking is widely used, most teachers still report a wide range of abilities in their classes. Interestingly, Japanese teachers tended to attribute lack of progress on the part of their students much more to their own failings rather than to some weakness on the part of students. They also tended to regard teaching mathematics as much more difficult that did teachers of most other countries.

Some of the Difficulties

The excessive length of time it took for SIMS to be completed, 12 years from the initial planning meeting to the publication of the third volume of the international report, was one of its principle weaknesses. The longitudinal version of SIMS has proved to be a very fertile ground for investigating links between growth in student achievements and teaching practices. Although SIMS used twice as many items as did FIMS, there were still not enough items to provide a thorough coverage of the curriculum across countries. The classroom-processes questionnaires, although useful and interesting, did not correspond adequately to the content items. It has been left to TIMSS to correct and improve on these shortcomings.

References

HUSÉN, T. (ed.) (1967) *International Study of Achievement in Mathematics (Vols. I and II)*, Stockholm: Almqvist & Wiksell.
McKNIGHT, C.C., CROSSWHITE, F.J., DOSSEY, J.A., KIFER, E., SWAFFORD, J.O., TRAVERS, K.J. and COONEY, T.J. (1987) *The Underachieving Curriculum*, Champaign, IL: Stipes Publishing Company.

ROBITAILLE, D.F. and GARDEN, R.A. (1989) *The IEA Study of Mathematics II: Contexts and Outcomes of School Mathematics*, Oxford: Pergamon Press.

TRAVERS, K.J. and WESTBURY, I. (1990) *The IEA Study of Mathematics II: Analysis of Mathematics Curricula*, Oxford: Pergamon Press.

WILSON, J.W. (1971) 'Evaluation of learning in secondary school mathematics', in BLOOM, B.S., HASTINGS, J.T. and MADAUS, G.E. (eds) *Handbook on Formative and Summative Evaluation of Student Learning*, New York, NY: McGraw-Hill, pp. 643–96.

3   An Overview of the Third International Mathematics and Science Study

Albert E. Beaton and David F. Robitaille

The Third International Mathematics and Science Study, an IEA-sponsored study which was carried out in over 40 countries in 1995, examined the achievement of students at five grade levels in a wide range of content and performance areas in mathematics and science. In addition to performance data, TIMSS collected contextual information from students, teachers and school principals. This chapter discusses the conceptual framework, research questions and design of the study. In addition, results from the mathematics achievement survey at the Grade 4 and Grade 8 levels, as well as plans for future analyses, are presented.

Introduction

Educational policymakers around the world recognize the need for more and better information about the effectiveness of schools. Some feel that their schools are not educating students well enough to be competitive in the knowledge and technologies that will be essential for progress in the next century. Many countries are involved in major educational reform movements, and they need good information about their own school systems as well as about those in other countries of interest to them. This sort of quest for more and better information is driven by a need to know how well their students compare to students from other countries in terms of the outcomes of schooling and in terms of how their educational systems differ from others. The Third International Mathematics and Science Study (TIMSS) was designed to address these information and research needs and to provide information which all educational stakeholders could use in their efforts to improve the teaching and learning of mathematics and science.

Participating countries may have had other reasons for involving themselves in TIMSS. Many believe that their country can best compete in the global economy only if their children are well educated. Mathematics and science education, with their perceived links to success in industry and technology, are of particular concern to both developed and developing nations. Other motivations might include a wish to compare a country's educational system and practices with those of other countries, both to gain some insight into potential changes in education policy and to explore possible improvements in curriculum design and instructional practice. The impact of participation in a cooperative international study may occur at any level, from the system as a whole to the individual classroom.

TIMSS is the largest international assessment that has been conducted to date in the field of education — the study measures student proficiency in mathematics and science in over 40 countries. Its tests and questionnaires were translated into over 30 languages, and testing was done at 5 different grade levels. Over a half-million students were tested, using many different types of tasks, including hands-on performance tasks; many of the teachers of these students and the principals of their schools filled out detailed questionnaires. Most of the data have been coded, checked and scaled, and several international reports have been published. The publication of the first report for Population 2 — focusing on the achievement of 13-year-olds — was featured in newspapers, magazines, radio and television around the world, and that level of interest underscores the importance which many countries attach to international comparisons in education.

The usefulness of any information for policy purposes depends heavily upon its quality. It is important that any comparisons be seen to be fair. For example, when comparing the mathematics or science achievement of students in different countries, it is important that the students be of more or less the same age, have the same number of years of schooling, and so on. It is also important to ensure that the tests the students write are designed to assess topics which are important in the curricula of the participating countries. This presents a challenge, because educational systems vary so extensively around the world; children in different countries start school at different ages, are exposed to different curricula, experience different degrees of parental involvement, and so on. In fact, clarifying the nature and scope of such differences is part of TIMSS mission. TIMSS has approached the task of making cross-national comparisons as comparable as possible by developing reasonable rules for the selection and testing of students by documenting its procedures thoroughly and ensuring that the participating nations follow those rules and procedures carefully. In this way, reasonably accurate international comparisons can be made and the cross-national differences can be described.

TIMSS as an IEA Project

TIMSS is a collaborative international project with participants from every part of the world working together to bring the project to a successful conclusion. The sponsoring agency for the study is the International Association for the Evaluation of Educational Achievement (IEA), a consortium of research centers, universities and ministries of education from more than 50 countries based in the Netherlands.

Four previous IEA studies focused on mathematics and science:

- First International Mathematics Study, FIMS   1959–1967
- First International Science Study, FISS   1966–1973
- Second International Mathematics Study, SIMS   1976–1987
- Second International Science Study, SISS   1980–1989

TIMSS incorporates a number of aspects from the designs of these earlier studies, giving prominent roles to a number of variables explored in them. In particular, TIMSS has focused a great deal of attention on curriculum documents, in the hope that these would yield the kind of information needed to develop a more comprehensive model of factors influencing learning in schools. An important influence on the study design was the degree to which the variables involved could be effectively measured or described. Many factors cannot be measured directly, and the TIMSS student surveys include some items that act as proxies for the social and economic backgrounds of students.

The headquarters for TIMSS is located in the International Study Center at Boston College in Boston, Massachusetts. The International Study Center maintains a close relationship with the International Coordinating Centre at the University of British Columbia and with its major subcontractors — the Australian Council for Educational Research in Melbourne, Statistics Canada in Ottawa, and the IEA Data Processing Centre in Hamburg, Germany. The TIMSS curriculum analysis is housed at Michigan State University.

In all, over 50 countries have participated is one or more aspects of TIMSS and, of these, 41 took part in the Population 2 study. The names of the 45 countries that carried out achievement testing at one or more of the population levels involved are shown below.

Argentina	Germany	Korea	Russian Federation
Australia	Greece	Kuwait	Scotland
Austria	Hong Kong	Latvia	Singapore
Belgium	Hungary	Lithuania	Slovak Republic
Bulgaria	Iceland	Mexico	Slovenia
Canada	Indonesia	New Zealand	South Africa
Colombia	Iran, Islamic Rep.	Netherlands	Spain
Cyprus	Ireland	Norway	Sweden
Czech Republic	Israel	Philippines	Switzerland
Denmark	Italy	Portugal	Thailand
England	Japan	Romania	United States
France			

Design of the Study

The conceptual framework for TIMSS evolved from that of earlier IEA studies. SIMS was the first study to examine the distinction among the intended curriculum, the implemented curriculum and the attained curriculum — what society would like children to be taught, what they are actually taught and what they actually learn. This framework provides an effective means for discussing different views of curricula and addressing the contexts of education within the participating countries.

Student achievement is affected by both the implemented curriculum and societal contexts. It is also a function of factors under the control of individual students, including effort, attitude and personal interests. All of these variables are addressed in the design of TIMSS.

TIMSS measured student achievement using a variety of kinds of achievement items. The design and approval of the items was a three-year process involving the input of several committees and the final approval of National Research Coordinators. All participants were anxious to ensure that the items represented their national curricula fairly, ensuring that international achievement comparisons would be based on valid data. As is traditional in IEA studies, TIMSS employed numerous multiple-choice items in the testing, but a large number of constructed response items were also included. Finally, TIMSS also included a set of performance tasks in both mathematics and science, and these were administered to a subset of the students who participated in the achievement survey.

Four research questions underlie the study design. These were chosen as the best means of exploring the relationships between the intended, implemented and attained curricula.

Research Question 1: The Intended Curriculum

TIMSS describes the intended curriculum as the concepts, processes, skills and attitudes used in mathematics and science. The first research question explores the ways in which countries vary in the intended learning goals for mathematics and science. The characteristics of the educational systems, schools and students, and the ways in which these factors influence the development of educational goals, are explored.

The ways in which the curriculum is articulated are particularly important. The locus of decision-making in this area varies considerably among countries — some issue a detailed, mandatory curriculum, others offer general guidelines that allow for local variation, and others issue goal statements that require full development at the regional level.

In all types of systems, an examination of the intended curricula reveals significant information about the differences and priorities of the educational systems. Official documents often reveal critical information such as teaching credentials, budget allocations and the numbers of years students spend in school. All these documents together reveal a wealth of detail about the intended curriculum, or what it is that society expects students to learn.

Research Question 2: The Implemented Curriculum

The implemented curriculum may be described in terms of concepts, processes, skills and attitudes, thereby enabling direct comparison between the intended and implemented levels of curriculum. Differences between the intended and the implemented curriculum are the result of numerous factors, including the physical and social conditions within which teachers work, the characteristics and needs of the student they serve, and the teachers' experiences and beliefs. TIMSS obtained information of this type by means of questionnaires administered at the school, classroom and individual student levels. Details were elicited about class size, school size, courses, student selection, community influences, social problems, professional qualifications and experience of teachers, pedagogical beliefs, preparation time, access to computers and availability of calculators.

Research Question 3: The Attained Curriculum

The attained curriculum relies heavily on factors pertaining to the individual student — the amount of homework the student does, the effort the student expends, the student's classroom behaviour patterns, and other details. Societal and school factors are also influential, and vary from student to student. Such factors include attitudes about education, aspirations, perceptions of their ability to succeed, parental expectations of success and the economic status of their families. TIMSS gathered information of this type through student questionnaires.

At the level of the attained curriculum, it is important to consider the overall structure of TIMSS — that is, the consideration of the variables of three kinds of content in the light of three levels of institutional arrangements, within three societal contexts. This framework then allows analysts to perform comparisons between countries and between subsets of students within countries.

Research Question 4: Relationships between Curricula and
Social and Educational Contexts

Finally, TIMSS explores the relationship between the intended, implemented and attained curricula with respect to the contexts of education, arrangements for teaching and learning, and outcomes of the educational process. This information will be invaluable to education researchers in providing accurate data about a complex set of interrelated factors. The findings from the study will be of interest to educators and decision-makers in the education process. TIMSS may reveal new information about curriculum structure, goals, teacher education or other factors that influence students' achievement.

Populations and Sampling

TIMSS has defined three internationally desired student populations for its assessment.

- *Population 1*: All students in the two adjacent grades that contain the largest proportion of 9-year-olds at the time of testing. These students are in Grades 3 and 4 in most countries.
- *Population 2*: All students in the two adjacent grades that contain the largest proportion of 13-year-olds at the time of testing. These students are in Grades 7 and 8 in most countries.
- *Population 3*: Students in their final year of secondary education. In addition, countries could test subpopulations consisting of students taking advanced courses in mathematics or physics.

TIMSS countries were required to assess Population 2, but the other populations were optional, as was participation in the performance assessment component of the study of Populations 1 and 2. Countries were allowed some freedom in adapting these definitions according to their national needs, as long as their nationally defined populations did not exclude more than 10 per cent of the nationally desired population.

Sampling was done using a carefully specified, two-stage, random sampling procedure, and each national plan was reviewed and approved by Statistics Canada. In the case of Populations 1 and 2, intact classrooms were sampled, usually from at least 150 schools. In each participating school, one or two classes from each of Grades 3 and 4 or Grades 7 and 8 were selected. For Population 3, the design called for selecting 40 students from each of approximately 120 schools.

Sampling standards for TIMSS were high and required, among other things, that at least 85 per cent of the selected schools agreed to participate. The sampling procedures were carefully documented so that the probability of selecting each student is known, making it possible to calculate sampling weights for estimating national achievement levels more accurately.

The Mathematics and Science Tests

TIMSS was designed to measure student achievement in mathematics and science. The tests were developed to cover a very wide spectrum of content, performance expectations and perspectives. The mathematics content areas were as follows: numbers; measurement; geometry; proportionality; functions, relations and equations; data analysis, probability and statistics; and analysis. The science content areas were: earth science; life science, physical sciences; science, technology and society; history of science and technology; environmental issues; nature of science; and science and other disciplines. The content areas, performance expectations, and perspectives are shown in Figure 3.1.

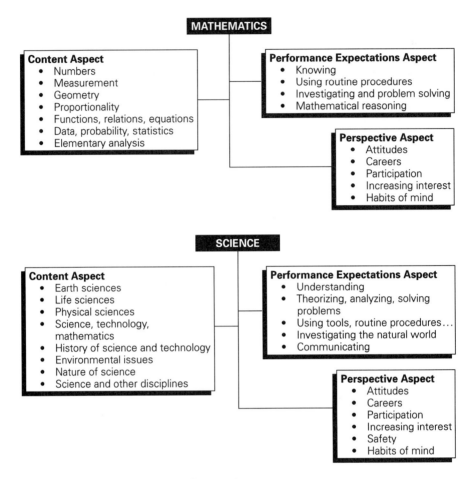

Figure 3.1: The TIMSS curriculum frameworks

The curriculum frameworks, the test specifications and the test items themselves were developed through the collaboration of mathematicians, scientists, mathematics educators, science educators, the National Research Coordinators and testing specialists.

The intended test coverage was so large that having all students answer all items would have overrun the available testing time. Instead, the test items for Populations 1 and 2 were distributed across eight overlapping booklets, each booklet containing some mathematics and some science items. The items for Population 3 were arranged in nine booklets, with some booklets appropriate for all students and others designed for students taking physics or advanced mathematics courses. No single student was administered all of the test items for his or her population level, and yet TIMSS was able to encompass broad coverage of topics in mathematics and science. The testing time was about an hour for Population 1 students and 90 minutes for students in Populations 2 and 3.

Scoring rubrics were developed and piloted for each open-ended item, and these included detailed instructions about how the items should be graded. For some items the scoring consisted simply of marking the item correct or incorrect, but some students' responses were assigned one, two, three, or no points depending on the degree of correctness. Open-ended items were also coded for the type of approach or error made by the student. Scoring training sessions were held at various sites around the world. In addition, after the data had been collected and the items scored, random samples of students' papers were selected for a second, independent scoring for estimating within-country reliability. The comparability of scoring among countries was investigated in an experiment using English-speaking coders from 20 countries.

The tests were administered in over 30 languages. Detailed specifications for translating the TIMSS tests were developed, and each translation was checked independently by persons who were fluent in English and the language in which the items were written, as well as familiar with the subject matter. Translation verification was carried out both within each country and by an organization in Vancouver working under contract to the International Coordinating Centre.

Contextual Information

Contextual information is an essential component of the TIMSS design, as it is with all IEA studies. Students were asked to complete a questionnaire about their backgrounds, attitudes, interests and study practices. In Populations 1 and 2, their mathematics and science teachers were asked to fill out questionnaires about their backgrounds and teaching practices. School principals in the participating schools were asked to fill out questionnaires about their schools' characteristics and about the community they served.

Administration

Detailed manuals designed to standardize the testing situation were developed, and test administrators were trained to meet international standards. The southern hemisphere countries tested Populations 1 and 2 in October/November 1994, and Population 3 in August 1995. The northern hemisphere tested all three populations between February and May 1995. Each country was responsible for coding the responses of its students on the open-ended items and for entering all information into an electronic database. In nearly all countries, a quality assurance monitor was selected, trained, and then sent to observe how well countries maintained TIMSS administrative standards.

Database Formation

TIMSS provided software so that countries could make internal consistency checks on their data. When each country completed its own database, copies of the data and the accompanying documentation were sent to the IEA Data Processing Center in Hamburg. Extensive checks of the data were made there, including matching the teacher and school data with the student data. Unusual or irregular data entries for any country were noted and the National Research Coordinator concerned was asked to confirm or correct the values. This process was repeated until each data file met the international standards.

Making population estimates from TIMSS data requires sampling weights for each student and school. For this purpose, each country's data was sent to Statistics Canada, which developed the weights. At this point, many checks were made on the sample to judge its adequacy as a representative sample of a country's population of students.

Since the TIMSS tests contained so many mathematics and science items, the TIMSS data were then sent to the Australian Council for Educational Research (ACER) in Melbourne for scaling. Scaling is a useful method of summarizing a student's responses to test items into one or a few test scores. It is especially useful for TIMSS since all students in a country are given scores which are comparable even though the students were assigned different test booklets. ACER also performed extensive checks on the quality of the TIMSS tests. After weighting and scaling, all of the data from each country were sent to the International Study Center in Boston College for further checking, analysis, interpretation and reporting.

Results

TIMSS is a very ambitious project that has gathered a huge amount of information about the students who were tested, their teachers and schools, as well as the countries in which they studied. Addressing all of the research questions which these data might address is clearly a formidable task.

The TIMSS strategy has been to address the four research questions in two phases. The first phase is to produce and publish basic data about student performance in a timely manner, including other basic information about the students, their teachers, schools, and countries. This phase has already produced 6 volumes: *Mathematics Achievement in the Middle School Years* (Beaton et al., 1996a); *Science Achievement in the Middle School Years* (Beaton et al., 1996b); *Performance Assessment in IEA's Third International Mathematics and Science Study* (Harmon et al., 1997); *Science Achievement in the Primary School Years* (Martin et al., 1997); *Mathematics Achievement in the Primary School Years* (Mullis et al., 1997); *Mathematics and Science Achievement in the Final Year of Secondary School: IEA's Third International Mathematics and Science Study* (Mullis et al., 1998).

The reports in this initial round contain information not only about students' performance but also about their teachers, class sizes, use of computers and many other topics of educational importance. To assist in the interpretation of these results, TIMSS has also published *National Contexts for Mathematics and Science Education* (Robitaille, 1997), which describes similarities and differences in the educational systems of the participating countries. To help in understanding the underlying technology, TIMSS has also produced the *Technical Report (Vol. 1): Design and Development* (Martin and Kelly, 1996a) and a report, *Third International Mathematics and Science Study Technical Quality Assurance in Data Collection* (Martin and Mullis, 1996b).

Achievement Results: Population 1, Upper Grade

Six content dimensions were covered in the TIMSS mathematics tests administered to Population 1 students: whole numbers; fractions and proportionality; measurement, estimation and number sense; data representation, analysis and probability; geometry; patterns, relations and functions.

Singapore and Korea were the highest performing countries at both Population 1 grade levels. Japan and Hong Kong also performed very well at both grades, as did the Netherlands, the Czech Republic and Austria. Lower-performing countries included Iran and Kuwait. Population 1 results for the upper grade are summarized in Table 3.1.

Gender differences: For most countries, gender differences in mathematics achievement were small or essentially non-existent. However, the direction of the few gender differences that did exist favoured boys over girls. Within the mathematics content areas, there were few differences in performance between boys and girls, except in measurement, where the differences favoured boys.

Results by content area: Nearly all countries did relatively better in some content areas than they did in others. This is consistent with the idea of countries having different curricular emphases in mathematics.

Even though students in the top performing countries had very high achievement on many of the test items, students generally had the most difficulty with the items in the area of fractions and proportionality. The least difficult items involved whole number, proportional reasoning and recognizing pictorial representations of fractions. In contrast, the more difficult items involved decimals and students being asked to explain their reasoning.

In data representation, students had some difficulty moving beyond a straightforward reading of data in tables, charts and graphs to actually using the information in calculations or to graphically represent the data. For example, students were asked to use data from a simple table to complete a bar graph. On average, 40 per cent of fourth graders across countries drew the four bars to appropriate heights. There was, however, a very large range in

Table 3.1: Population 1 mathematics achievement — upper grade (fourth grade*)

Country	Mean	Years of formal schooling	Average age	Mathematics achievement scale score
Singapore	625 (5.3)	4	10.3	
Korea	611 (2.1)	4	10.3	
Japan	597 (2.1)	4	10.4	
Hong Kong	587 (4.3)	4	10.1	
Czech Republic	567 (3.3)	4	10.4	
Ireland	550 (3.4)	4	10.3	
United States	545 (3.0)	4	10.2	
Canada	532 (3.3)	4	10.0	
† Scotland	520 (3.9)	5	9.7	
†2 England	513 (3.2)	5	10.0	
Cyprus	502 (3.1)	4	9.8	
Norway	502 (3.0)	3	9.9	
New Zealand	499 (4.3)	4.5–5.5	10.0	
Greece	492 (4.4)	4	9.6	
Portugal	475 (3.5)	4	10.4	
Iceland	474 (2.7)	4	9.6	
Iran, Islamic Rep.	429 (4.0)	4	10.5	
Countries not satisfying guidelines for sample participation rates:				
Australia	546 (3.1)	4 or 5	10.2	
Austria	559 (3.1)	4	10.5	
¹ Latvia (LSS)	525 (4.8)	4	10.5	
Netherlands	577 (3.4)	4	10.3	
Countries not meeting age/grade specifications (high percentage of older students):				
Slovenia	552 (3.2)	4	10.9	
Countries with unapproved sampling procedures at classroom level:				
Hungary	548 (3.7)	4	10.4	
Unapproved sampling procedures at classroom level and not meeting other guidelines:				
¹ Israel	531 (3.5)	4	10.0	
Kuwait	400 (2.8)	5	10.8	
Thailand	490 (4.7)	4	10.5	

Percentiles of Performance
5th 25th 75th 95th

Mean and Confidence Interval

200 250 300 350 400 450 500 550 600 650 700 750 800 850

International Average = 529
(Average of All Country Means)

*Fourth grade in most countries.
†Met guidelines for sample participation rates only after replacement schools were included.
¹National Desired Population does not cover all of International Desired Population. Because coverage falls below 65 per cent, Latvia is annotated LSS for Latvian Speaking Schools only.
²National Defined Population covers less than 90 per cent of National Desired Population.
( )Standard errors appear in parentheses. Because results are rounded to the nearest whole number, some totals may appear inconsistent.
Source: IEA Third International Mathematics and Science Study (TIMSS), 1994–95.

performance from country to country. For example, three-quarters or more of the fourth graders completed the bar graph in Hong Kong, Japan, Korea and Singapore.

Students were more likely to be able to recognize simple patterns and relationships than they were to determine the operations underlying the relationships. About half the students internationally provided an answer showing that they understood what to do to get the next number in a subtraction series, where the numbers were decreasing by 4. When given two columns of four numbers, only about a quarter of the third graders and two-fifths of the fourth graders correctly determined that they needed to divide the number in Column A by 5 to obtain the number next to it in Column B.

Student attitudes: Those students who reported either liking mathematics or liking it a lot generally had higher achievement than students who reported disliking it to some degree. The overwhelming majority of fourth graders in nearly every country indicated they liked mathematics, but not all students feel positive about this subject area. In Japan, Korea and the Netherlands, more than a quarter of the fourth-grade students reported disliking mathematics.

In most countries, fourth graders of both genders were equally positive about liking mathematics. In Austria, Hong Kong, Japan and the Netherlands, boys reported a significantly stronger liking of the subject than did girls. However, girls reported liking mathematics better than did boys in Ireland and Scotland. Across countries, the majority of fourth graders agreed or strongly agreed that they did well in mathematics — a perception that did not always coincide with the comparisons of achievement across countries on the TIMSS test. Fourth-grade girls had lower self-perceptions than did boys in Austria, Hong Kong, Japan, the Netherlands, Singapore and Slovenia.

Achievement Results: Population 2

Middle-school students were tested in six content areas: fractions and number sense; measurement; proportionality; data representation, analysis and probability; geometry; algebra. About a quarter of the questions were in free-response format, requiring students to generate and write their answers.

Singapore was the top-performing country at both the lower and upper grades. Korea, Japan and Hong Kong also performed very well at both grades, as did Flemish-speaking Belgium and the Czech Republic. Lower performing countries included Colombia, Kuwait and South Africa. Results for the upper grade of Population 2 are summarized in Table 3.2.

Gender differences: For most countries, gender differences in mathematics achievement were small or essentially non-existent. However, the direction of the gender differences that did exist favoured boys over girls. For the mathematics content areas, few differences were found between boys and girls.

Table 3.2: Population 2 mathematics achievement — upper grade (eighth grade*)

	Country	Mean	Years of formal schooling	Average age	Mathematics achievement scale score
	Singapore	643 (4.9)	8	14.5	
	Korea	607 (2.4)	8	14.2	
	Japan	605 (1.9)	8	14.4	
	Hong Kong	588 (6.5)	8	14.2	
†	Belgium (Fl)	565 (5.7)	8	14.1	
	Czech Republic	564 (4.9)	8	14.4	
	Slovak Republic	547 (3.3)	8	14.3	
¹	Switzerland	545 (2.8)	7 or 8	14.2	
	France	538 (2.9)	8	14.3	
	Hungary	537 (3.2)	8	14.3	
	Russian Federation	535 (5.3)	7 or 8	14.0	
	Ireland	527 (5.1)	8	14.4	
	Canada	527 (2.4)	8	14.1	
	Sweden	519 (3.0)	8	13.9	
	New Zealand	508 (4.5)	8.5–9.5	14.0	
¹²	England	506 (2.6)	9	14.0	
	Norway	503 (2.2)	7	13.9	
†	United States	500 (4.6)	8	14.2	
¹	Latvia (LSS)	493 (3.1)	8	14.3	
	Spain	487 (2.0)	8	14.3	
	Iceland	487 (4.5)	8	13.6	
¹	Lithuania	477 (3.5)	8	14.3	
	Cyprus	474 (1.9)	8	13.7	
	Portugal	454 (2.5)	8	14.5	
	Iran, Islamic Rep.	428 (2.2)	8	14.6	
Countries not satisfying guidelines for sample participation rates:					
	Australia	530 (4.0)	8 or 9	14.2	
	Austria	539 (3.0)	8	14.3	
	Belgium (Fr)	526 (3.4)	8	14.3	
	Bulgaria	540 (6.3)	8	14.0	
	Netherlands	541 (6.7)	8	14.3	
	Scotland	498 (5.5)	8	13.7	
Countries not meeting age/grade specifications (high percentage of older students):					
	Colombia	385 (3.4)	8	15.7	
†¹	Germany	509 (4.5)	8	14.8	
	Romania	482 (4.0)	8	14.6	
	Slovenia	541 (3.1)	8	14.8	
Countries with unapproved sampling procedures at classroom level:					
	Denmark	502 (2.8)	7	13.9	
	Greece	484 (3.1)	8	13.6	
	Thailand	522 (5.7)	8	14.3	
Unapproved sampling procedures at classroom level and not meeting other guidelines:					
¹	Israel	522 (6.2)	8	14.1	
	Kuwait	392 (2.5)	9	15.3	
	South Africa	354 (4.4)	8	15.4	

Percentiles of Performance

5th 25th   75th 95th

Mean and Confidence Interval

200 250 300 350 400 450 500 550 600 650 700 750 800

International Average = 513
(Average of all Country Means)

*Eighth grade in most countries.
†Met guidelines for sample participation rates only after replacement schools were included.
¹National Desired Population does not cover all of International Desired Population. Because coverage falls below 65 per cent, Latvia is annotated LSS for Latvian Speaking Schools only.
²National Defined Population covers less than 90 per cent of National Desired Population.
( )Standard errors appear in parentheses. Because results are rounded to the nearest whole number, some totals may appear inconsistent.
Source: IEA Third International Mathematics and Science Study (TIMSS), 1994–95.

Again, the few differences that did occur favoured boys (except in algebra, where, if anything, the differences favoured girls).

Results by content area: Consistent with the idea of countries having different emphases in curriculum, those eighth graders that performed relatively better in fractions and number sense tended to be different from those that performed relatively better in geometry and algebra.

Even though students in the top-performing countries had very high achievement on many of the test items — both seventh and eighth graders, in most countries, had difficulty with multi-step problem solving and applications. For example, students were asked to draw a new rectangle whose length was one and a half times the length of a given rectangle and whose width was half the width of that rectangle. In only two countries (Korea and Austria) did at least half the eight-grade students correctly draw the new rectangle.

Students also found the proportionality items difficult. For example, one of the least difficult items in this area asked about adding 5 girls and 5 boys to a class that was three-fifths girls. On average, fewer than two-thirds of students across countries correctly answered that there would still be more girls than boys in the class.

In algebra, 58 per cent of the eighth-grade students across countries, on average, identified the expression $4m$ as being equivalent to $m + m + m + m$. There was however, a very large range in performance from country to country. Seventy-five per cent or more of the eighth graders answered this question correctly in the Czech Republic, Hong Kong, Japan, the Russian Federation, Singapore, the Slovak Republic and Slovenia.

Student attitudes: Within nearly every country, a clear and positive relationship was observed between a stronger liking of mathematics and higher achievement. Even though the majority of eighth graders in nearly every country indicated they liked mathematics, clearly not all students feel positively about the subject area. In Austria, the Czech Republic, Germany, Hungary, Japan, Korea, Lithuania and the Netherlands, more than 40 per cent of the students reported disliking mathematics.

In no country did eighth-grade girls report a stronger liking of mathematics than did boys. However, boys reported liking mathematics better than girls did in several countries, including Austria, France, Germany, Hong Kong, Japan, Norway and Switzerland.

Future Analyses

The second phase in the analysis of the TIMSS data involves a more in-depth investigation of the research questions. Detailed study of the relationships among the many variables associated with student performance will require more time for analysis and exploration of research hypotheses. TIMSS proposes to embark on a major research program with researchers from around the world when the first phase of analysis and reporting is completed. Many of the participating countries have already started to look for common relationships between school practices and student achievement.

The TIMSS data, of course address many more issues than any single group of educational researchers can address. Different research interests, hypotheses, models and perspectives can be expected to produce different, sometimes conflicting, interpretations of the data. To encourage the use of the TIMSS data by as many secondary researchers as possible, a well-documented database containing all TIMSS data for Populations 1 and 2 has been prepared and is available through IEA. The Population 3 database will be available later.

Producing a database for analysis and reporting, whether for TIMSS own reports or for other researchers, requires meticulous concern about accuracy in every detail. TIMSS was concerned about accuracy in every step in its process. The International Study Center at Boston College rechecked the data looking for unusual results or irregularities — a test item behaving unusually in one country might signal a mistranslation, and a peculiar distribution of parents' education might signal a flaw in the sampling process. When an unusual result occurred, the problem was presented to the National Research Coordinators for clarification. In some cases, the original student data had to be re-examined.

An important step in establishing the credibility of international comparisons is assuring that the countries selected comparable samples — that is, that the countries followed TIMSS detailed sampling procedures. Judgments about the adequacy of the national samples were made by a committee consisting of the sampling subcontractor (Statistics Canada), the sampling referee (Keith Rust), and senior members of the International Study Center staff, according to a policy agreed upon by the National Research Coordinators. Various national samples were classified according to whether or not they fully met the international standards or failed in some way. The judgments are described in detail in the published reports. All tables in these reports note the inadequacy of the samples from some of the countries.

An important factor in the credibility of TIMSS results is the appropriateness or fairness of the tests for the students in the participating countries. The development of the tests involved representatives of all of the countries, as well as subject matter and test specialists, and so the test construction process was fair — but were the results? To address this issue, each National Research Coordinator was asked to have each item in each test evaluated for appropriateness for that nation's curriculum. Using this information, the test data for all countries were rescored using the appropriate items selected for each particular country. The results of this research effort showed that the national selections of items had little effect on the ordering or national results. The details of these analyses are available in the published results.

Another factor in credibility is the accuracy of estimates made from survey data such as TIMSS. For example, we want to know the average mathematics achievement of all students in a given country. This unknown value is called is a population parameter. Surveys use small, carefully selected samples of students to estimate such parameters in a defined population. To make these estimates from the attained samples, sampling weights computed by Statistics Canada were used, along with the student data. Such estimates are not exact, and so it is important to estimate their standard errors — that is, how far off from the true parameter the sample estimate is likely to be. For each reported parameter estimate, an estimate was made of its standard error. Since a complex sampling procedure was used in all countries, a computationally-intensive method of error estimation called the *jackknife* was used.

Standard errors are very important in interpreting cross-national differences in achievement. Simply comparing countries on the basis of rankings is incorrect, and almost certainly misleading, since rankings exaggerate small differences near the middle of a group of countries and understate large differences at the upper and lower ends. For this reason, TIMSS does not report ranking, although the countries are ordered by estimated average performance in the international reports. Given the probable variability in results due to sampling and measurement error, a country might move up or down several rankings if a different, equally valid, sample of students had been selected. To facilitate cross-national comparisons, the reports contain multiple comparison tables that display significant differences among countries. For any particular country, these tables show which other countries achieved at a significantly higher level, which are at a significantly lower level, and which countries are so close in performance that different sample selections might reasonably change their rank-order. These tables take into account the fact that one country is likely to compare itself to each other participating country.

A decision was made to report major TIMSS results by grade, not age. At the primary-school level, grades three and four were reported for most countries, while at the middle-school level grades seven and eight were reported. Grade reporting was selected because most school policies are determined by grade, and whole classes could be selected to facilitate research into classroom processes. However, information about performance by age groupings is also important in understanding the net performance of national school systems. Using its adjacent grade-sampling information, TIMSS was able to make fairly accurate estimations of the median performances of 9- and 13-year-old students in most participating countries. The median performance and corresponding standard errors are shown in the reports.

Many of the results in the earlier reports display mathematics and science results as if mathematics and science were unitary concepts. The TIMSS tests actually measure several different content areas in both mathematics and science, as discussed above. Early analyses showed that there is much in common between performance in one content area and another, and so it was deemed useful to present single, overall summaries of mathematics and science. However, some countries performed relatively better in some content areas than in others, and so the test results are also reported separately by content area. A separate table is provided so that each country can identify the areas in which it is relatively stronger or weaker.

The analyses for the first reports produced a wealth of important information — not only about student achievement, but about other factors of educational importance such as gender differences, variations in school facilities and instructional factors. However, only a small portion of the available data has been explored and reported.

Reporting TIMSS results is a complex process, circumscribed by the requirements of the schedule, the available data, careful data interpretation and presentation, illuminating art work and available funding. For an international study like TIMSS, the process is slowed down — and improved — by the participation of the National Research Coordinators. The National Research Coordinators were given all results in advance, first for their own countries alone and then with all other countries present. Each was given an opportunity to review and recommend changes in the data or its interpretation. The many review phases have led to substantial confidence in the TIMSS results and their presentation. The composition and art work for the reports was done at the International Study Center.

The TIMSS reports and access to the database for Populations 1 and 2, as well as other information about TIMSS, are available on the World Wide Web (http://wwwcsteep.bc.edu/timss). Future reports will be placed on the internet as they become available. Information on how to get copies of the TIMSS data-base will be placed on this website when the database is documented for general distribution.

References

BEATON, A.E., MULLIS, I.V.S., MARTIN, M.O., GONZALEZ, E.J., KELLY, D.L. and SMITH, T.A. (1996a) *Mathematics Achievement in the Middle School Years*, Boston, MA: Center for the Study of Testing, Evaluation and Educational Policy, Boston College.

BEATON, A.E., MARTIN, M.O., MULLIS, I.V.S., GONZALEZ, E.J., KELLY, D.L. and SMITH, T.A. (1996b) *Science Achievement in the Middle School Years*, Boston, MA: Center for the Study of Testing, Evaluation and Educational Policy, Boston College.

HARMON, M., SMITH, T.A., MARTIN, M.O., KELLY, D.L., BEATON, A.E., MULLIS, I.V.S., GONZALEZ, E.J. and ORPWOOD, G. (1997) *Performance Assessment in IEA's Third International Mathematics and Science Study*, Boston, MA: Center for the Study of Testing, Evaluation and Educational Policy, Boston College.

HOWSON, G. (1995) *TIMSS Monograph No. 3. Mathematics Textbooks: A Comparative Study of Grade 8 Texts*, Vancouver: Pacific Educational Press.

MARTIN, M.O. and KELLY, D.L. (eds) (1996a) *Technical Report Volume 1: Design and Development*, Boston, MA: Center for the Study of Testing, Evaluation and Educational Policy, Boston College.

MARTIN, M.O. and MULLIS, I.V.S. (eds) (1996b) *Third International Mathematics and Science Study: Quality Assurance in Data Collection*, Boston, MA: Center for the Study of Testing, Evaluation and Educational Policy, Boston College.

MARTIN, M.O., MULLIS, I.V.S., BEATON, A.E., GONZALEZ, E.J., SMITH, T.A. and KELLY, D.L. (1997) *Science Achievement in the Primary School Years*, Boston, MA: Center for the Study of Testing, Evaluation and Educational Policy, Boston College.

MULLIS, I.V.S., MARTIN, M.O., BEATON, A.E., GONZALEZ, E.J., KELLY, D.L. and SMITH, T.A. (1997) *Mathematics Achievement in the Primary School Years*, Boston, MA: Center for the Study of Testing, Evaluation and Educational Policy, Boston College.

MULLIS, I.V.S., MARTIN, M.O., BEATON, A.E., GONZALEZ, E.J., KELLY, D.L. and SMITH, T.A. (1998) *Mathematics and Science Achievement in the Final Year of Secondary School: IEA's Third International Mathematics and Science Study*, Boston, MA: Center for the Study of Testing, Evaluation and Educational Policy, Boston College.

ROBITAILLE, D.F. (1997) *National Contexts for Mathematics and Science Education: An Encyclopedia of the Education Systems Participating in TIMSS*, Vancouver, Canada: Pacific Educational Press.

ROBITAILLE, D.F. and GARDEN, R.A. (eds) (1996) *TIMSS Monograph No. 2. Research Questions and Study Design*, Vancouver, Canada: Pacific Education Press.

ROBITAILLE, D.F., SCHMIDT, W.H., RAIZEN, S., McKNIGHT, C., BRITTON, E. and NICOL, C. (1993) *TIMSS Monograph No. 1. Curriculum Frameworks for Mathematics and Science*, Vancouver, Canada: Pacific Educational Press.

4   Explaining TIMSS Mathematics Achievement: A Preliminary Survey

Curtis C. McKnight and Gilbert A. Valverde

This chapter is a preliminary survey of the data from the Third International Mathematics and Science Study (TIMSS) for students studying mathematics in the final year of secondary school. TIMSS tested both a general population of all students in the final year of secondary school and a special population of those who were studying advanced mathematics in their final year. The former were tested on basic mathematics knowledge, the latter on advanced mathematics. National results for these two populations are compared for the countries who took part in both tests. The relation of each set of test results to earlier achievement results for 9 and 13-year-olds is also examined. These data are further investigated for more specific categories of mathematics topics. General knowledge seems significantly related to work through the upper grade for 13-year-olds. Advanced mathematics achievement seems especially related to secondary school mathematics. The chapter concludes by discussing the importance of carrying out these analyses with greater specificity rather than aggregating results for different types of items.

Introduction

Since at least 1965 (Husén, 1967), cross-national comparison of mathematics achievement has been a tool for investigating the effectiveness of mathematics education. More importantly, in almost every study information other than achievement results has been gathered, both to provide a context for those results and to provide at least some basis for understanding factors affecting mathematics teaching and learning. While achievement comparisons may be useful for those who set policies concerning mathematics education, the related data have been more important for those pursuing mathematics education research.

While Husén was reporting the results from the first IEA mathematics study, and later reports of the second IEA mathematics study (SIMS) were published two decades later (McKnight, Crosswhite, Dossey, Kifer, Swafford, Travers and Cooney, 1987), the final achievement results from IEA's third mathematics study, the Third International Mathematics and Science Study (TIMSS), have just been released. Given TIMSS extensive scope and the time necessary for data analysis, results were reported in a series of three reports (Beaton, Mullis, Martin, Gonzalez, Kelly and Smith, 1996; Mullis, Martin, Beaton, Gonzalez, Kelly and Smith, 1997; Mullis, Martin, Beaton, Gonzalez, Kelly and Smith 1998).

Three populations were tested. Population 1 consisted of students in the two adjacent grade levels in each country that contained the most 9-year-olds. Population 2 consisted of students in the two adjacent grade levels in each country that contained the most 13-year-olds. Population 3 consisted of students in their final year of secondary school. Population 3 included both a representative sample of all students in their final year of secondary school and also a representative sample of those who were taking an advanced mathematics course containing calculus and who had studied mathematics in all secondary school years.

With the recent release of TIMSS results for students in their final year of secondary school (Mullis, Martin, Beaton, Gonzalez, Kelly and Smith, 1998), attention can now turn to understanding the patterns among achievements for participating countries and for the various student populations. As these patterns become more clear, they can be related to information about mathematics curricula, textbooks and teaching to seek the concomitants of mathematics achievement — results that at least suggest possible explanations for those patterns. Some of the TIMSS data on curricula, textbooks, teaching and other systemic factors have already been published (Schmidt, McKnight, Valverde, Houang and Wiley, 1997; Schmidt, McKnight, and Raizen, 1997; Schmidt, Jorde, Cogan, Barrier, Gonzalo, Moser, Shimizu, Sawada, Valverde McKnight, Prawat, Wiley, Raizen, Britton and Wolfe, 1996). Other of these data remains yet to be reported, and explanatory analyses have only just begun. This chapter takes a preliminary look at patterns in the achievement data and suggests something of what must be done to seek their explanations.

A Tale of Two 'Yields'

This investigation begins with the mathematics achievement results for students in their last year of secondary school (Mullis et al., 1998). The first relevant question is whether high achievement yields for specialist students (those taking advanced mathematics in their last year) is associated with high achievement yields for the general population of those finishing secondary school. Specialists were tested on specialist content — calculus, elementary functions, advanced algebra and geometry, and aspects of the real number system. General students (including a representative proportion of specialists) were tested for basic mathematics 'literacy' and general knowledge.

The relation of these two sets of results are important, both for those responsible for mathematics education policy and research. Each represents a kind of mathematics attainment 'yield' of educational systems. It is an open question whether both kinds of yields, general mathematics literacy and advanced mathematics accomplishments, can be attained by a (national or sub-national) education system. The TIMSS data hardly yield a definitive answer to this question but do offer suggestive evidence.

Participating countries could elect the parts of TIMSS in which they wished to participate (beyond providing basic systemic and curricular information). As

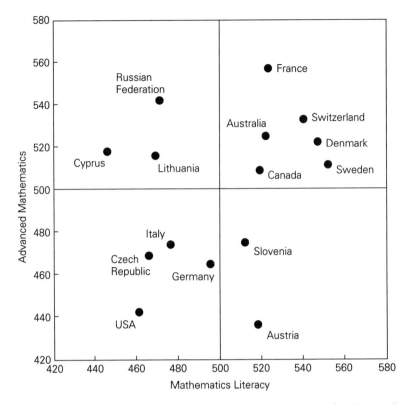

Figure 4.1: Mathematics literacy versus advanced mathematics results for 15 countries

a result, different sets of countries administered each of the four types of TIMSS mathematics achievement tests (Populations 1 and 2, Population 3 general, and Population 3 advanced) to their students. Twenty-one countries administered the mathematics 'literacy' tests to students in the last year of secondary school and 16 administered the advanced mathematics test. Fifteen countries administered both the mathematics literacy and advanced mathematics tests. Each test's results were scaled separately, and a score and international average reported for each test. The results are shown in Figure 4.1.

The actual numerical values of the scores (500, etc.) have no meaning except for establishing comparisons. The means of the participating countries differed slightly for the two tests (500 for the literacy test and 501 for advanced mathematics). The horizontal and vertical lines in Figure 4.1 mark the means of the advanced mathematics and literacy tests respectively. The actual distances between countries can be taken only as approximate, since the standard deviations for the two tests differed slightly. There were also some questions about the adequacy of the samples in certain cases (see Mullis et al., 1998) that are ignored here. Even with these limits, Figure 4.1 gives a reasonably accurate comparison of the two types of yields.

The mean lines divide this scatterplot into four quadrants. Each quadrant has a different substantive meaning (above average outcomes on both tests, above average advanced mathematics scores but below average literacy scores, etc.). First, note that there are points (countries) in all four quadrants with no obvious pattern in the scatterplot. This suggests that, for the set of 15 countries that administered both tests, relative standing on the two exams was relatively unrelated (r = 0.28). Second, the results for Australia, Canada, Denmark, France, Sweden and Switzerland (the 'high-high' quadrant) indicate that it is possible to have high comparative standing on both tests. Together these patterns suggest that it is possible to attain both high yields, but not particularly common (only one-third of the countries shown achieved twin high comparative standings).

This display suggests countries with approaches to mathematics education that might receive special attention. In particular, special attention should be paid to those countries that were extremes: France and Switzerland, which achieved comparatively high standings on both tests; the Russian Federation, which scored comparatively highly in advanced mathematics but much less so in literacy; Austria, which scored comparatively well in literacy but not advanced mathematics; and the United States, which scored comparatively poorly in both areas. Certainly the display also implies that explanations for the two types of yield should be investigated separately, at least initially.

A Closer Look at the Mathematics Literacy Scores

The results for the last year of secondary school are the third in a series of results. There were also previously reported results for Population 1 (9-year-olds), and Population 2 (13-year-olds) (Mullis et al., 1997 and Beaton et al., 1996 respectively). It is a reasonable conjecture that the attainments of these two earlier populations should have some predictive value for the mathematics literacy scores. In both Populations 1 and 2 all students still were required to take mathematics. The mathematics literacy results for the end of secondary school represented a mixture of levels of mathematics study in each country, since students differed among themselves and among countries in the grade at which they discontinued mathematics study (if they did). The two common denominator earlier populations represented measures of mathematics attainment that are likely to be representative of the prior, common attainments of those taking the literacy tests. However, they are separated from the literacy testing by four to eight additional years of mathematics study, schooling and maturation.

There are limits on how much predictive value should be expected for Population 3 literacy scores from Populations 1 and 2 results. TIMSS is not a longitudinal study. These are multiple cross-section measures of mathematics attainment. It is an assumption that the mathematics education and attainments of the Population 3 literacy sample tested were the same at ages 9 and

13 as those of the Populations 1 and 2 samples tested. Certainly broad similarities are to be expected. However, in a climate of world-wide reform and change in mathematics education, the fact that similar experiences and attainments are assumed, not empirically demonstrated, must be kept in mind.

Further, the achievement tests for each population were independent, and consisted of disparate items generally appropriate for the participating countries at each level but differing in their specific appropriateness for the mathematics curricula of each country. Achievement test scores, especially those scaled and reported at the most global level, aggregate these disparate items and are largely determined by whatever common factor underlies successful performance on the set of diverse items. Since these items also differ, not only among themselves but also in how appropriate they are to the curriculum for each country's students at each tested level, there is a trade-off between how global and aggregated the scores are and how sensitive they are to the curricular strengths and weaknesses of mathematics education in each country (see Schmidt and McKnight, 1995).

A Look at Trends

With these caveats in mind, what can we learn from the Population 1 and 2 results in comparison to the Population 3 literacy results? Populations 1 and 2 each include students from two adjacent grades. Attention here is limited to students in the upper of the two grades for each population (that is, for example, fourth and eighth grade in the United States and most other countries). There were again some concerns about the adequacy of the samples in some countries — these will be ignored for this preliminary survey but should be kept in mind in evaluating its results.

Only 12 of the 26 countries that administered the Population 1 test, and only 20 of the 41 countries that administered the Population 2 tests, also administered the literacy test. Of the 21 countries that administered the literacy test, only one (Italy) had neither Population 1 nor Population 2 results, although several did not have both. To examine the relation between the Population 1 and 2 scores and the literacy scores, attention must be restricted to those countries that had scores for at least one of the first two populations.

The full set of comparisons, even with the limits just described, shows a wide variety of trends among the three sets of test results. In fact, it is far clearer to represent the results in separate figures — those for which the trend was generally upward for all or part of the series, and those for which it was generally downward. Figure 4.2 shows the results for those with mostly improving levels of comparative achievement. Figure 4.3 shows the results for those with mostly declining levels of comparative achievement. The Netherlands, which showed an unusual pattern of decline from Population 1 to 2 but improvement from Population 2 to 3, is included in both figures.

The scores for each of the three tests were again independently scaled and had varying means. Further, the three tests also had somewhat differing

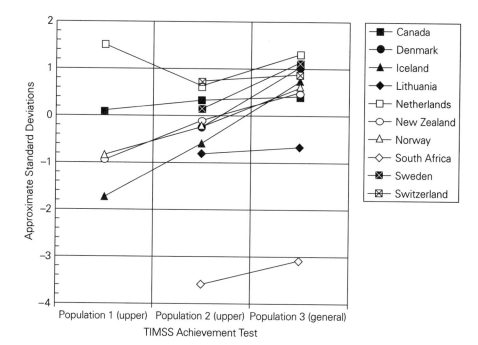

Figure 4.2: Countries with generally improving comparative scores from the upper grade of Population 1 to the upper grade of Population 2 to the general or literacy sample of Population 3

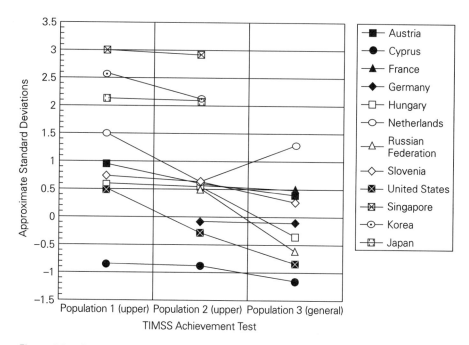

Figure 4.3: Countries with generally declining comparative scores from the upper grade of Population 1 to the upper grade of Population 2 to the general or literacy sample of Population 3

standard deviations. Since comparative attainments were to be examined across populations for each country, z-scores (score minus mean divided by standard deviation) were used rather than raw scaled scores. The standard deviations were approximated by using those for the countries included at each population. This is not the full set of countries, and thus not the standard deviation for all participating. The full range was not represented. While South Africa (which is shown) was generally the lowest scaled-score country, the higher scoring countries for the most part did not administer either the literacy or advanced Population 3 tests. For comparative purposes, the upper grade scores for Populations 1 and 2 for the three highest scoring countries (Singapore, Korea and Japan) are included in Figure 4.3.

Several things should be noted in comparing the data in these two displays. First, if one mentally superimposes the two figures, it can be seen that there is no clear pattern of general improvement or decline. There is enough variation in these trends to suggest that there is not a significant systematic relationship between the Population 1 and 2 scores and the Population 3 literacy scores. Some countries showed steady improvement in comparative standing while others showed steady declines.

Some Further Analyses of the Literacy Results

How do the trends of Figures 4.2 and 4.3 relate to the quadrants of Figure 4.1? All three countries with comparatively low standing on both Population 3 tests showed a pattern of declines. Figure 4.3 shows Germany and the US; the third country, the Czech Republic, maintained similar standing from Population 1 to Population 2 but dropped precipitously (almost two standard deviations) from Population 2 to the Population 3 literacy results. The pattern for Germany and the US suggest mathematics education arrangements that seem to create 'cumulative relative deficits' in general mathematics knowledge and literacy over the years. The Czech Republic's data suggest deficits in literacy more concentrated in secondary school. Of course, these results can only be interpreted by keeping in mind that these are multiple cross-sections, which may not be adequate substitutes for longitudinal assessment.

All of the 'high-high' countries show improving comparative standings. All but France and Australia are seen in Figure 4.2. France actually showed minimal changes in comparative standing across the populations; Australia showed only small changes, but compared slightly less favourably at Population 2 than at Populations 1 or 3 (literacy). The same education system arrangements that delivered comparatively high attainments in advanced mathematics also delivered improvements in something of a 'cumulative relative gains' model (although each country is compared at only three points) which suggests that one should not read too much into the term 'cumulative'.

The countries in the other two quadrants, with the exception of Lithuania, showed patterns of declines in comparative standings. The assumption of continuity and similarity in the multiple cross sections is, of course, particularly suspect in the case of Russia, Lithuania and Slovenia. To the extent that the data's pattern represents anything substantive, it suggests early mathematics education sufficiently strong in some cases (Slovenia, Austria) to leave comparatively above-average standings, but not in other cases (Russia, Cyprus). Of course, previous caveats must be kept in mind — for example, differences in how well the TIMSS tests matched the mathematics curricula of each of these countries.

Formally, the Population 2 and the literacy test scaled scores correlated fairly well ($r = 0.69$), as did the Population 1 and 2 results (0.92). There was almost no correlation between the Population 1 and the Population 3 literacy results. A simple linear regression model using the Population 2 results to explain the literacy results was significant ($p < 0.01$) and explained over 40 per cent of the variance in the literacy scores. The Population 1 results had no value in such a model. These results were, of course, based on a very small sample and on aggregate, scale scores and z-scores based on approximate standard deviations. Standard errors in the raw scale scores themselves were also not taken into account in this preliminary survey.

A Closer Look at the Advanced Mathematics Scores

The advanced mathematics results were also the third in a series of results. The same limitations of assumed continuity in multiple cross-sections, loss of curricular sensitivity through global scaling of disparate items, approximated standard deviations, and so on, hold as they did for the literacy results. The rationale for why the Populations 1 and 2 results should lead to comparatively strong performance in advanced mathematics differs somewhat. Such a rationale must assume either that gains are cumulative over all the years of schooling leading from early arithmetic to calculus, that pre-secondary mathematics curricula are aimed at preparation for advanced mathematics, or that these curricula create a strong foundation on which secondary schools can build attainments in advanced mathematics.

Are any of these rationales consistent with also preparing for a generally high level of comparative mathematics literacy? If the items on the literacy test and the advanced mathematics test drew on common stores of mathematical knowledge, there should likely have been a more consistent correlation of the two yields than the data showed. What kind of mathematics education prepares for both? Some countries' approaches obviously do, since they had comparatively high scores in both; other countries did not show such consistency. This is clearly a matter for further analysis. For the moment, it suggests that a look be taken at how Population 1 and 2 results relate to Population 3 advanced mathematics, one similar to the preliminary survey already presented for the literacy results.

Another Look at Trends

With the on-going caveats in mind, what can we learn from the Population 1 and 2 results in comparison to the Population 3 advanced mathematics results? Attention here is again limited to students in the upper of the two grades for each population (that is, for example, fourth and eighth grade in the United States and most other countries). There were again some concerns about the adequacy of the samples in some countries — these will be ignored for this preliminary survey but should be kept in mind in evaluating its results.

Only 7 of the 26 countries that administered the Population 1 test, and only 14 of the 41 countries that administered the Population 2 tests, also administered the Population 3 advanced mathematics test. Of the 15 countries that administered the advanced mathematics test, one (Italy) had neither Population 1 or Population 2 results, while the other 14 had Population 2 results and 7 of these also had Population 1 results. To examine the relation between the Population 1 and 2 scores and the advanced mathematics scores, attention must be restricted to those countries that had scores for at least one of the first two populations. While scores from 14 countries are available to examine the relationship between Population 2 and advanced mathematics, the full series of three is available for only seven countries.

As before it is useful to divide the trend results into those countries with generally improving comparative status and those with generally declining status. Owing to the limited number of countries with Population 1 and advanced mathematics scores, the series will often have only two data points. Figure 4.4 shows the results for those with mostly improving levels of comparative achievement, while Figure 4.5 shows the results for those with mostly declining levels of comparative achievement. Singapore, Korea and Japan again are included to indicate something of the full range of scores, although they did not administer the advanced mathematics test just as they did not administer the literacy test. The results for both samples of Population 3 are thus more restricted than the samples for Populations 1 and 2, since the top-scoring countries for the earlier two populations did not take part in Population 3. Analysis here must therefore focus on comparative status rather than on absolute scores.

As before, the scores for each of the three tests were independently scaled and had varying means. They also had differing standard deviations. Even allowing for this limitation, since comparative attainments were to be examined across populations for each country, z-scores were used rather than raw scaled scores. As before the standard deviations were approximated by using those for the countries included at each population.

Several things again should be noted in comparing the data in these two displays. First, if one mentally superimposes the two figures, it can be seen that there is no clear pattern of general improvement or decline. There is enough variation in these trends to suggest that there is not a significant systematic relationship between the Population 1 and 2 scores and the Population 3

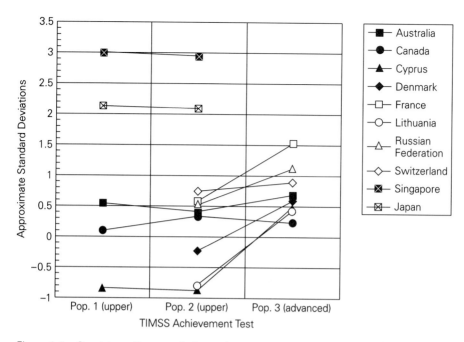

Figure 4.4: *Countries with generally improving comparative scores from the upper grade of Population 1 to the upper grade of Population 2 to the advanced mathematics sample of Population 3*

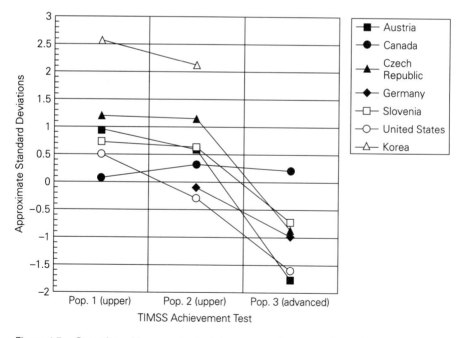

Figure 4.5: *Countries with generally declining comparative scores from the upper grade of Population 1 to the upper grade of Population 2 to the advanced mathematics sample of Population 3*

literacy scores. Some countries showed marked improvement in comparative standing while others showed marked declines.

Further Analyses of the Advanced Mathematics Results

How do the trends of Figures 4.4 and 4.5 relate to the quadrants of Figure 4.1? The pattern is quite clear in this case. All of the above-average countries for advanced mathematics showed improved comparative status, at least from Population 2 to Population 3, with the exception of Canada which showed little change in comparative status; Sweden's change was minimal. All of the below-average countries for advanced mathematics showed declines in comparative status. Thus improvements were paired with higher scores and declines with lower scores on advanced mathematics, regardless of the countries comparative performance on the Population 3 literacy test.

This pattern, although seen for a limited number of countries, suggests that high scores on advanced mathematics are strongly related to secondary mathematics, since virtually all comparatively high scores come after gains between Population 2 and the advanced mathematics tests. Assuming sufficient similarities to allow the multiple cross-section testing to stand as a surrogate for longitudinal testing, this places the key largely in secondary school. For some countries there was a gain between each pair of population tests, but that across secondary school was typically larger. The same can be said for the losses for countries that achieved less well in advanced mathematics. This suggests that mathematics education through the upper grade containing the largest proportion of 13-year-olds (roughly the eighth year of schooling) is mostly preparatory. The final positioning for comparatively-high or comparatively-low scores seems very likely to occur during mathematics study in secondary school.

Formally, the Population 1 and advanced mathematics test scaled scores correlated fairly well but negatively ($r = -0.62$). This seems to be an indication that, for the seven countries involved, high comparative scores on the Population 1 test were often associated with low comparative scores on the Population 3 advanced mathematics test. The significance of this result is limited by the small number of countries involved. Given what has already been noted about the consistency of increased status being associated with higher achievement, this may be nothing more than an artifact of having a comparatively-high initial score that allowed a decline. However, since there were no floor or ceiling effects on the scaled scores, this conjecture is far from certain.

Another interesting conjecture relates to test content. The Population 1 test focused heavily on arithmetic content and measurement. The Population 2 test continued to contain some of these topics, but included large proportions of geometry and algebra content as well. The advanced mathematics test focused on geometry, algebra (at least in the form of functions) and calculus. It may well have been that countries who did comparatively well on the arithmetic-oriented content of the Population 1 test continued to focus on that content, and were slower than other countries to move to geometry and algebra content that would serve as a better foundation for advanced mathematics. Evidence for this kind of conjecture must wait for more detailed linking of the TIMSS achievement results with its curricular content information. As stated earlier, the Population 1 and 2 results were strongly correlated ($r = 0.92$). This may suggest the persistence of arithmetic content into Population 2 or, perhaps more likely, the importance of an arithmetic foundation for successful work at the Population 2 level. This conjecture must also wait for more detailed curricular analysis.

Unlike the case for the literacy results, there was essentially a zero correlation ($r = -0.06$) between the Population 2 and the advanced mathematics scores. This is further evidence that the major concomitant of comparative success in advanced mathematics was mathematics work in secondary education. It appears that the first several grades (through Population 2) prepare the foundation for literacy attainments, even though these continue to change somewhat in secondary school, while secondary school serves as the primary locus for comparative success in advanced mathematics. Certainly these hypotheses are worth further exploration.

There was no simple linear regression model using the Population 1 or 2 results, or both, that helped explain the advanced mathematics results. No regression models even approached statistical significance. This is hardly surprising, given the very small number of data points and degrees of freedom for these models.

A Preliminary Closer Look at Mathematics Content

It has been suggested elsewhere (Schmidt and McKnight, 1995) that globally-scaled scores based on high-level aggregations of very disparate items at best measure only very general mathematics skills, and are thus essentially insensitive to curricular differences. Reports presenting further evidence of this suggestion are in press. In the meantime, it might be worth taking a closer look at content scores to see if, even at what is still a fairly global level, decreased aggregation can yield more curricularly related results.

The Population 3 advanced mathematics test contained a set of 17 real number and equation items that can be taken as a separate sub-test related to algebra content, and for which separate scaled scores were reported; a similar set of 23 items reflected geometry content. The Population 2 test had a similar separate set also of 23 geometry items, and an algebra set of 27 items for which separate scores were reported (as national average per cent of items correct rather than scaled scores). The Population 1 test had a 14-item geometry set with separate per cent correct scores reported but no algebra set. The Population 3 mathematics literacy test was not divided into separate subsets of items in the same way.

Sets of 14 to 27 items in areas as broad as geometry or algebra still involve aggregation of disparate items to get some measure of geometry or algebra skills that are still difficult to link to curriculum specifics. However, there are improvements over sets of 100 or more differing items. An examination of these category scores can allow a consideration of how well the topic-specific Population 1 and 2 scores are related to the topic-specific advanced mathematics scores and also to the more global advanced mathematics and literacy scores. Again what is presented here is only a preliminary survey.

The Geometry Strand

The three sets of geometry items may be considered a strand that relates specific aspects of the Populations 1, 2 and 3 (advanced mathematics) tests. The Populations 1 and 2 geometry sets can also be related to the overall scores for the Population 3 tests.

Advanced mathematics. Surprisingly, there is essentially no correlation between the z-scores for the Population 2 (upper grade) geometry results and those for the Population 3 advanced mathematics geometry items ($r = -0.03$). There is a mild but negative correlation between the Population 1 (upper grade) geometry results and those for advanced mathematics geometry ($r = -0.39$). Given the earlier conjecture, that comparatively higher scores at Population 1 may be related to fixating on more elementary content rather than moving on to more advanced content, this suggests that Population 1 geometry items may be substantively related to different mathematics skills and learning than the advanced mathematics geometry content. Further analyses are needed to know whether this supports the fixation hypothesis.

There is a modest positive correlation ($r = 0.53$) between the Populations 1 and 2 geometry results, suggesting some change of geometric substance mixed with some continuity and extension of previous geometry content. Both seem surprisingly irrelevant to the advanced mathematics geometry content. Unsurprisingly, no simple regression models yielded significant results. The Population 1 and 2 geometry scores correlated even less well with the full advanced mathematics scores ($r = -0.20$ and $r = -0.19$ respectively).

Mathematics literacy. There is no geometry sub-score for the Population 3 mathematics literacy test, but its overall scores can be related to the geometry scores for Populations 1 and 2. While there was a modest correlation between the Population 1 geometry scores and the literacy scores ($r = 0.19$), there was a modest but stronger negative correlation between the literacy scores and the Population 2 geometry scores ($r = -0.35$). As expected, no regression models yielded significant results.

One of the virtues of TIMSS, as will be discussed below, is that it collected a rich variety of curriculum and textbook information — especially for

Populations 1 and 2 and Population 3's advanced mathematics students. Even in this preliminary survey, it seemed worthwhile to examine whether some of these data were significantly related to the literacy results. Three variables were chosen here — the average age at which two-dimensional geometry was first studied in each country, the average age in which two-dimensional geometry was last studied, and the average grades devoted to studying a mathematics topic (geometry or otherwise, averaged across topics).

While none of these three factors related to the advanced mathematics total score or geometry score, the age at which two-dimensional geometry was begun and the average years per topic did correlate with the literacy scores ($r = -0.48$ and $r = +0.43$ respectively). Further, a simple linear regression model using the three factors yielded statistically significant results ($p < 0.025$). The three variables together accounted for almost 40 per cent of the variance in the literacy z-scores. Further, the regression coefficients for the year in which two-dimensional geometry study was begun and the average years per topic were significant ($p < 0.02$ and $p < 0.05$ respectively), while that for the latest average age at which two-dimensional geometry was studied was marginally significant (p approximately 0.10).

The coefficient for age when study was begun was negative, and that for average years per topic was positive. They suggested that for every year that study of two-dimensional geometry was delayed, the literacy results were about a quarter of a standard deviation lower. Similarly, they suggested that for every year longer spent on studying a typical mathematics topic, the literacy score was about a quarter of a standard deviation higher. For literacy (as opposed to advanced mathematics, for which there were no significant relations), studying geometry earlier seems to be linked to higher literacy results, as does spending longer on a typical mathematics topic. The data here are preliminary and approximate in some cases, but clearly the results are suggestive.

The Algebra Strand

The two sets of algebra items may also be considered a strand that relates specific aspects of the Populations 2 and 3 (advanced mathematics) tests. The Populations 2 and 3 algebra sets can also be related to the overall scores for the Population 3 tests.

Advanced mathematics. The Population 2 algebra item set was not significantly related to the Population 3 advanced mathematics algebra set ($r = -0.20$). As before, however, attention was turned to some simple curriculum variables. In this case, analyses explored the relation of the advanced mathematics algebra scores to the number of grades equations were studied, the age at which the earliest study of equations was begun, and the average number of grades devoted to study of a typical topic ($r = -0.19$, $+0.61$ and 0.11 respectively).

Although the score on the Population 2 algebra items was not significant, a simple regression model significantly related (p < 0.025) the other three variables to the national z-scores on the advanced mathematics algebra item set. The model accounted for about 60 per cent of the variance in those scores. All three variables had significant coefficients, and all were positive. Every additional grade equations studied were related to a national z-score about a quarter of a standard deviation higher. Every year that studying equations was delayed was related to a national z-score about 0.4 standard deviations higher. Every grade that was spent on additional study of topics in general (and not just equations specifically) was related to a score almost half a standard deviation higher.

This suggests quite a balancing act of devoting adequate time to the study of equations but not beginning such study too early. It is quite contrary to the findings for two-dimensional geometry and literacy. Again, these results are preliminary and approximate. If further analysis supports them, however, they will lead to several important questions for mathematics education. Is delay advisable for reasons of maturation? Is it related to curricular preparation through the mastery of prerequisite topics? If more definitive results are established, discussion of these questions may prove useful.

A similar pattern holds for the relation of these variables with the overall advanced mathematics scores. However, in a regression model, only the age of earliest study of equations remains significant (p < 0.05), accounting for about 30 per cent of the variance in overall scores. Again, delay of equation study (on average nationally) is related to slightly higher overall advanced mathematics scores, as was the case for national scores on the algebra item set of the advanced mathematics test. The other two variables do not significantly enter the picture for the overall test.

The similarity of the results for the overall advanced mathematics scores and the algebra scores is quite reasonable. The item sets (algebra and geometry) from the advanced mathematics set are highly correlated, and account for much of the variance in those overall scores. The algebra set is linked to the overall scores significantly in a regression model (p < 0.001) and accounts for about 80 per cent of the variance. The geometry item set is similarly significant in a regression model and accounts for almost 80 per cent of the variance used as a sole explanatory variable. The two item sets together account for over 90 per cent of the variance and are significantly related to the overall scores (p < 0.0001). The correlations of the algebra and geometry sets with the overall scores are 0.92 and 0.89 respectively. They also correlate highly (r = 0.73) with each other.

Mathematics literacy. The algebra item set for the Population 2 test and the related variables (grades equations are studied, average grades a typical topic is studied, and the age at which the study of equations is begun) are not significantly related to the national z-scores for the mathematics literacy test. The Population 2 algebra item set and the average grades a typical topic is studied are modestly correlated with the literacy scores (r = 0.32 and r = 0.43 respectively), but none of the variables is sufficiently related to the literacy scores to enter into a significant regression model. Geometry study, as discussed earlier, seems to have been far more relevant to the literacy results given these data.

Towards Truly Curricularly Sensitive Analyses

The preceding section was a quick sketch of the kinds of questions that may be raised by more carefully linked analyses of curricular and systemic mathematics education factors with less aggregated and more sensitive aspects of the TIMSS achievement results. This chapter has been a preliminary survey. Fortunately, the TIMSS data allow for far more than this and, more fortunately, these analyses are underway. TIMSS collected curriculum, textbook and teacher data from over 40 countries. It is these data, along with curricularly-sensitive achievement analyses linked to them, that hold considerable hope for using TIMSS data both to enlighten mathematics education policies and research.

Considerable time went into designing the resulting data collection methods, piloting them in a smaller set of countries, revising them, and giving them a field trial in most TIMSS countries. This process took almost two years, including documenting each method in usable manuals and conducting regional face-to-face training meetings. Curriculum data collection took more than another year. Analysis and reporting are on-going, and will take far more than two years. The resulting curriculum data are extremely rich sources for analyses, and will be so for years to come.

The final array of data collection procedures consisted of five separate methods. General topic-trace mapping was the method that documented — through expert opinion — which topics were covered in which grades, and whether they were the focus of special instructional attention. This provided essential longitudinal context. Expert questionnaires provided qualitative information on other key contextual issues for mathematics curricula — reform, past and proposed changes, incorporation of computational technology, and so on.

Curriculum guide analysis analyzed entire curriculum guides, but only at the grade levels at which TIMSS would conduct achievement testing. Textbook analysis also examined entire textbooks, but only at those same selected grade levels. In both of these cases, the full range of mathematics topics was included. Certain topics common to most of the TIMSS countries at the grade levels to be tested, and of particular interest, were designated in-depth topics. In-depth topic-trace mapping analyzed textbooks and curriculum guides, at all grade levels, to identify segments that dealt with each in-depth topic. An English-language summary description of each segment was provided, as well as country identification and labels of important content starting points and instructional milestones for these segments. Thus, for selected mathematics topics, document-based longitudinal data were obtained. Detailed descriptions of all methods exist in technical reports (McKnight and Britton, 1992;

McKnight, Valverde and Schmidt, 1992; McKnight, Britton, Valverde and Schmidt, 1992; and SMSO, 1993) and as background in volumes reporting mathematics curriculum analysis results (Schmidt, McKnight, Valverde, Houang and Wiley, 1997).

Before any of these methods could be developed, and to aid in TIMSS test development and linking the various components of TIMSS, a mathematics framework was developed. Detailed discussions of this framework (and its science counterpart) are available elsewhere (see McKnight, 1992; McKnight and Swafford, 1991; Robitaille, Schmidt, Raizen, McKnight, Britton, and Nicol, 1993; Schmidt et al., 1996; Schmidt, McKnight, Valverde, Houang and Wiley, 1997; and SMSO, 1992).

Essentially the mathematics framework consists of organized sets of categories for three aspects of curriculum documents — textbooks, questionnaires and tests. The first, content, deals with actual mathematics topics. An extensive topic list across the grades was rearranged into a smaller, more inclusive set of 44 topics. These 44 topics were grouped under one of 10 main mathematics categories (number, measurement and so on).

It was also considered important not only to capture what content students had opportunities to learn but what students were expected to be able to do with these contents. These are represented as performance expectations, a second set of categories. These specify about 25 specific kinds of tasks students can be expected to do with a mathematics content. They are grouped into five major categories (knowing, problem solving, reasoning, etc.). A third set of categories, perspectives, has yet to prove particularly useful.

Any test item, textbook segment or content-related questionnaire item can be identified (and coded) as involving one or more mathematical contents, one or more performance expectations and one or more perspectives. This complexity allows for complex characterizations of mathematics content, appropriate to more complex integrated content and multi-faceted demands on students that characterize many recent mathematics reform recommendations.

As a result of these methods, rich and detailed curriculum data are available for analyses of achievement outcomes. While some of these data have appeared elsewhere already (Schmidt, McKnight, Valverde, Houang and Wiley, 1997), others are forthcoming. It is hard to convey the flavour of the findings possible from these data, and their richness as a source of explanatory variables for achievement outcomes. Figures 4.6 and 4.7 show two typical kinds of results for a restricted set of countries.

Figure 4.6 shows how broad mathematical topics can be represented, while Figure 4.7 shows that more specific topics can also be represented. A variety of indices can be constructed from the data underlying these displays. They may be used to portray how focused textbooks are in each country and at each population; they may be used to investigate textbook attention to broad or specific topics or sets of topics that may relate to sets of items from achievement tests. These data deal only with mathematics content and do not include what performances are expected of students, a dimension richly captured

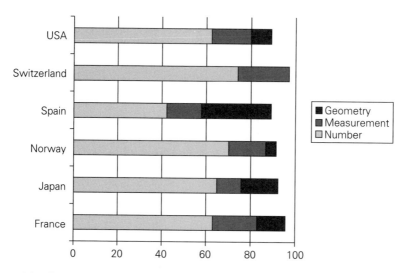

Figure 4.6:   Percentage of Population 1 mathematics textbooks devoted to three major topics in six selected countries

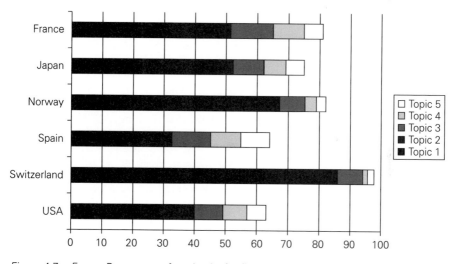

Figure 4.7:   Focus: Percentage of textbooks for five most emphasized topics for Population 2 mathematics in six selected countries

in the TIMSS data. They also focus only on textbooks — but data are also available for mathematics curricula and teacher reports of instructional practices, as well as far more textbook data.

This chapter was intended as a preliminary survey. It does reveal several suggestive aspects of the TIMSS achievement data. It also illustrates the kinds of questions these may raise for mathematics education researchers and policy-makers. However, as this last section has outlined, the TIMSS curriculum and context data are very rich and have great explanatory potential. Forthcoming analyses will seek to unlock some of this potential and to carry out achievement analyses and linkages with unprecedented sensitivity to mathematics curricula and the substantive questions of how best to conduct mathematics education. Comparatively soon, many of these data will also be made broadly available for others to analyze. The TIMSS data would seem to be a rich source of insight and insightful questions to involve mathematics education researchers for many years.

References

BEATON, A.E., MULLIS, I.V.S., MARTIN, M.O., GONZALEZ, E.J., KELLY, D.L. and SMITH, T.A. (1996) *Mathematics Achievement in the Middle School Years: IEA's Third International Mathematics and Science Study (TIMSS)*, Boston, MA: Boston College.

HUSÉN, T. (ed.) (1967) *International Study of Achievement in Mathematics. (Vols. I and II)*, New York: John Wiley and Sons.

MCKNIGHT, C.C., CROSSWHITE, F.J., DOSSEY, I.A., KIFER, E., SWAFFORD, J.O., TRAVERS, K.J. and COONEY, T.J. (1987) *The Underachieving Curriculum*, Champaign, IL: Stipes.

MCKNIGHT, C.C. (1992) *Explanatory Notes for the Mathematics Framework (SMSO Research Report 41)*, East Lansing, MI: Michigan State University.

MCKNIGHT, C.C. and BRITTON, E.D. (1992) *Training Manual for Document Analysis and In-depth Topic Trace Mapping for TIMSS Regional Training Meetings (SMSO Research Report 44)*, East Lansing, MI: Michigan State University.

MCKNIGHT, C.C. and SWAFFORD, J.A. (1991) *Mathematics Curriculum Framework, Draft 1 (SMSO Research Report 2)*, East Lansing, MI: Michigan State University.

MCKNIGHT, C.C., VALVERDE, G.A. and SCHMIDT, W.H. (1992) *In-depth Topic Trace Mapping, Draft 4 (SMSO Research Report 43)*, East Lansing, MI: Michigan State University.

MCKNIGHT, C.C., BRITTON, E.D., VALVERDE, G.A. and SCHMIDT, W.H. (1992) *Document Analysis Manual, Draft 4 (SMSO Research Report 42)*, East Lansing, MI: Michigan State University.

MULLIS, I.V.S., MARTIN, M.O., BEATON, A.E., GONZALEZ, E.J., KELLY, D.L. and SMITH, T.A. (1997) *Mathematics Achievement in the Primary School Years: IEA's Third International Mathematics and Science Study (TIMSS)*, Boston, MA: Boston College.

MULLIS, I.V.S., MARTIN, M.O., BEATON, A.E., GONZALEZ, E.J., KELLY, D.L. and SMITH, T.A. (1998) *Mathematics and Science Achievement in the Final Year of Secondary School: IEA's Third International Mathematics and Science Study (TIMSS)*, Boston, MA: Boston College.

ROBITAILLE, D.F., SCHMIDT, W.H., RAIZEN, S., MCKNIGHT, C., BRITTON, E. and NICOL, C. (1993) *Curriculum Frameworks for Mathematics and Science*, Vancouver, BC: Pacific Educational Press.

SCHMIDT, W.H. and MCKNIGHT, C.C. (1995) 'Surveying educational opportunity in mathematics and science: An international perspective', *Educational Evaluation and Policy Analysis*, **17**(3), pp. 337–53.

SCHMIDT, W.H., MCKNIGHT, C.C. and RAIZEN, S. (1997) *A Splintered Vision: An Investigation of US Science and Mathematics Education*, Dordrecht, Boston, London: Kluwer Academic Publishers.

SCHMIDT, W.H., MCKNIGHT, C.C., VALVERDE, G.A., HOUANG, R.T. and WILEY, D.E. (1997) *Many Visions, Many Aims: A Cross-national Investigation of Curricular Intentions in School Mathematics*, Dordrecht, Boston, London: Kluwer Academic Publishers.

SCHMIDT, W.H., JORDE, D., COGAN, L.S., BARRIER, E., GONZALO, I., MOSER, U., SHIMIZU, Y., SAWADA, T., VALVERDE, G., MCKNIGHT, C., PRAWAT, R., WILEY, D.E., RAIZEN, S., BRITTON, E.D. and WOLFE, R.G. (1996) *Characterizing Pedagogical Flow: An Investigation of Mathematics and Science Teaching in Six Countries*, Dordrecht, Boston, London: Kluwer Academic Publishers.

SURVEY OF MATHEMATICS AND SCIENCE OPPORTUNITY (SMSO) (1992) *Mathematics Curriculum Framework, Draft 4 (SMSO Research Report 38)*, East Lansing, MI: Michigan State University.

SURVEY OF MATHEMATICS AND SCIENCE OPPORTUNITY (SMSO) (1993) *TIMSS Curriculum Analysis: A Content Analytic Approach (SMSO Research Report 57)*, East Lansing, MI: Michigan State University.

5 An Examination of Instructional Practices in Six Countries

Leland S. Cogan and William H. Schmidt

A multi-national research team conducted observations in the mathematics and science classrooms of 9 and 13-year old students to inform the development of survey instruments to be used in the Third International Mathematics and Science Study. The research team employed an iterative, discourse methodology in analysing the classroom observations made in each of the participating countries of France, Japan, Norway, Spain, Switzerland and the United States. A consensus emerged that there appeared to be typical patterns of instructional and learning activities in each country's set of observations. These typical patterns appeared to result from the interaction of curriculum and pedagogy. The group coined the term Characteristic Pedagogical Flow (CPF) to refer to these typical patterns which is presented as an extended hypothesis for further investigation and elucidation. Differences in mathematics lessons from the six countries illustrate the key aspects of the CPF concept. A brief description of the CPF for each country's mathematics lessons is presented, and the origin of this concept is explained, illustrated and situated within the context of the larger conceptual model of educational opportunities.

Introduction

Around the world, classrooms are common sites in which a common goal is pursued — the development of new understandings and competences in students that will equip them for new and important roles in society. Instructional practices refer to those classroom goals and activities designed to achieve this end — they are the factors most proximally related to the learning that occurs there. This chapter presents the results of a study that examined classroom instructional practices in the course of developing survey instruments for use in a subsequent large scale, international survey of education. These classroom observations were conducted to obtain illustrations of typical classrooms from a range of countries in order to develop truly appropriate instruments for revealing cross-national distinctives and variation in education.

Since the characterizations presented in this chapter were an emergent product of a multi-national collaborative instrumentation development research group, they must be considered extended hypotheses for further investigation and validation. Accordingly, this first describes the research project that led to these characterizations. Second, the conceptual model the group developed to guide all its developmental activities is presented briefly. In the last part of the chapter, we present some of the issues that emerged from discussions of the cross-national differences found in the observed mathematics and science classrooms and introduce a new construct, characteristic pedagogical flow (CPF). Brief descriptions of the comparatively determined characteristics of each country's instruction are presented illustrating key aspects of CPF. We conclude by situating the CPF construct within the larger conceptual model of educational opportunity.

Project Description

The Survey of Mathematics and Science Opportunities (SMSO) was a small research and development project charged with developing the research instruments and procedures that would be used in the Third International Mathematics and Science Study (TIMSS). The TIMSS was the latest in a series of international comparative surveys of mathematics and science education sponsored by the International Association for the Evaluation of Educational Achievement (IEA).

Analyses from the IEA's Second International Science Study (SISS) and Second International Mathematics Study (SIMS) had identified curriculum and instructional practices as important explanatory factors in cross-national comparisons of student achievement — factors that were deserving of further, in-depth investigation (see, for example, McKnight, Crosswhite, Dossey, Kifer, Swafford, Travers and Cooney, 1987; Schmidt, 1992; Wiley, Schmidt and Wolfe, 1992; Wiley and Wolfe, 1992). Consequently, the goals of the SMSO project were to develop measurement approaches supporting a greater consideration of these areas. More specifically, the SMSO goals were to develop curriculum frameworks for mathematics and science, a methodology for an in-depth analysis of curriculum, improved measures of instructional practices and students' opportunity to learn specific curricular topics and survey instruments for schools, teachers and students that assessed important background factors related to students' opportunity to learn. In these development activities, the SMSO focused on 9 and 13-year-olds, the two younger TIMSS student populations.

For more than four years, a group of researchers from six countries worked together on the SMSO project, in a collaborative effort to identify and begin to understand the key elements of mathematics and science teaching and learning as it occurs in the classrooms of 9 and 13-year old students, and to incorporate this understanding into a comprehensive set of research instruments. The SMSO conducted a number of activities to inform and guide this process, which included interviews and surveys with experts and teachers, formal and informal instrument pilots and classroom observations. Conducting and analyzing these observations emerged as a defining part of the project. Observations were undertaken in order to uncover instructional practices that held promising potential to explain international variation in student achievement, and to clarify what occurs in classrooms as intended curriculum goals are transformed into potential learning experiences for students. From 1991 to 1993, over 120 classroom observations were made in the six SMSO countries — France, Japan, Norway, Spain, Switzerland and the United States — and native researchers from each country made classroom observations and wrote detailed summaries. In accord with the goal of obtaining illustrations of typical instructional practices in their country, native researchers were asked to observe a convenience sample of both mathematics and science classrooms. While all aspects of the project were informed to some degree by these observations, the survey instruments — the school, student and, particularly, the teacher questionnaires — were fundamentally influenced by the analyses and discussion of the observations.

Among the early products of the project were the Mathematics and Science Curriculum Frameworks and the Curriculum Analysis procedures. These frameworks, together with their relationship to classroom instruction, are more fully explained in Chapter 4 (see McKnight and Valverde). Several recent volumes have presented portraits of mathematics and science curricula across nearly 50 countries based on the detailed document analyses that employed these frameworks and analysis procedures (Schmidt, McKnight and Raizen, 1997; Schmidt, McKnight, Valverde, Houang and Wiley, 1997a; Schmidt, Raizen, Britton, Bianchi and Wolfe, 1997b). The SMSO also developed achievement test blueprints for TIMSS based on preliminary curriculum analysis data from several countries.

Conceptual Model

The relationship among the many SMSO products and the constructs imbedded in them is not transparent nor immediately obvious. SMSO began with the IEA's tripartite curricular model first explicated in SIMS (Travers and Westbury, 1989). This working model assumes that various factors influence the educational process at three different levels — system, classroom and student — and represents three faces or conceptions of curriculum — the *intended*, the *implemented* and the *attained*. Briefly stated, the *intended* curriculum refers to an educational system's goals and means, while the *implemented* curriculum refers to practices, activities and institutional arrangements within the educational context of schools and classrooms. The *attained* curriculum refers to the outcomes of schooling — what students have actually attained through their educational experiences (see, for example, Robitaille, Schmidt, Raizen, McKnight, Britton and Nicol, 1993 and Schmidt, Jorde, Cogan, Barrier, Gonzalo, Moser, Shimizu, Sawada, Valverde, McKnight, Prawat, Wiley, Raizen, Britton and Wolfe, 1996 for further discussions of the IEA model).

In the developmental process, these three curricular dimensions were crossed with the four research questions framing the TIMSS effort: what are students expected to learn, who delivers the instruction, how is instruction organized and what have students learned. This crossing of educational system levels with specific questions suggested areas for which measurements should be developed, but did not provide a particularly easy way for understanding how all these various pieces might fit together. What was needed was a coherent conceptual model illustrating the potential relationships among the factors of interest in a way that highlighted the importance of curriculum and the classroom, since the classroom is the educational focal point where curricular intentions are transformed into potential learning opportunities by teachers which may be realized by students in their own experiences.

The model of educational opportunity (Figure 5.1) lays out key aspects of the educational opportunities any system may provide to its students. The rows represent various levels of focus within a system, roughly corresponding to the IEA curricular dimensions, while the columns correspond to the four TIMSS research questions. These are essential questions to pose in any cross-national investigation of education and are useful organizers for briefly explaining the model.[1]

What Students are Expected to Learn

A description of students' possible learning experiences or what they have learned needs to begin with a consideration of the knowledge and skills students have been expected to attain. These goals and expectations are commonly determined and modified at three main levels of the educational system: the national or regional level, the school level and the classroom level. This first question encompasses not only defining the learning goals for a system or country as a whole but also differentiating them for any subdivisions within the larger system — regions, tracks, school types, grade levels and so on. These learning goals may be specified at any level in the model. Using the IEA curricular dimensions, the *intended* curriculum specifies these goals at the national or regional level while learning goals specified at the school or classroom level are part of the *implemented* curriculum.

Who Delivers the Instruction?

Students' learning experiences are undeniably moulded by the teachers who select, prepare and present a variety of instructional activities. Many structural factors influence the preparedness and approaches teachers bring to these tasks. Among these factors are a system's official teacher certification qualifications such as specific educational degree requirements, practical internship requirements, and types of licenses awarded including subject and grade level specifications. Other structural factors include how teachers' environments are organized to encourage or facilitate the accomplishment of professional

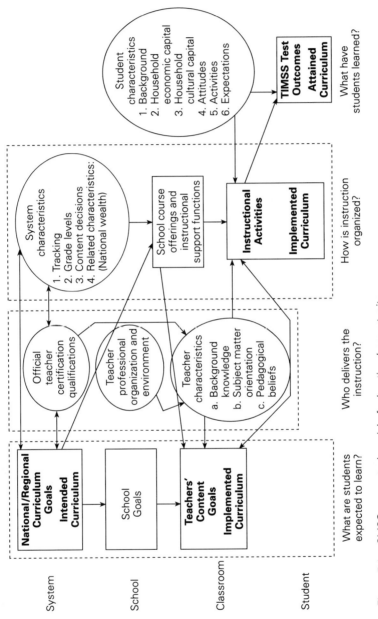

Figure 5.1: SMSO conceptual model of educational opportunity

activities such as individual and cooperative planning, the amount of time available for various types of planning, and specific course and subject matter assignments (Doyle, 1986; Lockhead, 1987).

Teacher characteristics such as their backgrounds and beliefs also influence instruction and thus the quality of students' educational experiences. Important background variables include a teacher's age, gender, education, subject taught and teaching experience. Teachers' beliefs about subject matter and subject matter-specific pedagogy also influence their instructional practices and student achievement (Peterson, 1990; Putnam, Heaton, Prawat and Remillard, 1992; Thompson, 1992).

How is the Instruction Organized?

The manner in which instruction is organized affects the implementation of curriculum and students' learning experiences. Decisions about this organization are widely distributed from the very top of the educational hierarchy to classroom teachers. Major organizational aspects include variations in the age–grade structure of educational systems, the collection and organization of grades within schools, and the various curricular tracks or streams into which students are placed (Oakes and Guiton, 1995). These decisions also include classroom instructional activities such as textbook usage, lesson structure, instructional materials, student assessment, teacher and student interaction, homework and in-class grouping of students. Economic resources influence all of these organizational decisions as well as teachers' qualifications, the array of instructional resources available to them, and the time and material resources available for students.

What have Students Learned?

Each student has unique characteristics that influence their learning beyond the influence of curriculum goals, teachers and instructional organization. These are, therefore, an important part of understanding what and how students learn. A few examples of these characteristics are listed in the model and include such important factors as students' academic histories, their self-concepts and how they use their time outside of school.

Discussion

Here we emphasize several important notions that informed and shaped the model. One was the idea that students' curricular experiences reflect the complexity of the educational system as a whole and are not merely functions of the individual and the individual's immediate learning environment. There are many factors that have an impact on education, even at the classroom and student level, which are systemic — stemming from the broader context of the education system and the specific cultural setting. An implication of this systemic view of education is that efforts to identify the effects of a single, isolated aspect of the system are likely to fail because of the extensive interrelated nature of education systems. In addition, the role and function of each system aspect may not be invariant across systems.

Another notion was the central role classrooms and teachers have in schooling and students' experiences. Embedded in the model is the backbone of curricula giving shape and definition to educational experiences. As teachers choose particular instructional topics, ignore or minimize others, and make many other decisions about how topics are presented and what students will be expected to do with these topics, teachers become the final arbiters of curricular intentions. In this sense, they serve as brokers or midwives of students' content-related learning experiences (Schmidt and McKnight, 1995; Schwille, Porter, Belli, Floden, Freeman, Knappen, Kuhs and Schmidt, 1983). The systemic view and the recognition of the dual importance of curriculum and teachers' instructional treatments of the curriculum embedded in the SMSO model presaged the development of an extended hypothesis regarding teachers' instructional practices in classrooms.

An Extended Hypothesis Concerning Instructional Practices

The SMSO research team employed an iterative, discourse methodology in analyzing the classroom observations made in each of the six countries. Team members read and discussed each observation, noting similarities and differences with instructional practices in their own countries. Questions were addressed to the native researchers who had made the classroom visits to clarify issues and to verify the accuracy of the developing perspectives and conjectures. As insights and conjectures were shared, discussed and refined, a consensus emerged regarding the existence of typical patterns. These typical patterns of instructional and learning activities did not appear to be simply the unfolding of a set of curriculum goals, documented in curriculum frameworks and textbooks, in parallel with a teacher's instructional activities and interactions with students. On the contrary, observations indicated that specific dimensions of the curriculum's content were interacting with aspects of classroom activity to yield specific lessons that differed qualitatively from one another.

The team coined the term 'characteristic pedagogical flow' (CPF) to refer to the recurrent patterns that were discerned across a set of classroom lessons. These were described as 'characteristic' because they were believed to stem from a constellation of perspectives on students, teaching, learning and subject matter that most likely stemmed from shared experiences and values embedded in the professional training and development of teachers. These patterns were 'pedagogical' because the observable part of this phenomena consisted of pedagogical strategies and approaches. Finally, the term 'flow' was included because these patterns did not appear to be consciously effortful but rather flowed as teachers moved through familiar territory — familiar activities, topics and interactions with students (Csikszentmihalyi, 1990).

The conjecture reached by the SMSO team was that there were country-specific patterns, or country-specific CPFs, that stemmed from unique ways in which teachers' instructional practices and subject matter interacted to produce qualitatively different classroom experiences. The balance of this chapter illustrates some of these differences. CPF and the accompanying conclusions about the specific qualitative differences across SMSO countries should be viewed as a working hypothesis. As intriguing and inherently appealing as these ideas may be to many, they were developed from a somewhat limited collection of classroom observations and deserve and require further investigation.

Typical Pedagogical Patterns

As the SMSO research team focused upon the instructional practices evident in the observations, a major reorientation in conceptualization and methodology was prompted. The team reached the conclusion that the focus for cross-national studies of contextual factors behind student achievement should not be primarily on concepts that differ *quantitatively* or *distributionally* across countries, but rather on concepts that exhibit significant *qualitative* or *categorical* differences. This shift was necessitated because two key assumptions undergirding the initial instruments were rejected. First, the prototypes had assumed implicitly that certain common instructional practices would be found cross-nationally. Second, they assumed implicitly that differences in the frequency and timing of these practices would relate to differences in student achievement. However, early in discussions about classrooms, the very notion of common practices became suspect. Practices are embedded in complex task environments and thus vary qualitatively depending on many factors — including views of teaching and learning, articulation with other practices within and across lessons, how subject matter is defined and others.

The way in which students work in their seats during lessons provides an example. Inherent in the US sense of 'seatwork' is the idea that students work individually and independently on paper and pencil tasks with a minimum of teacher supervision. Seatwork is a time for students to do independent, individual practice or review without additional information or guidance from the teacher, even though some guidance may be occasionally provided. Although students in other countries independently worked on tasks it did not fit the US 'seatwork' concept.

In some lessons, as teachers developed a topic, they paused and assigned students a brief exercise or problem to work on immediately. Teachers would give students enough time to think through the problem, if not complete it, and then continue with their presentation incorporating any insights or difficulties students may have encountered with the problem into the teacher's topic development. This type of seatwork involves and motivates students during lesson development and serves as a kind of advance organizer for the content yet to be presented. It also provides teachers with some initial information about students' understanding.

Qualitative differences in pedagogical practices were also evident in lessons' instructional content — the way mathematics was represented, presented and utilized as a basis for teacher–student discussion during lessons. In classroom explanations, illustrations and discussions, mathematics topics may be represented and considered in ways that more or less closely relate to students' immediate or concrete experiences. Content presentation is more a function of lesson structure — how content is distributed within a lesson by teachers' choices of pedagogical strategies. Closely related to this is lesson discourse — or the manner in which students and teachers interact with each other and the lesson's content. A series of examples can both clarify these concepts and illustrate differences.

Differences in content representation may be seen in two geometry lessons for 13-year-olds. In a Swiss lesson, the teacher had students form a circle and then, with string, form the sides and diagonals of a series of polygons, noting for each the number of sides, corners and diagonals. Students then worked in small groups, to find a general rule that would describe the relationship among these numbers. In a French lesson the teacher had students evaluate the sizes of parts in several different figures. The students needed to draw on their knowledge of definitions and rules for how various parts of the geometric figures related. As students worked, it became apparent that the teacher had assigned impossible values to at least one part of each figure because the assigned values violated the rules of relationship among the figures' parts. Both lessons connected to student experiences but did so in very different ways.

Two lessons for 9-year-olds illustrate differences in content presentation which refers to the logic and coherence of a lesson. In one Japanese lesson, the teacher presented two sets of numbers, one an exact count of the previous day's attendance at soccer games and the other an estimate of the previous day's attendance at baseball games. The entire lesson consisted of discovering which method of rounding (by tens, hundreds, thousands, etc.) could be used with the soccer numbers to show that the previous day's soccer attendance was greater than the baseball attendance. In a US lesson, students practiced addition orally, practiced other arithmetic operations at the blackboard, reviewed telling time with a worksheet, and explored metric measurements by reading and answering questions from the student textbook. Both lessons employed a variety of activities but, in the first lesson, all were related to a single, central problem. In the second lesson, no central content focus existed.

Lesson discourse reveals the specific cognitive demands placed on students during a lesson. The thinking a student is required to do can be quite different depending on the type of question asked by a teacher or the nature of the an assignment's required tasks. Questions such as 'How many millimeters in a centimeter?' or asking students to respond to basic number fact prompts (six times four, two times three, etc.) require little thought. Simple retrieval from memory is all that is required or expected. In contrast to this is a Spanish lesson in which the teacher drew two pictures on the board, one containing ten flowers and the other containing six flowers, and then asked 'What is the difference between these two bunches of flowers?' The students were told to draw a copy of the two original flower bunches and a third representing the difference between the two bunches. The teacher's phrasing of a basic arithmetic operations problem reminded students that they could reason their way to a solution and use meaningful representations and associations in doing so.

Perspectives on Mathematics

Analyses of the SMSO observations suggested that not only is teaching an activity embedded in culture but, so is what is taught. It is likely that few people doubt that teaching language, history or civics is highly influenced by culture — countries are expected to have unique perspectives on these subjects. However, most people probably would expect school mathematics to be relatively unaffected by such cultural influences. Although some research has focused upon the effect of social and cultural settings on the development of mathematical concepts (see Saxe, 1988; Saxe, Guberman, and Gearhart, 1987), the idea that the mathematics encountered in school is essentially the same across countries is probably an idea many people may still hold. Few would expect, for example, a French or Norwegian dialect of mathematics. Mathematics, unlike culturally embedded subjects such as history and language, is often thought to be acultural. For example, many believe 'numeration is numeration' — the concept is the same across all contexts — but these common expectations are false.

Not only did instruction differ qualitatively among the SMSO countries but, in each, culture influenced mathematics teaching in a way that is comparable to the teaching of language and history. The implications of this go far beyond the commonplace notion that countries emphasize different elements in instruction — the idea that students do less homework in Japan, for instance, or that they are evaluated through rigorous, external examinations in France. The presence of qualitative differences in mathematics instruction across the six countries points in a different direction, suggesting that more complex factors than are typically assumed may lie behind instructional differences. Countries have developed their own ways of engaging students in the substance of mathematics.

These differences were observable in mathematics topic selection — those topics that were the focus of lessons, and in cognitive complexity — what students were expected to do as they studied these topics. In addition to differences in mathematics topic selection and cognitive expectations, differences

The types of solutions teachers use in teaching students how to solve specific types of problems are very important. **WHAT TYPE OF SOLUTION WOULD YOU SUGGEST TO STUDENTS AS ONE OF THE BETTER WAYS TO SOLVE EACH OF THE PROBLEMS BELOW?**

Please detail all the steps you would expect to see on a student paper.

A building that is 24 m high casts a shadow of 18 m. At the same time, a flagpole casts a shadow of 15 m. How high is the flagpole?

Solution Steps

Teacher A's Response
(In geometric problems we recommend a drawing.)

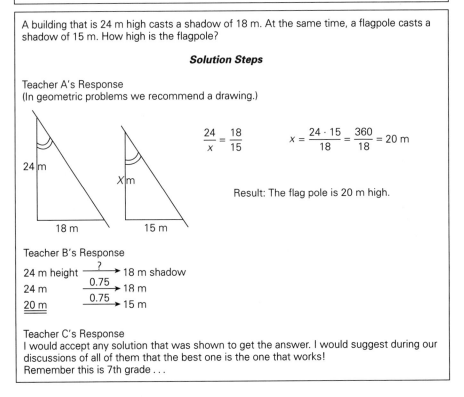

$$\frac{24}{x} = \frac{18}{15}$$

$$x = \frac{24 \cdot 15}{18} = \frac{360}{18} = 20 \text{ m}$$

Result: The flag pole is 20 m high.

Teacher B's Response

24 m height $\xrightarrow{\ \ ?\ \ }$ 18 m shadow

24 m $\xrightarrow{\ 0.75\ }$ 18 m

<u>20 m</u> $\xrightarrow{\ 0.75\ }$ 15 m

Teacher C's Response
I would accept any solution that was shown to get the answer. I would suggest during our discussions of all of them that the best one is the one that works! Remember this is 7th grade . . .

Figure 5.2: Three teachers' responses to an ideal student response item

in how mathematics topics are developed or sequenced have been documented through the detailed analyses of curricular documents that support classroom instruction (Schmidt et al., 1996; Schmidt et al., 1997a) suggesting that countries have different perspectives on what constitutes school mathematics. For example, in several Swiss lessons, 9-year old students were studying set theory and practicing classification schemes. In other countries, these topics were reserved for older students or were not included in the mathematics curriculum at all.

Convinced that these differences in perspectives and student expectations were important, the SMSO developed an item for the teacher questionnaire that asked teachers to write out what they would consider to be an exemplary response to a mathematics problem. The purpose was to document and characterize the different subject matter perspectives and approaches that were so striking from analyses of the classroom observations.

Figure 5.2 presents one such item from the piloted version of the teacher questionnaire, along with the responses of three teachers from three SMSO countries. Each teacher approached the problem in a different manner — one geometrically, one through a more informal or *ad hoc* approach, and one in a more pragmatic manner that may be indicative of a more procedural orientation. In any case, the different perspectives on mathematics illustrated by these teachers' responses would most probably lead to different types of student understanding and, later, differences in students' achievement.

Country-specific Interactions of Mathematics and Pedagogy

The preceding discussion highlighted some of the differences found among SMSO countries in lesson pedagogy or instruction and in the perspectives on mathematics apparent in their lessons. The previously introduced concept of CPF was defined as the interaction of these two elements — subject matter and pedagogy — in an inextricable manner. Not too surprisingly, countries' different approaches to mathematics and pedagogy interacted to yield qualitatively different lessons.

The next section presents brief characterizations of each SMSO country's CPF. Team members did not set out to create such country level descriptions. These grew out of the comments and observations non-native researchers had concerning each country's set of classroom observations. Initial characterizations were refined according the informed perspective of native researchers — often the same individuals who had conducted the lesson observations — and thus represent a consensus characterization. In addition, these descriptions are the result of a comparative analysis. What non-native researchers considered to be characteristic of a particular country's instruction was determined to a great extent by the character and nature of the observations from other countries. Thus while these descriptions might not be equally applicable to every mathematics lesson within any one country, the descriptions identify comparatively determined important aspects of mathematics lessons that contribute to a characteristic national approach.

SMSO Country CPF Descriptions

The French lessons were characterized by formal and complex subject matter that teachers actively organized and presented to students. More specifically, mathematics topics appeared more advanced than was typical in most of the other SMSO countries. Additionally, there was an emphasis on formal definitions, laws and principles, together with the expectation that students would engage in theoretical reasoning and problem solving. Blackboards frequently contained outlines of topics being considered that might span over several lessons. Included in the blackboard information were technical vocabulary, mathematical formulas and theorems. Within each lesson segment — review, exposition or development, and application — discussion was based on explorations and applications as well as mathematical theorems and principles. An illustration of this comes from an application lesson on exponents for which students were to have made up problems involving exponents. When one problem required changing meters into millimeters, the teacher took the opportunity to remind the students of the recently studied principle that when $a \neq 0$, $\dfrac{a^n}{a^m} = a^{n-m}$.

The Japanese lessons were characterized as built around a consideration of multiple approaches to carefully chosen practical examples or activities, through which the teacher led students into an understanding of mathematical concepts and relationships. For example, one lesson began by the teacher asking students to explore how many different ways 17 could be obtained on the calculator screen by using only the 5, +, −, ÷ and × keys. In another lesson the teacher introduced a new fraction form and had students work at their seats to devise ways of solving the problem. After students have worked on this, the teacher had several students present their solutions to the class. The complexity of the subject matter was due primarily to the way that the mathematics topics appeared to be carefully developed and sequenced throughout the curriculum, as well as to the relatively focused and coherent manner in which they were developed within lessons. Each lesson appeared focused on a single major concept. Topics were generally developed through subtly directed class discussions interspersed with periods for individual or small group reflection or practice.

Lessons from Norway were characterized by student activity, both individually and in small groups. Through teacher-prepared or selected activities students were expected to come to understand basic information and facts. This was evident in the relatively large amount of time students spent working on teacher-constructed worksheets or problem sets from the textbook and the rather brief periods on which teachers addressed comments to the entire class. What students were expected to do was central to the uniqueness of these lessons, emphasizing procedures and processes — performing operations in mathematics. During lessons students worked independently or in a small group much of the time with teachers available as needed. Such independent practice or exploration times tended to be longer, fewer and less integrated into the teacher's explanation of the lesson than in either France or Japan. An illustration comes from one seventh-grade lesson that began with the teacher addressing the whole class with review questions. After this, the teacher referred to the work plan for the week and had students work individually or in pairs for the remaining two-thirds of the lesson. Consistent with the cognitive emphasis found in textbooks (Schmidt et al., 1997a; Schmidt et al., 1997b), much of the discussion in lessons involved explanations about the learning activities and of basic facts and vocabulary (Schmidt et al., 1996).

Lessons from Spain were characterized by the teacher introducing formal and complex subject matter to students. Similar to lessons in France, the complexity of the subject matter stemmed from the topics selected, the emphasis on formal definitions, laws and principles, and the theoretical reasoning and problem solving expected of students. One of the more salient features of the lessons from Spain was the consistent linking teachers made between the principles being studies and their practical, real-life applications. In one third-grade class the teacher had students pretend to be bankers and used money to explore place value, examining the relationships between 1, 10 and 100 peseta coins and a 1000 peseta note. Unlike France, textbooks played an important role for both teachers and students in lesson topic development. In several lessons students read aloud from the textbook to introduce or review key concepts or definitions. Review of previously covered topics, especially as related to students' homework, occurred at a relatively conceptual level and played a significant role in the conceptual development and overall structure of lessons.

The Swiss lessons were characterized by students' exploration and investigation of mathematics through learning activities and teacher demonstrations. Similar to Norway, there was an emphasis on students' responsibility for their own learning. Many lessons mentioned a work plan the teacher had developed for students to follow over a period of one or two weeks. Students were expected to work on their own and to develop an understanding of mathematics facts through the specific learning activities the teacher had prepared. There was comparatively greater diversity in what students were expected to do than in some of the other countries. This impression was enhanced by the 'weekly plan' many teachers used. The weekly plan outlined topics and exercises that students were to complete, but students were allowed to choose the specific lesson they would work on during any particular class time. Textbooks, however, showed a preponderant emphasis on students' knowing, using and understanding information (Schmidt et al., 1996). Consistent with this emphasis, teachers often asked students for their observations, conjectures or conclusions during lesson development.

Lessons from the US were characterized by teachers presenting information and directing student activities and exercises. The multiplicity and diversity of both topics and activities was a unique feature of US lessons. Both teacher and student activity tended to emphasize the basic definitions and procedures of mathematics. For example, in one lesson when students were not getting homework problems correct, the teacher read the definition of proportionality from the textbook and reminded them of the necessary steps to solve proportionality problems. Consistent with the cognitive emphasis found in textbooks, the preponderance of lesson discussion involved information about procedures, exercises and basic facts (Schmidt et al., 1996). Content complexity in lessons stemmed from an emphasis on knowing technical vocabulary and definitions. Periods of independent student practice or application were common and appeared to function in a manner similar to that found in the Norwegian lessons. Such periods contributed to a low content visibility in some lessons such as those in which the teacher had students work on problems in their textbooks or on worksheets without any substantive discussion. These characterizations seem to have held despite a greater variability and diversity among the US lessons than among those from any other country.

Summary — CPF Dimensions

As the concluding comment about the US lessons illustrates, every country has diverse instructional practices within its classrooms — even when comparing classrooms for the same grade and subject matter — and these differences are never inconsequential. Nevertheless, intra-country similarities were so great compared to inter-country differences that there appeared to be culturally distinct and nationally characteristic patterns in which curriculum and pedagogy intertwined within classrooms — a *characteristic pedagogical flow* (CPF). These differences reflected, at least in part, particular stances toward pedagogy and classroom activity that were expressed in certain recurrent patterns. What has been highlighted by the preceding country-level description is a characteristic interaction between curriculum and pedagogy in lessons. Presumably, this interaction stems from certain national beliefs together with the particular training and experience teachers have had that lead them to share these beliefs.

The two important aspects of CPF — subject matter and instruction — are intimately related to the educational opportunity model introduced earlier. This relationship is made clear in Figure 5.3. The double-headed arrow between the implemented curriculum box (containing teachers' content learning goals) and the implemented curriculum box (containing teachers' instructional practices) may now be labeled CPF. We have claimed that the interplay between these two classroom factors gives rise to qualitatively different classroom lessons.

Differences in lessons' content — topic selection and emphasis, topic sequencing and cognitive expectations — contribute to these qualitative differences across countries. In addition, the way in which instructional content is represented, presented and discussed in student–teacher interactions equally contributes to these differences. CPF — the interaction of content and instruction — has been presented as an extended hypothesis having some empirical support yet requiring further investigation. It is our intent, along with our SMSO colleagues, to explore this concept more fully with TIMSS data. Whether the TIMSS instrumentation has been sensitive enough to capture all the subtleties of CPF remains to be seen. Nonetheless, the dimensions of CPF are important aspects of schooling that cannot be inconsequential to the quality of students' learning. They are important aspects to be considered in any comparative study of mathematics.

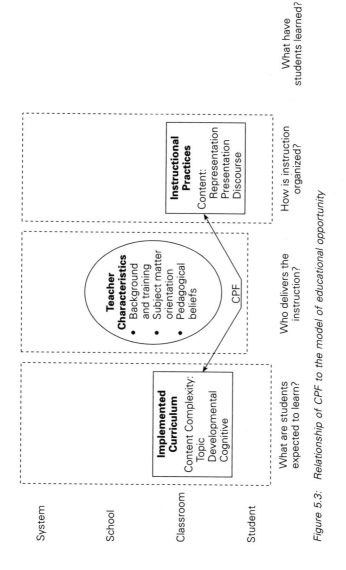

Figure 5.3: Relationship of CPF to the model of educational opportunity

Note

1 More extensive discussions of the model may be found in *Survey of Mathematics and Science Opportunities*, 1993; Schmidt and McKnight, 1995; Schmidt et al., 1996.

References

CSIKSZENTMIHALYI, M. (1990) *Flow: The Psychology of Optimal Experience*, New York: Harper and Row.

DOYLE, W. (1986) 'Classroom organization and management', in WITTROCK, M.C. (ed.) *Handbook of Research on Teaching*, 3rd ed, New York: Macmillan, pp. 392–431.

LOCKHEAD, M.E. (1987) 'School and classroom effects on student learning gain: The case of Thailand', paper presented at the American Educational Research Association, Washington, DC.

MCKNIGHT, C.C., CROSSWHITE, F.J., DOSSEY, J.A., KIFER, E., SWAFFORD, J.O., TRAVERS, K.J. and COONEY, T.J. (1987) *The Underachieving Curriculum: Assessing US School Mathematics from an International Perspective*, Champaign, IL: Stipes Publishing Company.

OAKES, J. and GUITON, G. (1995) 'Matchmaking: The dynamics of high school tracking decisions', *American Educational Research Journal*, **32**, pp. 3–33.

PETERSON, P.L. (1990) 'Doing more in the same amount of time: Cathy Swift', *Educational Evaluation and Policy Analysis*, **12**, pp. 216–80.

PUTNAM, R.T., HEATON, R.M., PRAWAT, R.S. and REMILLARD, J. (1992) 'Teaching mathematics for understanding: Discussing case studies of four fifth-grade teachers', *The Elementary School Journal*, **93**, pp. 213–28.

ROBITAILLE, D.F., SCHMIDT, W.H., RAIZEN, S., MCKNIGHT, C., BRITTON, E. and NICOL, C. (1993) *Curriculum Frameworks for Mathematics and Science (TIMSS Monograph No. 1)*, Vancouver, Canada: Pacific Educational Press.

SAXE, G.B. (1988) 'Candy selling and math learning', *Educational Researcher*, **17**, pp. 14–21.

SAXE, G.B., GUBERMAN, S.R. and GEARHART, M. (1987) *Social Processes in Early Number Development*, Monographs of the Society for Research in Child Development, **52** (2, Serial No. 216).

SCHMIDT, W.H. (1992) 'The distribution of instructional time to mathematical content: One aspect of opportunity to learn', in BURSTEIN, L. (ed.) *The IEA Study of Mathematics III: Student Growth and Classroom Processes*, **3**, New York: Pergamon, pp. 129–45.

SCHMIDT, W.H. and COGAN, L.S. (1996) 'Development of the TIMSS Context Questionnaires', in MARTIN, M.O. and KELLY, D.L. (eds) *Third International Mathematics and Science Study: Technical Report*, **1**, Boston, MA: Boston College.

SCHMIDT, W.H. and MCKNIGHT, C.C. (1995) 'Surveying educational opportunity in mathematics and science: An international perspective', *Educational Evaluation and Policy Analysis*, **17**, pp. 337–53.

SCHMIDT, W.H., MCKNIGHT, C. and RAIZEN, S. (1997) *A Splintered Vision: An Investigation of US Science and Mathematics Education*, Dordrecht: Kluwer Academic Publishers.

SCHMIDT, W.H., MCKNIGHT, C., VALVERDE, G.A., HOUANG, R.T. and WILEY, D.E. (1997a) *Many Visions, Many Aims: A Cross-National Investigation of Curricular Intentions in School Mathematics*, Dordrecht: Kluwer Academic Publishers.

SCHMIDT, W.H., RAIZEN, S.A., BRITTON, E.D., BIANCHI, L.J. and WOLFE, R.G. (1997b) *Many Visions, Many Aims: A Cross-National Investigation of Curricular Intentions in School Science*, Dordrecht: Kluwer Academic Publishers.

SCHMIDT, W.H., JORDE, D., COGAN, L.S., BARRIER, E., GONZALO, I., MOSER, U., SHIMIZU, Y., SAWADA, T., VALVERDE, G., MCKNIGHT, C., PRAWAT, R., WILEY, D.E., RAIZEN, S., BRITTON, E.D. and WOLFE, R.G. (1996) *Characterizing Pedagogical Flow: An Investigation of Mathematics and Science Teaching in Six Countries*, Dordrecht: Kluwer Academic Publishers.

SCHWILLE, J., PORTER, A., BELLI, G., FLODEN, R., FREEMAN, D., KNAPPEN, L., KUHS, T. and SCHMIDT, W. (1983) 'Teachers as policy brokers in the content of elementary school mathematics', in SHULMAN, L.S. and SYKES, G. (eds) *Handbook of Teaching and Policy*, New York: Longman, pp. 370–91.

SURVEY OF MATHEMATICS AND SCIENCE OPPORTUNITIES (1993) *TIMSS: concepts, measurements and analyses (Research Report Series 56)*, East Lansing, MI: Michigan State University.

Thompson, A. (1992) 'Teachers' beliefs and conceptions: A synthesis of the research', in GROUWS, D.A. (ed.) *Handbook of Research on Mathematics Teaching and Learning*, New York: Macmillan, pp. 127–46.

TRAVERS, K.J. and WESTBURY, I. (1989) *The IEA study of mathematics I: analysis of mathematics curricula. (Vol. 1)*, Oxford, England: Pergamon Press.

WILEY, D.E., SCHMIDT, W.H. and WOLFE, R.E. (1992) 'The science curriculum and achievement', in POSTLETHWAITE, T.N. and WILEY, D.E. (eds) *The IEA Study of Science II: Science Achievement in Twenty-Three Countries*, New York: Pergamon, pp. 115–24.

WILEY, D.E. and WOLFE, R.E. (1992) 'Opportunity and achievement: What they tell us about curriculum', in POSTLETHWAITE, T.N. and WILEY, D.E. (eds) *The IEA Study of Science II: Science Achievement in Twenty-Three Countries*, New York: Pergamon, pp. 115–24.

6 Studying Mathematics Classrooms in Germany, Japan and the United States: Lessons from the TIMSS Videotape Study

Takako Kawanaka, James W. Stigler and James Hiebert

This chapter describes the video component of the Third International Mathematics and Science Study (TIMSS), which involved detailed analyses and comparisons of eighth-grade mathematics classrooms in three countries — Germany, Japan and the United States. It also describes the struggle that our research group experienced in attempting to analyse systematically a large number of videotaped lessons from three cultures. Observing classroom practices in other cultures provides us with opportunities to notice how we teach and learn mathematics, as well as how the members of other cultures teach and learn mathematics. The results of our videotape study have shown that mathematics is indeed taught and learned differently in Germany, Japan and the United States. The kind of mathematics studied, the way mathematical concepts and procedures are presented, the kind of work expected of students, the role of the teacher and the nature of classroom discourse are a few of the many differences we found across the three countries.

Introduction

Efforts to improve mathematics education should be based on a deep understanding of teaching and learning, but such a deep understanding is difficult to achieve because both teaching and learning are cultural activities (Gallimore, 1996). Over time, each culture has developed norms and expectations for teaching and learning that are passed along from one generation to next. Since these norms and expectations are so widely shared and so familiar, they become nearly invisible to members within a culture. When we observe classroom practices in other countries, these accepted and unquestioned cultural models are revealed.

In the following sections we present the video component of the Third International Mathematics and Science Study (TIMSS), which involved detailed analysis and comparison of eighth-grade mathematics classrooms in three countries — Germany, Japan and the United States. We first describe the background and goals of the study and discuss the advantage of using videotapes to study classroom processes. Next we describe our approach to the task of analysing systematically a large number of videotaped lessons from three cultures. Finally, we present some of our numerous findings that illustrate cross-cultural differences in classroom practices. A full description of the study can be found in Stigler, Gonzales, Kawanaka, Knoll and Serrano (1998).

Background and Goals of the Study

As planning commenced for the TIMSS, there was a great interest in being able to go beyond the cross-national achievement data to focus on the underlying processes that produce achievement. Classroom processes were seen as a likely important cause of student learning. For this reason, the National Center for Education Statistics funded two studies to complement the main TIMSS study — the comparative Case Study and the Videotape Study. The primary goal of the Videotape Classroom Study is to provide a rich source of information regarding what goes on inside eighth-grade mathematics classes in the three countries. Aside from this general goal, the study had three additional objectives.

- To develop objective observational measures of classroom instruction to serve as quantitative indicators at a national level of teaching practices in the three countries.
- To compare actual mathematics teaching methods in the US and the other countries with those recommended in current reform documents and with teachers' perceptions of those recommendations.
- To assess the feasibility of applying videotape methodology in future wider-scale national and international surveys of classroom instructional practices.

To achieve these goals, we faced a number of logistical and methodological challenges. How could we describe and measure classroom processes on a large-scale?

Seeking a Method to Study Classroom Processes

One approach to studying classroom processes on a large scale is to ask teachers on a questionnaire to describe their instructional practices. Although such a questionnaire had been administered as part of the *Second International Mathematics Study* (SIMS), there are problems with this approach. Even within the same culture, we lack shared meanings for the words we use to describe teaching. One teacher will call something 'problem solving' and her colleague next door will call the same thing a 'routine exercise'. The problem of no shared language is compounded in a cross-cultural questionnaire study — the responses are nearly impossible to interpret.

Another approach is to go into classrooms and observe actual lessons with a predeveloped coding scheme. Although the meanings of the categories may be more comparable across observers than across questionnaire respondents — assuming that observers are carefully trained — they still provide a view of the classroom that is narrowly relevant to the investigator's specific purpose. For this reason most data resulting from coding schemes applied by live observers are not of interest to researchers working from other theoretical perspectives or to anyone who wants a full description of teaching and learning in the classroom context.

We needed data that could be analyzed and re-analyzed objectively by researchers working from a variety of perspectives. The idea of using videotapes began to emerge, and the final decision was made to collect direct information on classroom processes by videotaping instructional practices.

Use of Video for Studying Classroom Processes

There are many advantages of using video as data. Unlike questionnaires, video data provide information about classroom processes that does not rely on a teacher's own descriptions. They allow us to view the events and interactions that occur during the lesson from multiple perspectives. Video data also allow for discovery of new ideas about teaching and learning, whereas questionnaires mainly provide us with the information that was elicited by questions.

When doing live observation in classrooms, an observer must have a coding scheme that has already been constructed based on some previous qualitative analyses. What takes place is that the observer implement the coding scheme in the classroom, followed by re-evaluation of previous qualitative analyses. With video data, on the other hand, it is possible to move much more quickly between the two modes of analysis. Once a code is applied, the researcher can go back and look more closely at the video segments that have been categorized as similar. This kind of focused observation makes it possible to see, for example, that the segments differ from each other in some significant way, and this difference may form the basis for a new code.

Classrooms are complex environments and instruction is a complex process. Live observers are necessarily limited in what they can observe, and this places constraints on the kinds of assessments they can do. When there is a striking incident in a classroom, an observer tends to focus on that particular incident and fails to pay attention to other aspects of the classroom practice. Video provides a way to overcome this problem — observers can code video in multiple passes, coding different dimensions of classroom process on each pass. They can code striking incidents, but they can go back and observe other things also.

One may wonder if the camera has an effect on what happens in the classroom. Will students and teachers behave as usual with the camera present? Will a teacher prepare a special lesson just for the occasion that is unrepresentative of his or her normal practices? This problem is, however, not unique to video studies. Questionnaires have the same potential for bias — teachers' questionnaire responses, as well as their behaviour, may be biased toward cultural norms. On the other hand, it may actually be easier to gauge the degree of bias in video studies than in questionnaire studies. Teachers who try to alter their behaviour for the videotaping will probably show some evidence that this is the case. Students, for example, may look puzzled or may not be able to follow routines that are clearly new for them. It also should be noted that changing the way a teacher teaches is notoriously difficult to do, as much of the literature on teacher development suggests. It is highly unlikely that teaching could be improved significantly simply by placing a camera in the room. On the other hand, teachers will obviously try to do an especially good job, and may do some extra preparation for a lesson that is to be videotaped. We may, therefore, see a somewhat idealized version of what the teacher normally does in the classroom. This bias can be minimized by telling the teachers explicitly that the goal of the study is to videotape a typical lesson.

Methods

Sampling

The scope of the present study was limited to one of the three grade levels studied in TIMSS (eighth grade), and to three of the 41 TIMSS countries (Germany, Japan and the United States). Germany and Japan were chosen because both are viewed as important economic competitors of the US; Japan is of special interest because it has repeatedly scored near the top in international comparisons of mathematics achievement.

To compare classroom processes across cultures we needed to be sure that the videotapes we analyzed were representative of instruction in each country. Fortunately, the main TIMSS sampling plan was highly sophisticated, and it was possible to construct the video sample as a random sub-sample of national probability samples. Our original plan was to videotape 100 classrooms from each country. In the end, this plan was achieved in Germany, but only 81 classrooms agreed to participate in the United States. The number was reduced to 50 in Japan because national curriculum and absence of tracking across schools make the variability between classrooms low, and the Japanese collaborators felt that videotaping 100 classrooms would cause burden but no gain.

We also wanted to be sure that our sample was representative of the entire school year. This was especially important in Japan, where a national curriculum leads to different topics being taught at different times of the year across the entire nation. Although we succeeded in videotaping evenly across the school year in the United States and Germany, we were somewhat less successful in Japan, where our sample was skewed toward geometry and away from algebra. For some analyses, therefore, we selected balanced sub-samples of algebra and geometry lessons in each country.

Procedure

Two main types of data were collected in the video study — videotapes and questionnaire responses. A primary purpose of the questionnaire was to get teachers' judgments of how typical the videotaped lesson was compared to what we would normally see in their classrooms. We also collected supplementary materials (such as copies of textbook pages or worksheets) deemed helpful for understanding the lesson.

Standardized procedures for camera use were developed, tested and revised, and videographers were trained. Only one camera was used in each classroom, and it focused on what an ideal student would be focusing on — usually the teacher. Each classroom was videotaped once, on a date convenient for the teacher. One complete lesson — as defined by the teacher — was videotaped in each classroom.

Teachers were initially contacted by a project coordinator in each country, who explained the goals of the study and scheduled the date and time for videotaping. Since teachers were informed when the taping was to take place, we knew they might attempt to prepare in some way for the event. In order to mitigate any bias that might be caused by their preparation, we gave teachers in each country a common set of instructions. We told teachers that our goal was to see what typically happens in the mathematics classrooms of their country — what they would have done had we not been videotaping. After taping, teachers filled out a questionnaire describing the goal of the lesson, its place within the current sequence of lessons, how typical the lesson was, whether they had used methods recommended by the reforms, and so on.

Once the videotapes of lessons were collected, they were sent to project headquarters in the US and were digitized and stored on CD-ROM (to increase durability and random access). All the lessons were translated and transcribed in English, and the transcripts were linked by time codes to the video in a multimedia database.

Analyzing the Data

In deciding what to code, we kept two goals in mind — code those aspects that relate to our developing construct of instructional quality, and define codes that would yield valid and informative descriptions of mathematics lessons across the three cultures. For the first goal, we sought ideas of what to code from the research on teaching and learning in mathematics and from reform documents. We wanted to code both the structural aspects and the processes of lessons. The dimensions of lesson we judged most important included:

- *The nature of the work environment:* How many students are in the class? Do they work in groups or individually? How are the desks arranged? Do they have access to books and other materials? Is the class interrupted frequently?

- *The nature of the work in which students are engaged:* How much time is devoted to skills, problem-solving, and deepening of conceptual understanding? How advanced is the curriculum? How coherent is the content across the lesson? What is the level of mathematics in which students are engaged?
- *The methods teachers use for engaging students in work:* How do teachers structure lessons? How do teachers set up for seatwork and how do they evaluate the products of seatwork? What is the teacher's role during seatwork? What kinds of discourse do teachers engage in during classwork? What kinds of performance expectations do teachers convey to students about the nature of mathematics?

For our second goal — which was to portray accurately instruction in Germany, Japan and the United States — we were concerned that our description of classrooms in Germany and Japan made sense from within those cultures and not just from the US point of view. We convened a team of six code developers, two from each country, and spent the summer of 1994 watching and discussing a small sample of preliminary tapes from each country.

Early Impressions

We noted earlier that teaching and learning are cultural activities. Cultural activities often have a routineness about them that ensures a degree of consistency and predictability. Lessons are the daily routine of teaching and learning and are often organized in a certain way that is commonly accepted in each culture. As we watched the field-test tapes, we began to see patterns that underlie lessons in the three countries. The differences in the patterns undoubtedly follow from different instructional goals, and are probably based on different assumptions about the nature of mathematics, the way in which students learn, and the appropriate role for the teacher.

The US lessons seemed to be organized around two phases — an acquisition phase and an application phase. In the acquisition phase, the teacher demonstrates or leads a discussion on how to solve a sample problem — the aim is to clarify the steps in the procedure so that students will be able to execute the same procedure on their own. In the application phase, students practice using the procedure by solving problems similar to the sample problem. During this seatwork time, the teacher circulates around the room, helping students who are having difficulty. The problems that are not completed by the end of the lesson are often assigned for homework.

The Japanese lessons seemed to follow a different script. The lesson tended to focus on one or sometimes two key problems. After reviewing the major point of the previous lesson and introducing the topic for today's lesson, the teacher presents the first problem. The problem is usually one that students do not know how to solve immediately, but for which they have learned some crucial concepts or procedures in their previous lessons. Students are asked to work on the problem for a specified number of minutes, using any method they want to use, and then to share their solutions. The teacher reviews and highlights one or two aspects of the students' solution methods or presents another solution method. Sometimes this cycle is repeated with another problem; at other times students practice the highlighted method or the teacher elaborates it further. Before the lesson ends, the teacher summarizes the major point for the day; homework is rarely assigned.

The German lessons seemed to follow a different script again. At the beginning of the lesson, the teacher presents a simple situation or concept on the board, which will be expanded through a series of question–response sequences, and leads a discussion to arrive at some general principle at the end of the lesson. For example, the teacher draws a triangle on the board, asks the students what kind of a triangle it is, what they know about its properties. The teacher asks many more questions and students contribute a great deal in verbal exchanges. In the end, they may arrive at the conditions of congruence or Pythagorean theorem. The characteristics of German style are that the teacher and students spent a lot of time elaborating on a particular topic, but the lesson goals are not always stated by the teacher at the beginning of the lesson and the summary of the major points of the lesson is not always provided at the end of the lesson.

The patterns we detected seemed to be typical, but we needed to have more than subjective impressions. How could we capture these patterns reliably and objectively?

Translating Impressions into Codes

As noted earlier, we had the impression that mathematics was taught and learned differently in the three counties. We wanted to translate these subjective impressions into objective codes that represent and quantify various dimensions of classroom processes. Categorizing complex cultural practices such as classroom processes is not an easy task, even within the same culture. The challenge for us was to develop categories that capture the aspects of classroom processes that help us understand mathematics teaching and learning at deeper level, and the categories had to be meaningful within each culture and yet applicable across the three cultures.

One of the most salient features of classroom processes is that there is a teacher and a group of students, and the teacher interacts with the students sometimes as a whole class and other times individually. We first thought distinguishing whole-class interaction, which we called *classwork*, from individual interaction, which we called *seatwork*, would be easy, but we found that this was not true. US teachers often talked to the whole class while the students were doing seatwork — the teacher repeats instructions, gives hints about the problems, makes announcements, and so forth. Usually the interactions last only for a short period of time, and most students do not stop working while the teacher is talking, but sometimes interaction lasts for a certain amount of time. It was simple to say that whenever the teacher was interacting with the whole class it was coded as classwork, and everything else was seatwork. However, this could give us as many as 50 classwork and 50 seatwork segments in some of the US lessons. We thought of identifying a shift between classwork and seatwork when an interaction lasts for a certain number of seconds, but the duration of time did not seem to be the most important criterion in characterizing the organization of interaction. When a teacher gives hints to the whole class while students are doing seatwork, the teacher's intention is not to stop seatwork and move to classwork. Likewise, when a teacher asks a question and waits for a while so that students can figure out the answer, the teacher's intention is not to shift from classwork to seatwork. We realized that teachers give clear enough signals to students that they know what they are supposed to be doing at any given moment. Our decision was to take into account teachers' intentions and identify the cues that signal classwork or seatwork. We found that this could be done reliably, once we defined those cues. The key to this was that a coder imagines himself or herself in the classroom as a student — if the students could assess the teacher's intention, so could the coder.

Another feature of classroom practice is that there are a variety of activities during a lesson that are organized and controlled by the teacher. Teachers in all three countries guide students to review previous lessons, check previously assigned homework, learn new concepts and procedures, work on example problems as a class or independently, share the results from seatwork, and so forth. However, we found out that there were enormous differences in how these activities were done. For example, after students had worked individually on solving some problems for a while, a Japanese teacher would ask several students to present their solution methods at the chalkboard or at their seats. The teacher and the rest of the class rarely interrupt the students' presentation, but a brief summary is often provided by the teacher after each student presentation. On the other hand, a German teacher would ask one student to go to the chalkboard and work on a problem and explain as he or she works on it. The teacher and the rest of the class constantly interact with the student at the board. A US teacher, after students had worked individually for a while, would elicit answers from the students by asking a series of questions, and the exchanges are mostly controlled by the teacher. The Japanese case is more student centered, the German case is more collaborative, and the US case is more teacher guided. Although they all occur after seatwork, one can argue that the activities are very different, and they are not quite comparable. However, if we label these three cases differently, we lose the basis for cross-cultural comparisons, which defeats one of our purposes for the study. After a tremendous amount of discussion, we finally decided to call the activity *sharing* when it occurs after seatwork, disregarding who is presenting the results and how the results are presented. In this way, we are able to go back and compare all the sharing segments, both within and between cultures, which will enable us to go beyond our belief about what supposed to occur after seatwork.

Another feature of classroom practices that we cannot ignore is the content. Teachers and students interact in certain ways, and engage in various activities, so that students acquire intended knowledge and skills. So our next task was to decide how to describe mathematical content of lessons. One of the well recognized facts is that students learn mathematics through problem solving — but what do we actually mean by problem solving? Both English and German language have the term *problem*, and the concepts are virtually the same. *Problem* can readily be translated into Japanese as *mondai*, and the general concept of the term is equivalent to those of *problem*. However, we were faced with a difficulty when we tried to define what constitutes a *problem* in a mathematics lesson in the three countries. For example, US teachers often distribute worksheets to students that contain a single task (for example, 'Solve a linear equation') and many situations (such as equations with different numerals). The example below shows one task and four situations.

---

1. Solve for x.
a. $3x = 9$ b. $2x + 5 = 11$ c. $5x - 3 = 22$ d. $x + 3x = 16$
e. $4x + 10 = 50$

German teachers, on the other hand, often assign a series of tasks starting with one simple situation at the beginning. The initial situation evolves and produces new situations. In the example below, there are seven tasks and four situations.

Teacher: Someone go to the blackboard and draw any triangle. (Task 1)

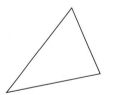

(Situation 1)

Teacher: Label the vertexes. (Task 2)

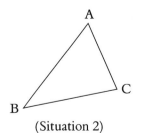

(Situation 2)

Teacher: Label the sides. (Task 3)

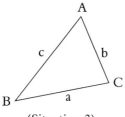

(Situation 3)

Teacher: Explain why which side is where. (Task 4)
Answer: It is always the opposite side to the vertexes.

Teacher: What is missing? (Task 5)
Answer: Angles.

Teacher: Fill them in. (Task 6)

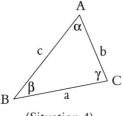

(Situation 4)

Teacher: Could somebody summarize why we use here capital letters, here lower case letters, here foreign letters? (Task 7)

Japanese teachers often present one situation and one task, which require students to invent solution methods rather than to simply apply routine procedures. The example below contains one situation and one task.

It has been one month since Ichiro's mother has entered the hospital. He has decided to pray with his younger brother at a local church every morning so that she will be well soon. There are 18 ten-cent coins in Ichiro's wallet and just 22 five-cent coins in his brother's wallet. They have decided to take one coin from each wallet and put them in the offertory box, and continue the prayer until either wallet becomes empty. One day after they were done with their prayer, when they looked into each others' wallet, the brother's amount of money was greater than Ichiro's.
How many days has it been since they started the praying?

We could say that there are four problems in the US example and one in the Japanese example, but are there seven problems in the German example because there are seven tasks, or four problems because there are four situations, or one problem because they are all related? After many lengthy discussions and repeated trials, we decided to do without the term *problem*, and code the content of lessons by identifying tasks and situations.

The dilemmas such as the ones we described above occurred constantly, and led us to have an extensive time — and energy — consuming discussion each time, but this struggle gave us an important lesson. That is, we could not take for granted any terminology to signify the same concept in different cultures, just because there is a translation in a dictionary. That schemas of every event or entity differ greatly across cultures was revealed when a multicultural group of observers attempted to generate categories together to capture various phenomena in the three countries.

By the fall of 1994, our initial coding system finally emerged. The system was refined regularly as the primary coding team began applying it to the actual study tapes, and as inter-coder reliability checks indicated that categories needed further definition.

Lesson Tables

As the coding process unfolded, we found it essential to construct an intermediate representation of each lesson, which we called lesson tables. These lesson tables were skeletons of each lesson that showed, on a time-indexed chart, how the lesson was organized through alternating segments of classwork and seatwork, what pedagogical activities were used (such as setting up for tasks, teacher demonstration), what tasks were presented and the solution strategies for the tasks that were offered by the teacher and by the students. Some categories could be coded directly from the tables, some required reviewing the tapes.

The table included the following information.

- *Organization of class* — each videotape was divided into three segments: pre-lesson activities (Pre-LA), lesson, and post-lesson activities (Post-LA). The lesson needed to be defined in this way because lesson would be the basic unit of analysis in the study.
- *Outside interruptions* — interruptions from outside the class that take up time during the lesson (such as announcements over the public address system) were marked on the tables.
- *Organization of interaction* — the lesson was divided into periods of classwork (CW), periods of seatwork (SW) and periods of mixed organization. Seatwork segments were characterized as being Individual (students working on their own, individually), Group or Mixed.
- *Activity segments* — each classwork and seatwork segment was further divided, exhaustively, into activity segments according to changes in pedagogical function. We defined four major categories of activities:

Setting Up, Working On, Sharing, and Teacher Talk/Demonstration (each of which were divided into subcategories).

- *Mathematical content of the lesson* — the mathematical content of the lesson was described in detail. Content was marked, for analytical purposes, into units which are noted on the table: Tasks, Situations, Principles/Properties/Definitions, Teacher Alternative Solution Methods (TASM) and Student Generated Solution Methods (SGSM). In addition, frames from the video were digitized and included in the table to help illustrate the flow and content of the lesson.

An example of what the tables looked like is shown in Figure 6.1, which represents part of a Japanese lesson in our sample. The table contains five columns. The first column indicates the time code at which each segment begins as well as the corresponding page number from the printed lesson transcript. The second column shows the segmentation of the lesson by organization of interaction and the third column shows the organization of activity. The fourth and fifth columns show the symbolic description of the content and the concrete description of the content, respectively. Rows with lines between them show segment boundaries. Seatwork segments are shaded gray.

As mentioned above, the tables served two functions. First, they were used by subsequent coders to get oriented to the contents of the videotapes. Often it takes a great deal of time for coders to figure out what is happening in a lesson. The tables ease the way, providing an overview of the structure and content of each lesson. Second, tables were used as objects of coding themselves. Some aspects of the lesson can be coded from the tables without even going back to the videotapes. Examples of such codes include TIMSS content category, nature of mathematical tasks and situations and changes in mathematical complexity over the course of the lesson.

Illustrative Results

Having developed categories for coding and analysis, we then applied these codes to the full sample of tapes. Unfortunately we can not possibly present all the results of our analyses in this chapter. Instead we present below the results of just a few indicators that illustrate the characteristics of mathematics education in the three countries.

Differences in the Kind of Mathematics

The first question that occurs to most people is probably whether the students in different parts of the world are learning the same level of mathematics. To answer this question, we were able to make use of the TIMSS curriculum analyses (Robitaille, McKnight, Schmidt, Britton, Raizen, and Nicol, 1993). The average grade level of topics covered in the video sample based on the

Topic: 1.3.2 Two-dimensional geometry: basics
Material: Chalkboard; worksheet

*PPD: Principles/Properties/Definitions

Page # (Time)	Organization of interaction	Description of activity	Symbolic description of content	Description of content
1 (00:09)	Pre-lesson activity			
1 (00:54)	Classwork	Setting up	Task 1 Situation 1	Find the angle in the bend with any method from the three problem-solving methods (previously presented). (Worksheet #1)
1 (02:33)	Seatwork: Individual	Working on tasks/situations/PPD		
2 (04:23)	Classwork	Sharing tasks/situations	Student generated solution method 1 Student generated solution method 2	

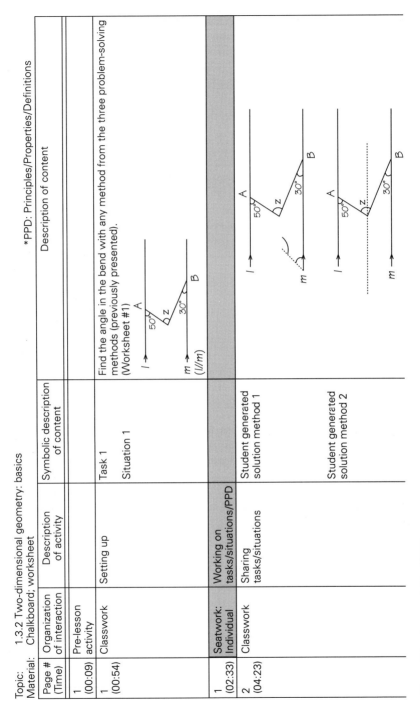

Figure 6.1: Lesson table JP007

Table 6.1: Average grade level of content by international standards

	Mean	SE
Germany	8.67	0.24
Japan	9.14	0.19
United States	7.41	0.29

curriculum analyses is shown in Table 6.1. By international standards, the mathematical content of US lessons was at a seventh-grade level, of German lessons was at the high eighth-grade level, and of Japanese lessons fell at ninth-grade level.

To see how advanced the mathematical contents of lessons are in a more concrete way, we coded a lesson as including a proof if an assumption was presented, a proof executed and the assumption confirmed as correct. The proof could be presented by the teacher, by a student or worked out collaboratively during classwork. As long as an assumption was presented and the strategy for proving it was discussed, it was still considered a proof, even if the proof was not executed. Likewise, if a proof was started but not completed due to running out of time in the lesson, we still coded the lesson as including a proof. The result was rather surprising. Ten percent of German lessons included proofs, while 53 per cent of Japanese lessons included proofs; none of the US lessons included proofs.

Differences in the Presentation of Mathematical Concepts and Procedures

Mathematical concepts and procedures can either be simply stated by the teacher or they can be developed through examples, demonstrations and discussions. We coded 'developed' if teachers made any attempt to motivate a procedure or explain why it worked. As shown in Figure 6.2, concepts and procedures were usually developed in German and Japanese lessons, but were usually just stated in US lessons.

Differences in the Work Expected of Students

What students were expected to do during seatwork differed across the three countries. Since it is not possible to know what students were doing during classwork, we coded the kinds of tasks students were assigned by the teacher to work on during seatwork. We coded tasks into three mutually exclusive categories.

- *Practice routine procedures* — this category was coded to describe tasks in which students were asked to apply known solution methods or procedures to the solution of routine problems.

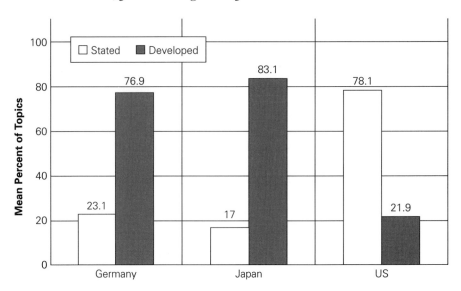

Figure 6.2: Average percentage of topics in each lesson that contained concepts that were developed vs. only stated

- *Invent new solutions/think* — this was coded to describe tasks in which students had to create or invent solution methods, proofs or procedures on their own or in which the main task was to think or reason.
- *Apply concepts in new situations* — this was coded whenever the seatwork task did not fall into one of the other two categories. The tasks coded into the category generally involved transferring a known concept or procedure into a new situation, hence the label.

The average percentage of seatwork time spent in each of the three kinds of tasks is shown in Figure 6.3. Clearly, this indicator differentiates Japan from both Germany and the United States. Japanese students spent less time practicing routine procedures and more time inventing new solutions or thinking about mathematical problems.

Differences in Discourse

We have shown above that eighth-grade mathematics lessons differ between Germany, Japan and the United States in the presentations of concepts and procedures, performance expectations, lesson designs and lesson scripts. Since classroom practices are carried out through the medium of language, we may expect differences in who talks what, when, how much and to what end. To analyze these differences, we coded the speech of teacher and students that were spoken publicly during the lesson in our samples into 12 mutually exclusive categories based on the speaker and the function in the interaction. The results indicated that there were both similarities and differences across the

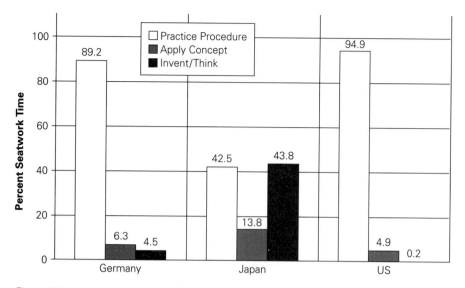

Figure 6.3: Average percentage of seatwork time spent in three kinds of tasks

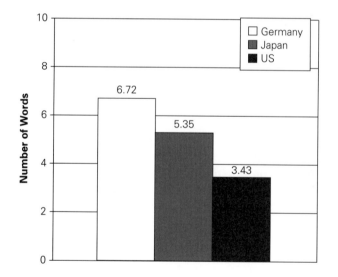

Figure 6.4: Average length of student responses as measured by number of words

three countries. In all three countries, classroom discourse was dominated by teacher. As shown in Figure 6.4, the most common type of student utterance was *response* in all three counties. German students responded more often than Japanese and US students, but when we compared the length of responses as measured by number of words, the difference between German and Japanese students was not significant. US students' responses were significantly shorter than those of German students (see Figure 6.4).

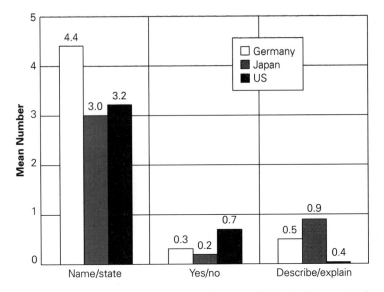

Figure 6.5: Average number of utterances (out of 30 sampled) coded into each of three categories of content elicitations

As we have just seen, students' opportunities to communicate mathematics are given by teacher questions in all three countries. We decided to see if there were differences in teachers' questions. We categorized teacher questions into three types, based on what teachers are asking students to do — to say yes or no, to name or state, and to describe or explain: yes/no questions request simple yes or no responses from students; name/state questions request relatively short responses, such as naming objects or stating a rule; describe/explain questions request relatively long responses, such as description of a mathematical object or explanation of solution method. As shown in Figure 6.5, US teachers asked significantly more yes/no questions than did Japanese teachers; German teachers asked significantly more name/state questions than did Japanese or US teachers; German and Japanese teachers asked significantly more describe/explain questions than did US teachers.

Not only did the teachers in the three countries ask different types of questions at different rates, they seemed to have different strategies in the use of questions during lessons. German teachers tended to ask questions to elicit information from students while they were developing concepts together by working out example problems. Japanese teachers tended to ask students to explain their own thinking methods after students had some time to work individually on a given problem. US teachers tended to ask questions to check if students knew mathematical rules and vocabulary, or if they were able to execute rules to produce correct answers.

Conclusion

The impressions about the characteristics of mathematics lessons in Germany, Japan and the US that all members of our research team shared in the summer of 1994 remain unchanged after we viewed more tapes from the main study data. After implementing extensive coding and analyses, our impressions were confirmed and reliably illustrated by numerous indicators. Mathematics is indeed taught and learned differently, and the roles of teachers and students are different across the three countries. We can now say this with confidence to any researcher or to any individual, and video data allow anyone to look at the videotapes to see if they see what we saw. We believe that there are many aspects of lessons that we could not analyze in our study, and we hope our data will be used and re-examined by people from various disciplines and interests.

It is tempting to conclude here that German and US teachers should teach more like Japanese teachers, given the high mathematics achievement of Japanese students. In fact there are some educators in the United States who believe that we should use particular indicators to improve our mathematics education. Although there probably are many ideas in the Japanese videos that could prove useful in the classrooms in other countries, systems of teaching are not easily transported from one culture into another. Teaching and learning, as cultural activities, fit within a variety of social, economic and political forces in our society. Every single aspect of mathematics education, from a particular teacher behaviour to national policy, must be considered and evaluated within a socio-cultural context. Another point we wish to make in conclusion to our study is that, in our efforts to improve mathematics education, our primary focus should always be on students' learning. It is far more important that our students will be given better opportunities to make sense of mathematics out of classroom instructions than simply to raise our ranking in international achievement tests.

References

GALLIMORE, R. (1996) 'Classrooms are just another cultural activity', in SPEECE, D.L. and KEOGH, B.K. (eds) *Research on Classroom Ecologies: Implications of Inclusion of Children with Learning Disabilities*, Hillsdale, NJ: Lawrence Erlbaum.

ROBITAILLE, D.F., McKNIGHT, C., SCHMIDT, W.H., BRITTON, E., RAIZEN, S. and NICOL, C. (1993) *Curriculum Frameworks for Mathematics and Science, TIMSS Monograph No. 1.* Vancouver, Canada: Pacific Educational, Press.

STIGLER, J.W., GONZALES, P., KAWANAKA, T., KNOLL, S. and SERRANO, A. (1998) *Methods and Findings of the TIMSS Videotape Classroom Study*, Washington, DC: US Government Printing Office.

US DEPARTMENT OF EDUCATION (1996) *Pursuing Excellence: A study of US Eighth-grade Mathematics and Science Teaching, Learning, Curriculum, and Achievement in International Context*, NCES 97–198, Washington, DC: US Government Printing Office.

7   The Case Study Project of TIMSS

Harold W. Stevenson

The Case Study Project was initiated to provide information that would be helpful in the interpretation of other quantitative data from TIMSS. Hundreds of interviews and conversations were held with teachers, parents, students, administrators and education policymakers in Germany, Japan and the United States. Observations were conducted in science and mathematics classes in grades 4, 8, and during the last year of high school. The information was entered into the computer (in English) and coded, using a software system developed for descriptive data. Four topics about which data were believed to be needed were the focus of the project: dealing with differences in students' ability, place of secondary school in students' lives, teacher training and working environments, and national standards.

Introduction

The publication of the Third International Study of Mathematics and Science (TIMSS) sponsored by the International Association for the Evaluation of Education Achievement (IEA) has aroused world-wide interest. Its size (it included 41 countries, a much larger number than had participated in the First and Second IEA International Studies of Mathematics and Science), and its breadth (it contained a much broader array of test and questionnaire items than had been used in the earlier studies) led the author of one of its reports to describe TIMSS as '. . . the largest, most comprehensive, and most rigorous international comparison of education ever undertaken' (Peak, 1996). In addition to its size and breadth, TIMSS differed from earlier studies in other important ways as well. Among the innovations were the analyses of the content of textbooks, videotaping of classrooms, hands-on tests of science and the inclusion of a Case Study Project, the aspect of TIMSS with which we are concerned here.

The Case Study Project of TIMSS was funded by the US Department of Education and involved three countries — the United States, Germany and Japan — which are often considered to be leading economic competitors. We hoped that the case studies would augment what is already known about the education systems in the three countries by providing detailed accounts of everyday practices and perceptions of students, parents, teachers and education authorities. Although equal attention was given to all three of the countries involved in the case studies, our focus was on those aspects of the situation in

Germany and Japan that would be most useful in understanding what is oc-curring in the United States during the elementary and secondary school years.

One of the primary goals of international comparative studies of achieve-ment has been to evaluate the level of achievement of students in various countries. An equally important goal is to attempt to understand the bases of the differences among countries in students' academic achievement. In an effort to provide information that would be helpful in interpreting the results, the organizers of TIMSS asked teachers, principals and students to respond to questionnaire items related to such matters as the mathematics curriculum, opportunities to learn and the use of devices such as calculators. Question-naires reveal useful information, but they are insufficient, both in their com-prehensiveness and depth, to offer appropriate opportunities for understanding more than a few of the possible interpretations of why students in some nations perform so well and students in other nations perform so poorly.

Questionnaires make it possible to gather quite cheaply large amounts of information from many persons, on a wide variety of topics. However, one of the problems with questionnaires is that respondents may provide answers that are difficult to interpret. Deprived of the opportunity to question the respondent about the meaning of certain responses, to probe for more com-plete answers, or to ascertain if the respondent understands the questions, the investigator can only conjecture about what the respondent might have meant. The personal interactions that occur in case studies offer opportunities to obtain more complete, comprehensible and interpretable answers.

Rationale for the TIMSS Case Study Project

Case studies — which involve observations, long conversations and interviews — are much more time-consuming, require more highly trained examiners, and are necessarily more expensive than are questionnaire studies. However, they do help us to understand the context and relationships which lie behind quantitative data. This advantage is especially important in studies involving international comparisons, for it is here that the need for bridging the perspect-ives of the outsider and the insider are most urgently needed.

The advantages of ethnographic studies have been summarized succinctly by the Board on International Comparative Studies in Education (Gilford, 1993:22).

> There is a great need for small, in-depth studies of local situations that would permit cross-cultural comparisons capable of identifying the myriad of causal variables that are not recognized in large-scale surveys. In fact, much survey data would remain difficult to interpret and explain without the deep under-standing of society that other kinds of studies provide. Given that research in cross-national contexts benefits from increased documentation of related con-textual information, it would be useful to combine large-scale surveys and qualitative methods.

In other words, studies can be planned so that a complementary relation exists between the results emanating from studies employing both quantitative and qualitative methods. Each method can benefit from the findings of the other.

Case studies were included in TIMSS in the hope that they would provide in-depth information about the beliefs, attitudes and practices of students, parents and teachers that would complement and amplify information obtained through the questionnaires used in the main TIMSS study. The case studies employed a methodology that relies on the interaction of experienced researchers with respondents and on observations made by the researchers during school hours and before and after school. Although the time required for such interactions and observations limits the number of persons with whom contacts can be made and of situations that can be observed, the rich descriptive information obtained by experienced interviewers and observers helps to isolate and clarify many of the factors underlying cross-national differences in academic achievement in mathematics and science.

Background Information

There is no reason to investigate topics about which a great deal is already known. The first step in designing a study such as the one undertaken was to conduct a thorough review of background information. To accomplish this task it was necessary to have access to up-to-date books and journals, but gaining this access did not prove to be an easy task. We were fortunate to be able to rely on colleagues in Germany and Japan to provide us with lists of current publications that they considered to be essential for inclusion in a contemporary review of the literature.

In addition to reviewing what had already been published, we consulted with leading researchers in each of the countries to obtain any additional information that they might have available. A volume has been written in which the results of these conversations and the bibliographic material are integrated (Stevenson, Lee and Nerison-Low, in press).

Collaboration

The Case Study Project was considered to be a collaborative venture between the United States, Japan and Germany from its inception. Representatives from Japan's National Institute for Educational Research, Germany's Max Planck Institute for Human Development and Education, and the National Center for Educational Statistics and the National Science Foundation in the US participated in all the major decisions concerning the conduct of the project.

From the beginning, the Case Study Project was considered to be a descriptive study employing a quasi-ethnographic methodology. It is termed a quasi-ethnographic study for several reasons. Although researchers spent several months in each country, were fluent in the language, and had participated in ethnographic research in the country they visited, they followed a semi-structured interview that focused attention on a series of predetermined topics rather than follow free-flowing interactions with participants from each country. Since a total of 17 persons served as researchers in the study, it was necessary to use this type of interview in order to standardize the work of multiple researchers — of these researchers, 8 were primary researchers who spent two or three months in the country, and 9 were part-time researchers who participated in the study for shorter periods of time.

Research Topics

The overall purposes of the study were clear — we were to gather and integrate information related to the correlates of academic achievement of elementary and secondary school students in Germany, Japan and the United States. Even with extensive involvement in the three cultures, it is impossible to cover all aspects of education. It became necessary, therefore, to limit the number of topics to which primary attention would be given.

The major criterion for selection of topics was that they be of interest to US policymakers who deal with elementary and secondary schooling. After extensive discussions, the topics ultimately chosen by the National Center for Education Statistics were national standards, teachers' training and working conditions, attitudes toward dealing with differences in ability and the place of school in adolescents' lives.

To understand these topics it is obviously necessary to have a good grasp of the organization of the education systems in each of the countries that were visited. Thus, in addition to covering the four topics mentioned above, we sought out policymakers and education administrators to obtain accurate descriptions of the structure of education in each country, including the organization of educational institutions, types of schools, student characteristics, school governance and funding, and characteristics of the school day and the school year.

Decisions also had to be made about the grade levels and types of schools that would be visited. Since the TIMSS study involved students at grades 3–4, 7–8, and at the end of schooling, we limited our case studies to grades 4, 8 and 12, close approximations to the grade levels included in the major TIMSS study.

The Locations

Regional differences within each country made it necessary for us to visit more than a single site within each country. We decided that visits to one primary and two secondary sites in each country would be sufficient to evaluate the degree to which we could generalize findings from the primary research site. In meetings with representatives from each country, we selected research sites that were as comparable as possible among countries in terms of factors such as size, geographic distribution and economic base. The sites were located in three different sections of each country: East, Central and West in the United States; East, Central and Southwest in Germany; and North, Central and South in Japan.

We selected schools at each site in consultation with local education authorities, and with reference to data about such characteristics of the school as size, level of student achievement, socio-economic status of the families and minority representation. We sampled the full range of primary and secondary schools, including successful, average and less successful schools. In selecting parents within each classroom we relied on school personnel, mainly the principal and teachers, to advise us about which families to approach in order to obtain representative parents and students for inclusion in our study.

Researchers

In doing comparative research involving other countries, researchers must not only have strong research skills but must also possess a high degree of facility in the language and a broad understanding of the culture they are studying. In this project, for example, we had to locate researchers who were fluent in German, Japanese or English, and who had previously conducted research in the country under study. They were also required to have a background in education or the social sciences, experience in qualitative research, and the time available to spend several months in residence at the research sites.

The full-time researchers in each country spent between two and three months at the major research site and were responsible for covering one of the four topic areas. As well as completing their research in the major research site, they spent shorter periods (sometimes only a few weeks) at one of the secondary research sites. Visits to the secondary research sites were necessarily shorter than those to the major sites, so researchers who made visits to the secondary sites had to cover more than a single topic and had a smaller number of contacts with students, parents, teachers and education authorities.

Major Topics

We began our discussions of the topics on which we were to focus our attention by considering the following general concerns about what should be covered.

National Standards

An understanding of the background and current status of education standards in Germany and Japan, and of reactions to the prospect of establishing national standards in the United States, should be especially helpful to policymakers concerned with this topic. In investigating education standards it is necessary to understand the type of standards set for students, the curriculum that reflects the standards, and the examinations used to evaluate the degree to which students meet these standards. Setting national standards is but the first step in a long process that involves other important issues — opportunities to learn, linguistic and cultural differences within a country, differences among children in the rate with which they learn, accommodating students who prove to be unable to attain the standards, and other issues that involve some of the most fundamental tenets of democratic societies in terms of equity.

Teachers' Training and Working Environment

One of the unfortunate reactions to the results of some international comparative studies is that teachers are often blamed when students fail to perform effectively. While the skill and knowledge of individual teachers are of obvious importance to students' academic achievement, such charges often fail to recognize the more fundamental reasons why teaching practices may sometimes be less than optimal. The social and financial support of teachers provided by a society has an important influence on who become teachers, who remain teachers and who are successful teachers. Societies differ in the degree to which teachers are esteemed and to which teaching is viewed as a critical profession for the society's welfare and progress.

A second aspect of the study of teachers concerns the improvement of instruction, by developing new instructional approaches and by helping teachers improve their classroom practices. Each of the countries is experimenting with different innovations in methods of instruction and, to varying degrees, with efforts to provide teachers with opportunities for developing more effective instructional practices. Included under this topic, therefore, are considerations of teachers' personal characteristics, their working environments, their education and in-service training, and the role of teachers' unions in teachers' daily lives.

Dealing with Differences in Students' Ability

Regardless of a society's philosophy about the contribution of ability and effort to students' academic achievement, every teacher must cope with the problem of meeting the needs of students representing a wide range of knowledge and skill. Schools in the United States respond to this problem at various times during the students' schooling by using learning groups, tracks and special programs. Japan separates students into learning groups only after entrance to high school, and prohibits any type of separation of elementary-school students into ability groups. After fourth grade in Germany, students branch out into three different tracks that have different career goals. Knowledge about the beliefs, attitudes and practices related to differences in ability among students provides a necessary background for understanding each country's education system.

Research questions dealing with this topic must start with a consideration of the philosophical perspectives held in each nation about the sources and means of handling individual differences. Three main approaches exist. The first involves tracking of students, the second focuses on remedial programmes and programmes for gifted students, and the third deals with how teachers respond to the differences that exist within every classroom in students' abilities, motivation, interests and backgrounds.

Place of Secondary School in Adolescents' Lives

Several approaches are required to evaluate the role of secondary school in adolescents' lives. Perhaps the most revealing way of addressing this question is to ask adolescents to estimate the time they spend on academic-related endeavours, to compare this with the time spent on non-academic activities and to describe in detail how they spend this time. Other approaches include assessing the actual practices in which students are engaged, the attitudes and values regarding education held by adolescents and their parents, the nature of parental involvement in their children's education and the extent to which the peer group in each society supports academic excellence.

The Research Method

Protocols

General descriptions such as those just summarized offered insufficient guidelines for researchers who were asked to focus their attention on the four topics. We realized that, even though interactions were to be relaxed and informal, it was necessary to provide more detailed descriptions of the areas that the researchers were expected to cover. Researchers were not instructed to follow any particular order in gaining information — they were expected to let the interactions flow naturally. The only requirement was that in the course of their interactions they obtained information about each of the topics.

It is important to emphasize that, in view of the paucity of our knowledge about these topics, it would have been premature to develop a project derived from an explicit set of hypotheses. Rather than defining the information we would seek, we assumed that hypotheses would be generated by our data — we did not attempt to test a particular set of hypotheses, the topics of primary concern had to be developed empirically.

When a case study involves only a single individual or a single setting it is difficult to evaluate the degree to which the results constitute a valid indication of what may exist beyond the individual setting. We believed it was necessary, therefore, not only to conduct the study in different locations within each country, but also to include different schools within each location. It was also necessary to seek the participation of a reasonably large number of persons within each location. Replication across individuals and across settings provides the basis for making claims of the applicability of explanations in both similar and dissimilar settings.

Each researcher was assigned one of the four topics of investigation and was responsible for two things — first, for conducting a minimum of roughly 80 encounters (meaning a total of 80 observations, interviews or conversations, each lasting an hour or more) and second, for providing weekly field notes that would be of interest and assistance to the other researchers and to the ultimate understanding of the situation in each site. The sampling procedure resulted in a minimum of 960 of these encounters, conducted over the equivalent of at least three full years of field work. The encounters included nearly 500 hours of interviews in Japan, over 500 hours in the US and over 350 hours in Germany. Transcriptions of these field notes and encounters filled thousands of pages of text. Supplementing the interviews and conversations were over 250 hours of observations of science and mathematics classes in the three countries.

Amounts of information as large as we gathered can be retrieved efficiently only through the use of computers — it would be nearly impossible otherwise to organize the content of interviews. Not only is the information more readily accessed, but the use of computers also makes it possible to establish trends with much greater confidence than if every statement required a new review of piles of field notes. Moreover, illustrating particular points by reference to especially vivid or characteristic examples can be accomplished much more readily through searches of computer files than by rereading many pages of original field notes.

Computer programs for the analysis of ethnographic data require that key words and concepts be tagged. To make retrieval possible, a list of tags was assigned to each topic prior to the beginning of field work. These lists were based on the items in the questionnaires and on the researchers' knowledge of the three cultures in which they would be working. Each list was developed by the field researchers assigned to investigate the same research topic. For example, field researchers dealing with parents' discussions of the role in school in adolescents' lives agreed upon approximately 16 tags for the material they were to cover. Other topics were supplied with 35 or more tags.

By retrieving information associated with the tags it was possible to assemble all of the researchers' notes about, for example, homework. We could then determine, among other things, the views of parents and teachers toward homework, and assess whether they were in accord with each other and with the views of students. We could compare the information about homework, gathered by researchers in the course of their interactions with the respondents, and establish the comparability of the information gathered by each researcher in their interviews with parents, teachers and students. In other words, it is possible through the use of the computer to review and organize an enormous number of written reports in ways that would otherwise be a hopelessly time-consuming task.

The Data

The plan from the beginning of the project was to obtain data that would be used not only for the immediate purposes of the TIMSS project but that would be available to other researchers for later analyses. As a result, we gathered vastly more information about each topic than could ever be summarized in a single chapter in the separate volumes that were planned for Japan, Germany and the United States. All identifying information concerning the schools visited and the persons interviewed has, of course, been deleted and pseudonyms have been substituted.

The data were not dependent upon later recollections of the researchers, for whenever possible the interactions were tape-recorded. In the case of the United States, the content of these tapes was entered directly into computer files. In Germany and Japan it was necessary to translate the content of the tapes so that they could be used by persons who were not fluent in German or Japanese.

Illustrative Findings

Although it is impossible here to present the wide array of findings described in the five volumes resulting from our study (described in Stevenson, Lee, and Nerison-Low, in press; and Stevenson and Nerison-Low, 1998), it is useful to provide some examples from each country of the types of information we obtained. These deal with factors that differentiate the educational systems and the practices, attitudes and beliefs of the participants in the education of primary and secondary students in the three countries. These comparisons reveal both remarkable commonalities and striking differences among the three countries in all aspects of education. The following examples are illustrative of the types of information obtained for each of the topics with which we were concerned.

Organization of Education

Public education in Japan consists of three levels — elementary, middle and high schools. Attendance at elementary and middle schools is compulsory. Although students are free to leave school after completing the ninth grade, over 97 per cent continue their education through the high-school years.

Beginning at age six, and ending four years later, German children are enroled in elementary school. In most states, students then transfer to one of three types of school that differ in the rigor of their curriculum: *Gymnasium*, for the most able students, *Realschule*, for students with average grades, and *Hauptschule*, for the least academically qualified students.

Students in the United States are expected to begin school by the age of six, and enrolment in most states is mandatory until the age of sixteen. There is no uniform configuration throughout the country in the organization of primary and secondary education.

Education Standards

Control by the Japanese Ministry of Education over education standards is exerted in several ways. The Ministry develops national curricular guidelines which define the education standards, but no effort is made in writing the curricular guidelines to define exactly what should be taught (the only exception concerns the Chinese characters (*kanji*) that are to be taught at each grade). Rather, the guidelines consist of general descriptions of what students are expected to accomplish during each year of schooling. The time and manner in which the material is presented are decided by the school administration or by the individual teacher. The Ministry of Education allows schools and local boards of education to modify national curricular guidelines in ways that are considered to be appropriate at the local level.

The German Conference of Ministers of Education is composed of representatives from each state, and is charged with overseeing the policies of all states within a framework of cultural sovereignty guaranteed by the German constitution. Through the Conference, the individual states coordinate the structures, institutions and school-leaving certificates of the education systems. The result is that Germany has developed a set of *de facto* national standards that form the basis for a degree of comparability across the states in the structure of schools, in the school-leaving examination, and in the credentials for certifying completion of school.

The United States government has created no mechanism at the federal level for developing and enforcing uniform standards of education throughout the country. State education standards include, in addition to content standards in core subjects, performance standards for students and standards related to students' opportunities to learn. Even as state guidelines and voluntary national standards have influenced school curricula, there has been a concurrent emphasis on the return of decision-making powers from the district to the school level.

Implementing the Curriculum

The major influence on the curriculum by the Japanese Ministry of Education is exerted through controlling the content of textbooks. The Ministry reviews all commercially produced textbooks in terms of their adherence to the curriculum guidelines and quality of presentation and must approve the books before they can be used. Teacher committees are then responsible for selecting textbooks from those approved by the Ministry.

Textbooks in Germany must conform to the state guidelines and must be approved by a state committee before they can be adopted by a state's schools. Grade-level committees often select the textbooks. Textbooks typically establish the content and organization of courses but, if a German teacher decides the textbooks are too difficult or otherwise unsatisfactory, the textbooks are used only for reference and the teacher develops separate course material.

Textbooks in the United States are published for the national market. Since there are no national guidelines, publishers have a wide degree of latitude to develop and market books which they believe will have the greatest sales. Even when a state does not make textbook recommendations, the textbooks selected by schools are often ones that incorporate topics covered in state assessment tests.

Homework

Some of the elementary schools in Japan explicitly forbid the assigning of homework. This does not mean that students are not expected to study. Rather than have the students complete homework assignments, it is expected that students will review the content of the past day's lesson and prepare for the next day's lesson. Parents and teachers believe studying is a very important aspect of the adolescent's development beyond the knowledge that it provides, for they also believe that it instills discipline, persistence and dedication — attributes admired by the Japanese.

According to teachers, *Realschule* and *Gymnasium* students are assigned homework every night, primarily to enable the teacher to evaluate how well the students understand their lessons. Students in *Gymnasium* reported spending the most time on homework, typically between two and three hours a day. In contrast, students in *Hauptschule* and *Realschule* said that their homework assignments ranged from 'none at all' to 'an hour at most'.

US teachers are given responsibility for deciding whether or not to assign homework. As a result there is wide diversity among schools, and even within schools, in the amount and frequency of homework that is assigned. According to our interviews and conversations, it is increasingly common in both middle schools and high schools that homework is done at school and simply represents work that teachers expect to be completed before the next class meeting.

Transition from High School to Work

Apprenticeships organized by the government or by schools are rare in Japan, and vocational high-school students usually gain work experiences through part-time jobs they arrange on their own. Even academic high-school students express a desire to find part-time employment during high-school. This symbolizes for them, as well as for the vocational high-school students, the independence to which Japanese adolescents aspire. However, their demanding schedules at school permit few students in academic high schools to have the time for any type of job.

Vocational apprenticeships are the most frequently attended form of upper-secondary education in Germany, with over three-quarters of German adolescents attending such a programme following graduation from one of the types of secondary school. During the two or three years of their apprenticeship, students spend one or two days a week at a vocational school attending classes, and work more than half-time as apprentices. German students can easily plot a course from school to work for any type of career, because of the ready availability of information about vocational decision-making.

Little is done in the American high schools we visited to prepare students for entry into the world of work. Students often lack information about careers, and are unaware of what is needed to achieve their career goals. For example, one student who wants to be a doctor regarded 'Decent grades — no Ds and no Fs' as the requirement for entering medical school. Most American adolescents must rely primarily on themselves in making a successful transition from school to work.

Becoming a Teacher

In Japan, those who want to be a teacher must take education courses and choose an academic area in which to specialize. During the four-year undergraduate programme, teachers-in-training visit schools, write lesson plans, and eventually spend from two to four weeks in closely supervised student teaching. Those who find a teaching position are assigned a mentor, a master teacher who is given a reduced teaching load for taking on these additional responsibilities. The mentor visits the new teacher's classroom frequently, and then discusses the strengths and weaknesses of the practices that were observed. The new teacher is also expected to visit a teachers' resource center a certain number of days each week.

Each of the 16 German states handles its own programme of teacher training, but the Conference of Ministers of Education from all German states establishes the fundamental requirements for becoming a teacher. After completing four or five years of university study, which includes several weeks of observation in a school, teachers-in-training must take the First State Examination. Those who pass the exam must complete a 24-month assignment as a student teacher. After completing the two-year period of practical training, teachers-in-training must pass the Second State Examination. They are then qualified to seek a regular teaching appointment.

The formal aspects of teacher training in the United States occur primarily in university classrooms. Individuals aspiring to become elementary school teachers typically enrol in a liberal arts programme for the first two years of their college training, and then transfer to a department or college of education to complete their undergraduate programme. Some complete a major or minor in the subjects they propose to teach, while others, especially those planning to become elementary school teachers, have only a minimal number of courses in the subjects for which they will be responsible. This is the most common path, but, as is the case in most aspects of the US education system, other paths are also available.

Teaching Practices

One teacher phrased the goal of Japanese teachers as 'Guiding students into being more fully developed human beings'. In pursuit of this goal, teachers in Japan seek to promote the students' academic progress and social development. Academic progress is fostered through an interactive style of whole-class teaching that seeks to involve all students; social development is promoted by providing students with ample opportunities for social interaction.

The goals of education in Germany depend on the type of school being discussed. Elementary school teachers are likely to subscribe to the belief that their job is to promote children's intellectual and social development. Secondary school teachers, in contrast, seek to provide students with the broad base of knowledge that is necessary to prepare them for future careers. Since the needs of students in the various types of schools differ, no single mode of teaching characterizes German educational practice, and all types of methods can be observed.

This is a time of great change in American education, a time when the public is engaged in a serious debate about the unique value of the general purpose elementary and secondary schools that have characterized American education in the past. Despite the questions being raised about education, most American students are still receiving whole-class instruction from a teacher who is in charge and who controls events in the classroom. Approaches in which students are engaged in cooperative learning or group learning experiences characterize the practices in some schools — as do individualized instruction, hands-on experiences and question-and-answer sessions — but the predominant mode of instruction is a sequence in which the teacher controls the interaction by asking questions, evaluating answers and frequently providing the explanation as well. Judging from the schools we visited, changes in the goals of education do not appear to have led to widespread changes in the teaching that goes on in most schools.

Ability Grouping

Japanese educators generally believe that grouping by ability within classrooms is discriminatory and may hurt students emotionally. When students are found to have trouble in keeping up with their classmates, teachers may spend time with the students outside of class or provide remedial homework assignments during the summer or winter vacations. Alternatively, students may choose to attend remedial *juku* (private school classes) that provide opportunities for review and practice related to the content of the textbooks used in the students' school.

German schools do not group students by level of ability within classes. It is a common practice to keep students and teachers together from first through fourth grade of elementary school. It is also a common practice in Japanese schools to keep the students and teachers together for more than a single year. In both countries the argument for this practice is that it enables teachers to know their students very well, and to be able to offer appropriate types of assistance before any problems become magnified.

In contrast to both Germany and Japan, no effort is usually made in American schools to keep a class, composed of students and teacher, together for more than a year. Two common responses to students of different levels of ability are the use of cooperative learning groups, where peer tutoring is possible, and the formation of subgroups of students who are taken out of the regular classroom to receive accelerated or remedial instruction in basic subjects.

Equity

An argument for equity in the Japanese school system was made by one of the students in a Japanese vocational high school, and shared by most of the other students we met.

> Those who are smart and those who are not smart study together in one class. No matter how smart or not, you can receive the same education, and this is true at any level of Japanese education — elementary, junior high, and high school. The education at this school is fair in the same way, and I think it's good (Stevenson, Lee and Nerison-Low, in press).

After the elementary school years the German school system is flexible, but upward mobility within the secondary level is less likely than lateral or downward mobility. Despite this, individuals we spoke to saw the separation of students into differentiated forms of schooling to be a way of providing an education that was appropriate for the students' capabilities and necessary for giving them the kinds of skills required to become productive members of society.

In general, the US education system supports the practice of tracking students by ability, and most parents with whom we spoke approved of the provision of instruction that parallels the student's levels of ability. Reservations were expressed about this practice, however, by parents who pointed out that narrow measures of ability, such as test scores, resulted in the over-representation of certain ethnic and racial minorities in the lower tracks.

Perception of Differences in Ability

Primary emphasis is given in Japan to the influence of effort on all forms of accomplishment. When a student has difficulty in school, Japanese parents and teachers typically attribute the problems to lack of effort or inadequate family support. Regarding children as diamonds in the rough, ready to be polished, various education agents must decide how much they would like to refine and strengthen the potential that is assumed to exist in every child.

In contrast to the Japanese focus on effort and hard work as paths to success, German respondents said the primary factors contributing to differences in academic ability were natural disposition (often referred to as innate intelligence and talent), the home environment and parental support. Parents and students also mentioned differences in innate ability as a primary factor contributing to differences in students' academic outcomes. It was normal, they explained, that not everyone could be good in all academic subjects.

Teachers, parents and students in the US readily acknowledged the existence of differences in academic ability among students, and often pointed out the magnitude and range of these differences. When asked to explain the basis of these differences, they cited family stability and family support as major factors. Socio-economic status also appeared to influence the respondents' beliefs about the role of innate ability — explanations focusing on innate ability occurred more frequently in affluent communities. Parents and teachers in poor communities seldom mentioned innate differences in intelligence or personality as major contributors to differences in academic ability.

Time Use

Japanese adolescents have a long school day. Arriving at school shortly after 0800, many leave at 1800 or even later in the evening. It is a mistake, however, to consider these long hours as reflecting time spent in academic courses. The daily schedule of classes departs no more than an hour from that found in many other countries, and it is in the after-school activities that the major differences arise. Japanese junior-high and high-school students are expected to participate in one of the school's clubs, and some Japanese students remain after school to study together or simply for social interaction.

School begins for German adolescents between 0730 and 0800, and lasts until 1300 or 1330; most students return home after this and eat lunch. During the school day, however, students in different types of schools do not have the same number of lessons. Depending on the state, the type of school and students' year in school, they may attend from 30 to 36 lessons per week. Few extra-curricular activities are organized by the school, and most teachers and students in schools other than the *Gymnasium* agreed that more extra-curricular activities should be offered, but they acknowledged that lack of financial and human resources seemed likely to make this impossible.

The length of the school day is much the same across the United States. Most adolescents described a formal school day of six or seven hours, typically from 0800 to 1430. Schools in affluent school districts offer the most extra-curricular activities, and the range is great — programs aimed at academic enrichment as well as at more traditional activities such as sports teams, musical groups and publication committees. In some inner city schools there were few after-school activities, primarily because of a lack of financial resources, but also because teachers and students were reluctant to stay after school in unsafe neighbourhoods.

Conclusions

The Case Study Project was a collaborative venture between the United States, Germany and Japan from its inception. As far as we can ascertain, the project is unique in that it involved systematically guided interviews, conversations and observations in three countries, and dealt with issues deemed to be of particular interest to policymakers and educators concerned with primary and secondary education.

Educational systems of different countries are embedded within the culture of that country. As a result of this close relationship, one cannot hope to learn how educational systems can be improved or academic achievement can be increased without understanding the actions, beliefs and attitudes related to education that exist within the culture. We tried to do this in the Case Study Project.

We sought to provide, through intensive study of four major topics within three cultures, a better idea of why students in some countries should fare better or worse in international comparisons of achievement in mathematics and science. We approached this goal by obtaining information about the daily lives of students, parents, teachers and policymakers, and by exploring their beliefs and attitudes about learning and development. We hope that some of the findings may be considered sufficiently reasonable and convincing to be considered as explanations; others may serve primarily as a fruitful source of hypotheses and suggestions for future exploration.

A fuller treatment of the information we obtained is included in four volumes (Stevenson, Lee and Nerison-Low, in press). There is one volume for each of the three countries, and the fourth describes the background of published research related to the four topics on which the study was focused. A fifth volume, *To Sum It Up* (Stevenson and Nerison-Low, 1998), is, as the title indicates, a summary and comparison of the major findings from the three countries. Information about ordering these volumes and about gaining access to the data can be obtained from the National Center for Education Statistics of the US Department of Education in Washington, DC.

I conclude from this comparative study that the Japanese, whose students' scores exceeded those of Germany and the United States in the mathematics and science tests of TIMSS, also demonstrate more of the positive attributes often considered to accompany high levels of academic achievement. Japan is characterized by the high standards and great importance it places on education, and by its highly involved parents, versatile and excellent teachers, and highly motivated students. Such conditions exist in some sections of the United States (especially in advantaged neighbourhoods) and in Germany (notably in many of the *Gymnasium*) but for the most part they appear to share fewer of the positive attributes involved in academic success evident in Japan.

Further investigation of the relevance of the information reached in our explorations will clarify the conditions that appear to result in successful achievement. The study of Singapore, Korea, Hong Kong and the Czech Republic — all high scorers on the TIMSS mathematics and science tests — would be especially informative. Case studies of particular schools or school systems in various countries that received the highest scores on the TIMSS tests would add further depth to our understanding of effective schooling. Both of these approaches would alert us to conditions that may be applicable to the widespread improvement of primary and secondary education.

References

GILFORD, D.M. (ed.) (1993) *A Collaborative Agenda for Improving International Comparative Studies in Education*, Washington, DC: National Research Council, National Academy Press.

PEAK, L. (1996) *Pursuing Excellence: A Study of US Eighth-grade Mathematics and Science Teaching, Learning, Curriculum, and Achievement in International Context*, Washington, DC: OERI, US Department of Education.

STEVENSON, H.W. and NERISON-LOW, R. (1998) *To Sum It Up*, Washington, DC: US Government Printing Office.

STEVENSON, H.W., LEE, S.Y. and NERISON-LOW, R. (eds) (In press) *Contemporary Research in the United States, Germany, and Japan on Four Education Issues: Standards in Education, the Role of School in Adolescents' Lives, Individual Differences Among Students, Teachers' Lives*, Washington, DC: OERI, US Department of Education.

8 Some Findings of the US–Japan Cross-cultural Research on Students' Problem-solving Behaviours

Jerry P. Becker, Toshio Sawada and Yoshinori Shimizu

This chapter presents descriptive data and results pertaining to the performance of Japanese and US students on certain problem-solving behaviours on four mathematics problems. The results are contrasted for the two national samples: Japanese students exhibit higher levels of mathematical sophistication in their problem-solving and a higher level of technical mathematical knowledge. Further, there is evidence that Japanese students are more able to solve a problem in more different ways than their US counterparts. Japanese students have a tendency to see mathematics as hard and feel that they are not good at it, whereas US students see it as easy and they like it. The results complement those of international comparisons and point to the potential of cross-national studies for improving instruction and learning in mathematics.

Procedures and Methodology in the Research

Background to the Research

This chapter reports on a project entitled US–Japan Cross-national Research on Students' Problem-solving Behaviours. The research had its origin in the US–Japan Seminar on Mathematical Problem-solving held at the East–West Center in Honolulu, Hawaii (Becker and Miwa, 1987). At the end of the seminar, future communication, exchange of materials and cross-national collaborative research were planned. Subsequently, the US group made visits to Japanese classrooms and observed numerous problem-solving lessons preliminary to conducting the research (Becker, Silver, Kantowski, Travers and Wilson, 1990). These visits and the related discussions set the stage for the research, which was further broadened and deepened by a visit to the US by the Japanese group, which made similar classroom visits followed by further discussions and planning.

The purpose of the study was to collect descriptive data pertaining to the performance of Japanese and US students on certain kinds of problem-solving behaviours. Contrasts in these behaviours between students in the two countries were also sought. The problems used in the study were as follows: marble arrangement — grade 4; matchsticks — grades 4 and 6; marble pattern — grades 6, 8 and 11; arithmogons — grades 8 and 11; area of squares — grade 11.

Grade Levels for Data Collection

The US and Japanese groups made decisions to collect problem-solving data at the 4th, 6th, 8th and 11th grade school levels. Data from several grade levels would provide a picture of students' performance on these behaviours over several grade levels, and would also provide a context for contrasting them. Problems were selected and administered as follows: one problem at the 4th grade only; one problem at both the 4th and 6th grades; one problem at the 6th and 8th (with a variation of the problem at 11th grade in the US); one problem at the 8th and 11th grades (two problems at the US 11th grade — a variation of one 8th grade problem); one problem at the 11th grade only. The problems were selected from a pool to which both groups contributed.

Subjects

Subjects were at least two classes of 4th, 6th, 8th and 11th grade students in each of several geographical areas of both countries. For all grade levels, students were attending school in large rural, small urban or large urban schools. Schools were purposely selected to provide this mix, although the selection of schools and classes within a school was not made in a random manner in order to be nationally representative.

Questionnaires

In addition to the problems, a questionnaire was developed to gather information about students 'liking' and 'good at' maths, their comparison of the problems to their textbook problems, and their reactions to each of the problems in the research. A questionnaire was also developed to collect information about the schools, teachers' views of their classes, their reactions to the problems, and their perceptions of how seriously students worked on the problems. In addition, a set of instructions was developed for use by proctors when the problem booklets were administered. All are included in the reports of the US–Japan Cross-national Research on Students' Problem-solving Behaviours (Miwa, 1991, 1992; Becker, 1992a). Due to space limitations only two sets of questionnaire results are presented in this chapter — those for the marble arrangement and the arithmagons.

Trials of Research Materials

The problem booklets and questionnaires were 'tried out' in classrooms at each grade level prior to collecting data. The results were tabulated, reported and discussed at the group's second meeting in Japan. Subsequently, the materials were revised and finalized for data collection, which occurred at about the same point in each country's school year (but note that the Japanese school year begins in early April, and the US one in late August).

Data Collection

In the formal data-collection phase, students were given 15 minutes to work on each of two problems (three at the 11th grade for the US — the time for the third problem was 10 minutes) and were asked to write down all their work and to 'line out' rather than erase writing. Each problem was read aloud by the proctor before students began, students were asked to read the problem themselves, and were stopped promptly after the time allowed on each of the problems. Students filled out the questionnaire during the last five minutes of the class period, and teachers filled out their questionnaire while the problems were being administered. The total time elapsed was 45 minutes for the 4th, 6th and 8th grades, and 55 for the 11th grade, the approximate length of class periods in the schools.

Analysis of the Data

Individual or pairs of researchers had responsibility for analyzing the data for one problem at each of the centers. The full results are given in Miwa (1991, 1992) and Becker (1992a).

Results and Analyses of the Marble Arrangement Problem

This section presents the results of a comparison of the results for the US and Japanese samples of students who solved the same problem (see also: Nagasaki, 1990; Nagasaki and Yoshikawa, 1989).

Students

A total of 151 students (83 boys and 68 girls) participated in this part of the study in the US. Most of these students (142) were fourth graders; the remaining students (9) were 5th graders from a combined 4th/5th grade class. All students attended classes that were judged to be of average ability, with the exception of the combined 4th/5th grade class which included gifted students. The Japanese sample included a total of 206 4th grade students (102 boys and 104 girls).

Task and Administration

Each student was given a workbook (called a script below) in which the marble arrangement problem (see Figure 8.1) appeared as the first of two problems. For this problem, students were instructed to determine the number of marbles in a given arrangement in as many different ways as they could. Nine copies of the marble arrangement, each with a separate solution space, were provided after the presentation of the problem and the instructions. The workbooks also included a questionnaire that students completed after working the two problems.

Comparison of US and Japanese Results

Students of both countries found the correct answer equally well, and could find it by various counting and grouping approaches (e.g. $4 \times 4 + 9 = 25$) or by changing the structure of the problem (e.g., moving the corner marbles to make a 5×5 square). The focii of the comparisons were responses, solution strategies and modes of explanation. In general, the comparisons were made by referring to the results reported by Nagasaki and Yoshikawa (1989). However, in a few instances, comparisons were made to results reported in a subsequent analysis by Nagasaki (1990), in which he used a more restricted sample by excluding the national school students, who were judged to be of higher-than-average ability.

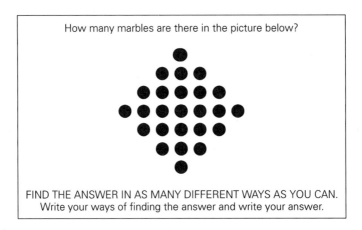

Figure 8.1:   The marble arrangement problem

Responses

Table 8.1 shows the distribution of scripts by gender and by national sample. In the Japanese sample there were no separate analyses on partially correct

Table 8.1: Per cent distribution of scripts by gender by national sample

	Boys	Girls	All students
US			
CC Scripts	48 (58%)	51 (75%)	99 (66%)
PC Scripts	77 (93%)	65 (96%)	142 (94%)
All scripts	83 (100%)	68 (100%)	151 (100%)
Japan			
CC Scripts	97 (95%)	100 (96%)	197 (96%)
PC Scripts	No attempt	No attempt	No attempt
All scripts	102 (100%)	104 (100%)	206 (100%)

(PC) scripts due to the large number of completely correct (CC) scripts. Students in the Japanese sample produced significantly more CC scripts than students in the US sample (US: 66 per cent, Japan: 96 per cent, z = 7.46; p < .001). It is interesting to note, however, that the percentage of PC scripts from the US sample was about the same as the percentage of CC scripts from the Japanese sample. The percentage of girls' CC scripts in the US sample was significantly higher than the percentage of boys' CC scripts. No gender-related difference was found in the Japanese sample.

Although there were significantly more CC scripts produced by students in the Japanese sample, US students produced a significantly greater number of solutions per CC script (US: 7.5, Japan: 5.8, t = 6.68; p < .001). The range of the number of responses produced by Japanese students was 1 to 15, in contrast to the range of 1 to 10 for the US students. Although there were some differences in response frequency, it is important to note an overall similarity — over 80 per cent of the students in both national samples provided 5 or more responses.

Solution Strategies

The distribution of solution strategies in the US sample was similar to the distribution in the Japanese sample. In both national samples, about 60 per cent of the students used *enumeration* (counting) at least once, 90 per cent used *find-a-structure* (grouping) at least once, and less than 5 per cent used *change-the-structure* (restructuring the arrangement, indicated by arrows or adding on and later subtracting) at least once.

Regarding solution shifts between the first and subsequent responses, the patterns were quite similar in the two samples. Most students in both samples continued to use the type of strategy they used on the first response. About 33 per cent of US students and about 50 per cent of Japanese students used a different strategy on the fifth response from that used on the first, and the change was more likely to be from *enumeration* to one of the other two 'structure' strategies.

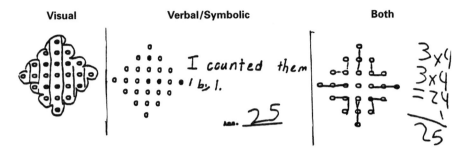

Figure 8.2: *Examples of explanation modes*

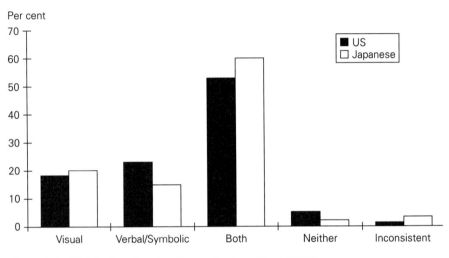

Figure 8.3: *Distribution of explanation modes by national sample*

Mode of Explanation

The comparison of the distribution of explanation modes was based only on the group of CC scripts. Examples of the explanation modes are given in Figure 8.2. Figure 8.3 shows the distribution of explanation modes by national sample. In both samples, most responses (about 60 per cent) were categorized as *both* (i.e., both *visual* and *verbal/symbolic* modes).

Table 8.2 can be used to compare the results on *verbal explanations* versus *mathematical expressions*, as given in the second report on the Japanese sample (Nagasaki, 1990). Two categories of non-visual explanations were used: Verbal Expressions (using words to describe the process — e.g., 'I counted them 1 by 1 to get the answer') and Mathematical Expressions (using symbols to show the process — for example $5 \times 5 = 25$) as in Silver, Leung and Cai, 1994.

Table 8.2: Per cent distribution of categories of non-visual explanations by national sample [n = number of non-visual responses involving explanations]

	Verbal explanations			Mathematical expressions	
	Counting	*Addition*	*Multiplication*	*Addition*	*Multiplication*
US (n = 849)	26%	45%	1%	17%	11%
Japan (n = 930)	22%	1%	18%	22%	37%

Discussion and Interpretation

For students in the US sample, the marble arrangement problem was thought to be non-routine in at least two ways. First, the nature of the problem-solving activity, in which a student answers a single problem a number of times, was thought to be somewhat novel. Moreover, the students were asked to provide explanations of their solution methods or justifications of their answers, which was also thought to be novel. Some reports of instructional activity in Japanese mathematics classrooms (see Becker et al., 1990) have suggested that students in that country are often given opportunities to solve problems in more than one way and to present different solutions to the same problem. In contrast, reports of such activity in US mathematics classrooms are rare.

In the light of expectations of task novelty for US students, it is somewhat surprising that about 60 per cent of the students reported having previously seen a problem similar to the marble arrangement problem. When asked whether the marble arrangement problem was similar to problems that appear in their textbooks, 42 per cent of the students in the Japanese sample reported that the problem was different (Nagasaki, 1990) while, in contrast, 61 per cent of the US students reported that the problem was different. These data suggest that the marble arrangement task may have been more familiar to the Japanese students than to the students in the US sample.

Although it is impossible to reach a definitive conclusion regarding task familiarity, and its impact on students' performance from the data obtained in this study, it is nevertheless interesting to examine some of the most salient findings. In many ways, students in both national samples behaved somewhat similarly with respect to the marble arrangement problem. Although there were differences favouring the Japanese students in the number of *completely correct* (CC) scripts, there was virtually no difference when the percent of Japanese CC scripts was compared with the per cent of US PC (*at-least-partially correct*) scripts. The occurrence of US scripts in which some but not all answers were correct may be a direct result of the US students' relative unfamiliarity with tasks in which one is asked to answer the same question many times. Students may have assumed that the marble arrangement was different at least some of the time, and treated each occurrence as a new problem rather than an occasion to display a new method of solving a problem whose solution was known. Moreover, the fact that the Japanese students were more likely to persevere beyond the limitations imposed by the workbook than the US students, by drawing additional figures in order to produce solutions after filling all the given answer spaces, may reveal their increased comfort and familiarity with this kind of task. Nevertheless, the majority of students in both national samples were constrained by the presentation format of the tasks and produced exactly the same number of solutions as there were answer spaces available in the workbook.

In most studies involving a comparison of the mathematical proficiency of Japanese and American children (for example Robitaille and Garden, 1990; Stevenson, Lee and Stigler, 1986) Japanese children far outperform their American counterparts. We note that the US and Japanese students in this study exhibited some similar behaviours — for instance, in both samples, over 80 per cent of the students produced 5 or more solutions, so the students in both countries were able to solve the problem and produce multiple solutions and explanations of their solutions.

The analysis of solution strategies also revealed some interesting similarities between the students in the two national samples. In particular, the solutions produced by the US students were easily analyzed, using a coding scheme developed by the Japanese researchers, to code responses from students. Moreover, the frequency and patterns of strategy use across-response occasions were almost identical in the two national samples. For example, in both countries, about 90 per cent of the student used the *find-a-structure* strategy at least once, about 60 per cent used *enumeration*, and less than 5 per cent used the *change-the-structure* strategy. The findings on strategy use suggest that the students in both national samples were comfortable with counting and grouping the objects in the figural display, but they were less comfortable moving the objects to create a new display.

An examination of the findings on students' mode of explanation suggests another similarity and some important differences between the two national samples. Students in both samples used the same kinds of explanations, although there was differential frequency of use in some categories. A similarity was the finding that approximately 60 per cent of the responses from students in both samples involved explanations that had both visual and verbal/symbolic features. It would appear that children in both national samples in this study occupy a middle position rather than either extreme on the hypothesized verbalizer-visualizer continuum (Richardson, 1977).

A very important difference between the two samples was the level of mathematical sophistication evident in the students' explanations. Although students in both samples were likely to provide explanations that combined the use of visual and verbal/symbolic features, Japanese students produced a much higher proportion of responses involving mathematical expressions than did their US counterparts, who tended to favour explanations involving verbal statements. Moreover, Japanese students produced a higher proportion of mathematical explanations that involved multiplication than US students, who were more likely to use explanations involving addition. This tendency to use mathematical expressions rather than verbal statements, and the tendency to use multiplication rather than addition, are both indications of the increased mathematical sophistication of the Japanese students' responses when compared to those provided by the US students. Another major difference in the findings for the two national samples is the detection of significant gender differences in the US sample, but not in the Japanese sample.

Results and Analyses of the Arithmogons Problems

This section presents a comparison of US students' results with those from a sample of Japanese students who solved the arithmogons problems (see Senuma, 1991; Senuma and Nohda, 1989). The arithmogons problem (McIntosh and Quadling, 1975) and its variation was the second of two problems administered during one class period at the 8th and 11th grade levels in both countries. Students proceeded to the arithmogons problem immediately after the proctor stopped work on the first problem in the booklet.

The Problems

The arithmogon problem (problem I) and its variation (problem II) are shown below. Students were provided with six different work spaces following the problem statement, in which they could write their different approaches to solving problem I. For problem II, students were given space as indicated in the figure that follows.

Problem I

Given a three-sided arithmogon as in the figure below. We put three numbers in the three □ — the number in each □ must equal the sum of the numbers in the two ○ on either side.
Find the numbers for ○ at each corner. The numbers in ○ may be negative numbers.

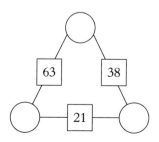

Do not erase anything you write down, just draw a line through anything you feel is in error.
FIND THE ANSWER IN AS MANY DIFFERENT WAYS AS YOU CAN.

Problem II

Now change to a square (four-sided) arithmogon as in the figure below. The number in each □ must equal the sum of the numbers in the two ○ on either side.
Try to find the numbers for ○ at each corner.

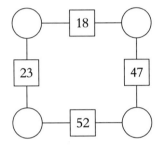

If you need more space, write on the back of this page.

Approaches to Solving the Problems

It was anticipated that students would exhibit from none to all of the following ways of solving the Problem I, and possibly others.

Problem I: Unique Solution

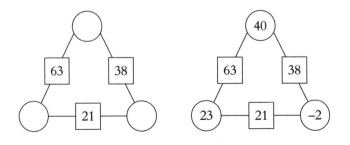

(1) Random trial and error
Here students might guess a number for the top ○ and, by subtraction and moving counterclockwise, see if they would end up with the same

number in the top ○. Alternately, students might either work clockwise or else work both clockwise and counterclockwise, starting with a guess in the top ○, to see if they end up in both directions with 21 at the bottom.

(2) Systematic trial and error
Here students might reason that the numbers in the top ○ and lower left ○ must add to 63. After picking a pair adding to 63, work around counterclockwise or clockwise, using subtraction, to see if they end up with the same number in the top ○. If not, pick a different pair and proceed similarly.

(3) One equation in one unknown
Let x represent the number in the top ○. Then the lower left ○ is $63 - x$ and the lower right ○ is $38 - x$. The two must add to 21; so

$$(63 - x) + (38 - x) = 21$$

(4) System of two equations in two unknowns
Here students might let x represent the number in the top ○ and y the number in the lower right ○. Then $x + y = 38$ and $63 - x = 21 - y$; so

$$x + y = 38$$
$$x - y = 42$$

(5) Three equations in three unknowns
Here students might let x represent the number in the top ○, y the number in the lower right ○, and z the number in the lower left ○; so

$$x + y = 38$$
$$x + z = 63$$
$$y + z = 21$$

(6) By adding 63, 38, 21 (seeing a structure)

$$63 + 38 + 21 = 122$$
$$122 \div 2 = 61$$
$$61 - 63 = -2$$
or
$$61 - 38 = 23$$
or
$$61 - 21 = 40$$

(7) Difference of the two smallest □s (seeing a structure)
a. Find the difference of the numbers in the two smallest □s.
b. Subtract the difference from the number in the largest □.
c. Divide the second difference by 2, which is one of the numbers in the ○s.

d. Add this number to the first difference to get the number for the next ○.
e. Determine the number for the third ○.

(8) General solution (changing perspective and solving a 'bigger' problem first)
Let *x* represent the number in the top ○ and let the numbers in the □s be represented by *a*, *b*, and *c*. Then, work counterclockwise.

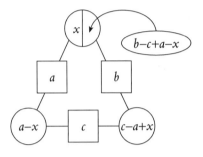

then, $x = b - c + a - x$

so, $x = \dfrac{a + b - c}{2} = \dfrac{63 + 38 - 21}{2} = 40$

so, 40, 23, and −2 is the solution.

Problem II: One non-unique solution

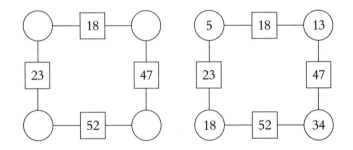

It was anticipated that students would exhibit one or more of the following approaches to solving problem II.

(1) Trial and error
Let the top left ○ be 5 (or any integer). Then the lower left ○ is 18; then the lower right ○ is 34; then the upper right ○ is 13; and 5 + 13 = 18.
   Note: Will students recognize that starting with any number in any ○ will lead to a solution, and that there is more than one (infinitely) many solutions?

(2) Four equations in four unknowns
Let x, y, z, w represent the numbers in the four Os. Then

$$x + y = 23$$
$$y + z = 52$$
$$z + w = 47$$
$$x + w = 18$$

(3) Two equations in two unknowns
Let x represent the number in the upper left O and y the number in the lower right O.

Then, $18 - x = 47 - y$
$23 - x = 52 - y$
So, $x - y = -29$
$x - y = -29$

Therefore, there are infinitely many solutions.

(4) Addition of pairs of numbers in opposite □s.
Will students see that $23 + 47 = 52 + 18$ and, therefore, there are infinitely many solutions, or reason as follows?

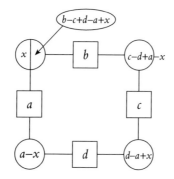

So, $x = b - c + d - a + x$
So, $a + c = b + d$ (condition for a solution to exist)

Samples

In the US sample, there were 368 (178 male and 190 female) 8*th* grade students and 246 (124 male and 122 female) 11*th* grade students. In Japan, at the 8*th* grade level, there were 189 students (96 male and 93 female), and at the 11*th* grade level, there were 234 students (135 male and 99 female). In both countries, students were attending schools in large rural, small urban or large urban schools that were purposely selected to provide this mix, although the selection of schools and classes within a school was not made in a random manner.

Comparison of US and Japanese Results

For Problem I, 39 per cent of Japanese 8*th* grade students got the correct answer, in contrast to 15 per cent for US students; 90 per cent of Japanese 11*th* grade students got problem I correct, compared to 46 per cent of US students. Thus, more than twice as many Japanese 8*th* grade students than US students, and nearly twice as many Japanese 11*th* grade students than US students, got the correct answer to problem I.

For problem II, 38 per cent of Japanese 8*th* grade students compared to 26 per cent of US got one correct answer. Only one US 8*th* grade student indicated there were infinitely many solutions, compared to 1 per cent of Japanese students. However, the results for 11*th* grade students are different, where 24 per cent of Japanese students got one correct answer compared to 55 per cent of US students, and 1 per cent of Japanese 11*th* grade students indicated that there were infinitely many solutions compared to 0 per cent for the US. A probable explanation for the reverse results on problem II for 11*th* grade students is that since 15 minutes were allowed for students to do both problems, and Japanese students far more commonly used simultaneous equations for the first problem (83 per cent in Japan and 9 per cent in the US), they quite naturally used simultaneous equations for the second problem (which are not linearly independent and therefore do not have a unique solution) and ran short of time. Since 64 per cent of Japanese students used the same approach for problem II as problem I, this time with four variables, in contrast to US students who commonly used trial and error (and it is an approach that would work starting with any integer), Japanese students had a low success rate than their US counterparts.

If the above contrasting results are interesting and show big differences in overall performance between US and Japanese students, then approaches to solving problems I and II provide even more interesting and contrasting results. The results showed clearly that Japanese 8*th* and 11*th* grade students, in aggregate for each level, used *all the approaches* listed compared to US students who very predominantly used only trial and error and, in particular, did not use some of the approaches at all. Though Japanese 8*th* grade students use trial and error fairly commonly too (44 per cent), they also use simultaneous equations in two and three variables (24 per cent), in contrast to US students (1 per cent, all incorrect). The results for 11*th* grade students are even more striking in contrast: 83 per cent of Japanese students use simultaneous equations compared to 12 per cent of US students (8 of 28 US students were incorrect 28 per cent); far fewer Japanese student use trial and error (8 per cent) than US students (58 per cent) — 58 of 143 US students were incorrect (41 per cent). For the Japanese sample, 8*th* and 11*th* grade students begin study of algebra in grades seven and eight and have algebraic techniques to work with, in contrast to US students who commonly begin study of algebra in grades 8 or 9. Moreover, Japanese 8*th* and 11*th* grade students, in aggregate at each grade level, in contrast to US students, exhibit a propensity to use all the various approaches to problem I accurately, whether the approaches involve reasoning, computation (including negative numbers), or algebraic techniques. For this sample, Japanese students appear to have acquired algebraic knowledge and an ability to apply it very effectively. A large number of US 8*th* grade (158 or 43 per cent) and 11*th* grade (61 or 25 per cent), in contrast to Japanese students, did not understand what to do. US students more than Japanese also showed difficulty in working with negative numbers, though this difference was more prominent at the 8*th* grade level. Japanese mathematics education exhibits clearly that students can learn algebra, beginning in grade 7.

Similar contrasting results emerge for problem II. The results show that US students (57 per cent) use 'try a number' very commonly along with Japanese students (42 per cent) at the 8*th* grade level; but, at the 11*th* grade, Japanese students far more commonly (64 per cent) than US students (7 per cent — used correctly or incorrectly) use simultaneous equations. Further, 11*th* grade Japanese students far less frequently than 8*th* grade students use trial and error. While only 21 per cent of Japanese 11*th* grade students used simultaneous equations correctly, this may be due to the time factor discussed above — given more time they may have been able to work on the system of four equations in four variables and see that, perhaps, there are infinitely many solutions.

There are other results that, for both problems I and II, provide still further contrasts. Here 9 per cent of US 8*th* grade students compared to 25 per cent of Japanese students got both problems correct (one correct answer or indicated infinitely many solutions for problem II), but far more US students (67 per cent) got both problems incorrect than Japanese (14 per cent). These results seem consistent with other overall results. For 11*th* grade students in both samples, more US students (34 per cent) than Japanese (22 per cent) got both problems correct. Also, more US students (33 per cent) than Japanese (2 per cent) got both problems incorrect. These results reflect earlier discussion of the reversal of results for the two samples from problem I to problem II, but are otherwise consistent with earlier results for the two samples. Moreover, for both grade levels, the number of 'no attempts' for problem II are about the same — 8*th* grade, 40 per cent in Japan and 42 per cent in the US, and 11*th* grade, 20 per cent in Japan and 26 per cent in the US. There is a uniformity in performance among male/female students in this Japanese sample. In contrast, the results vary and differ among males/females in this US sample, though not consistently. Perhaps this reflects clear expectations of performance for both male and female students in Japanese education.

The results of the questionnaire data are consistent with findings of other researchers (see Becker, 1992b; McKnight, Crosswhite, Dossey, Kifer, Swafford, Travers and Cooney, 1987) in which Japanese students, more than

US ones, dislike maths and feel they are not good at it; however, they perform better. Though their results are for 1st and 5th grade students, Stevenson, Lee and Stigler (1986) and Stigler et al., 1990:13 report that the status of Japanese students' achievement remains high and relatively constant across grade levels and the relative status of US students shows a striking decline.

Discussion and Interpretation

There are several considerations deriving from these analyses that mathematics educators in both countries must address. Looking at the US results, there is a need to be concerned about the overall performance of students at both grade levels on these problems. For the US sample, students frequently show little ability to understand the problems, see any kind of structure in them, or are able to reason about them. Reading and understanding the problems as well as learning more algebraic techniques earlier in the curriculum that can be applied in their solutions would seem reasonable. Also, students at these grade levels should not, in any marked degree, have difficulty operating on negative numbers.

Students in the US sample also show remarkably little mathematical sophistication in their solutions of the problems (use of mathematical expressions, equations, simultaneous equations and seeing some structure in the problems). As indicated earlier, however, trial and error predominates and students show little fluency in dealing with the problems — there is little evidence that students can think about the problems in different ways. As is well known, US students believe that there is one and only one solution and way to get the solution to a problem — and there is evidence of this in these results. Further, US students have a tendency to see math as easy and have a feeling that they are good at math, but this is entirely inconsistent with their performance. Where these attitudes come from and how they are formed are questions that need to be addressed in the US. Finally, we need to address the problem of student work habits — there needs to be more order and neatness in students' work.

From the Japanese perspective, for this Japanese sample, it is seen that students have rather marked knowledge of and sophisticated algebraic techniques which they bring to problem-solving situations. At the same time, they seem unable, at the 11*th* grade level, to switch from a sophisticated approach to a more naïve one in transition from problem I to problem II — more flexibility was needed to cope with the situation. Further, Japanese students have a strong tendency to dislike maths and express feelings of not being good at maths. Here again, exactly why this is the case is not known, but it is something that is being addressed as a big problem by Japanese mathematics educators. The results given here, for both national samples, are consistent with the findings in the SIMS and TIMSS studies.

Conclusion

Probably the most important reason for carrying out this kind of cross-national descriptive research is that it may contribute towards understanding and improving the approaches to mathematics teaching. As such, it may be viewed as a complement to other studies such as the NAEPs in the US and similar studies in Japan, and the international comparisons such as FIMS and SIMS (see Bradburn and Gilford, 1990).

Though we do not know from these research results exactly why the differences exist, for various cultural, societal and other factors may play a role, there is increasing evidence that what goes on in the Japanese mathematics classrooms is different from that in the US. Japanese classroom lessons may be characterized as carefully crafted, organized and teacher-managed, and also coherent, with a focus on one main idea. Further, drawing on students' thinking is part of the pedagogy along with a lot of teacher–student and student–student interaction. Very frequently, lessons begin with a carefully developed problem situation and the teacher, far from being a dispenser of knowledge, acts as a guide in the lessons using student input, aware of how much time remains for the lesson and what the teacher wants accomplished by the end of the lesson. Classroom management is critically important. Even when the problem around which a lesson plan is constructed is more 'mathematical' than it is real-life, the teacher knows the characteristics of the problem (for example, knows that the problem lends itself to multiple approaches to its solution or to multiple correct answers) and can therefore draw upon students' solutions for discussion. However the lesson unfolds, the teacher ends the lesson with a summary of what the problem was to begin with, how various approaches contribute to its solution, and what was learned in the lesson. This kind of 'lesson closure' is critically important.

There are still other considerations. The mathematics curriculum is set by the Ministry of Education in Japan, in terms of overall objectives, content and the teaching of the content. Teachers must, to a very large extent, teach the prescribed mathematics curriculum — textbooks used in classroom must first be approved by the Ministry of Education. It would be valuable for US mathematics educators to see and study what mathematical content is in the curriculum, how it is organized and how it is taught (philosophy, approaches, materials and classroom management). This requires translation of these books and related materials for US curriculum developers to study and see what might be useful and adapted to the US. A translation of one Japanese book that reports research on open-ended problem-solving has been published by the National Council of Teachers of Mathematics (Becker and Shimada, 1997), and a second such translation of a book on problem formulation (from problem-to-problem) will also be available in the near future (Becker, Sawada and Takeuchi, in preparation).

It would also be useful to continue research carried out in the US–Japan Cross-national Research on Students' Problem-solving Behaviours described here. While there are no absolute standards of achievement in mathematics education, in any country, comparative types of studies like the one reported here have potential for improving instruction and learning in both countries, setting attainable standards, and monitoring progress in achieving those standards. Further, instances are increasing in which having a one-country only sample is not efficient for developing improvements in effective delivery of education. As Bradburn and Gilford (1990:3) mention, the issue here is not whether an observed pattern is typical, but rather whether something that exists in one country, but not in the other, would be useful in the first. This notion is an important one to consider along with the one of how typical an observed pattern is in a country.

Acknowledgments

The Seminar and subsequent research was supported by the US National Science Foundation (Grants INT-8715950, INT-8514988 and MDR-8850546) and the Japan Society for the Promotion of Science. Any opinions, findings, conclusions or recommendations contained herein are those of the authors and do not necessarily reflect the views of the funding agencies.

Members of the groups were as follows. US: Jerry P. Becker, Edward A. Silver, Mary Grace Kantowski, Kenneth J. Travers, and James W. Wilson. Japan: Tatsuro Miwa, Shigeru Shimada, Toshio Sawada, Tadao Ishida, Yoshihiko Hashimoto, Nobuhiko Nohda, Yoshishige Sugiyama, Eizo Nagasaki, Toshiakira Fujii, Shigeo Yoshikawa, Hanako Senuma, Junichi Ishida, Toshiko Kaji, Katsuhiko Shimizu, and Minoru Yoshida.

This report is based on the reports of the research given in Miwa (1991) and Becker (1992a).

References

BECKER, J.P. (ed.) (1992a) *Report of US–Japan Cross-national Research on Students Problem-solving Behaviors*, Columbus, OH: ERIC/SMEAC Clearinghouse. (ERIC Clearinghouse Documentation Reproduction Service No. ED 351 204).

BECKER, J.P. (1992b) 'Cross-national mathematics achievement results and observations concerning problem solving and creativity of American and Japanese students', *Journal für Mathematik-Didaktik*, **13**(2/3), pp. 99–141.

BECKER, J.P. and MIWA, J. (eds) (1987) *Proceedings of the US–Japan Seminar on Mathematical Problem-solving*, Columbus, OH: ERIC/SMEAC Clearinghouse. (ERIC Documentation Reproduction Service No. ED 304315).

BECKER, J.P. and SHIMADA, S. (eds) (1997) *The Open-ended Approach: A New Proposal for Teaching Mathematics*, Reston, VA: National Council of Teachers of Mathematics.

BECKER, J.P., SAWADA, T. and TAKEUCHI, Y. (in preparation) *From Problem to Problem: Toward an Improvement of Arithmetic/mathematics Through Teaching Based on a Developmental Treatment* (Translation from Japanese to English by NAGATA, H.).

BECKER, J.P., SILVER, E.A., KANTOWSKI, M.G., TRAVERS, K.J. and WILSON, J.W. (1990) 'Some observations of mathematics teaching in Japanese elementary and junior high schools', *Arithmetic Teacher*, **38**(2), pp. 12–21.

BRADBURN, N.M. and GILFORD, D.M. (eds) (1990) *A Framework and Principles for International Comparative Studies in Education*, Washington, DC: National Academy Press.

McINTOSH, A. and QUADLING, D. (1975) 'Arithmogons', *Mathematics Teaching*, **70**, pp. 18–23.

McKNIGHT, C.C., CROSSWHITE, F.J., DOSSEY, J.A., KIFER, E., SWAFFORD, J.O., TRAVERS, K.J. and COONEY, T.J. (1987) *The Underachieving Curriculum — Assessing US School Mathematics from an International Perspective*, Champaign, IL: Stipes Publishing Company.

MINISTRY OF EDUCATION (1984) *The Report of Comprehensive Survey of the State of Enforcement of the Course of Study — Elementary School, Arithmetic.* (In Japanese)

MIWA, T. (1991) *Report of the Japan–US Collaborative Research on Mathematical Problem-solving. Report submitted to the Japan Society For the Promotion of Science*, Tokyo, Japan (in Japanese, with English abstracts for each part).

MIWA, T. (1992) *Teaching of Mathematical Problem-solving in Japan and the US*, Tokyo: Toyokanshuppan. (In Japanese)

NAGASAKI, E. (1990) 'An analysis on the results of common survey on "marble arrangement"' in *Japan–US Collaborative Research on Mmathematical Problem-solving*, Tokyo: National Institute for Educational Research.

NAGASAKI, E. and YOSHIKAWA, S. (1989) Analysis of Japanese results on 'marble arrangement', in *common survey*, Tokyo: National Institute for Educational Research.

NATIONAL INSTITUTE FOR EDUCATIONAL RESEARCH (1981) *Mathematics Achievement of Secondary School Students*, Tokyo: Daiichi-Houki. (In Japanese)

RICHARDSON, A. (1977) 'Verbalizer-visualizer: A cognitive style dimension' *Journal of Mental Imagery*, **1**, pp. 109–26.

ROBITAILLE, D.F. and GARDEN, R.A. (1990) *Second International Mathematics Study (SIMS) of IEA: Contexts and Outcomes of School Mathematics*, New York: Pergamon Press.

SAWADA, T. (1987) 'Comparisons of achievement in problem-solving on SIMS between the United States and Japan', in BECKER, J.P. and MIWA, T. (eds) *Proceedings of the US–Japan Seminar on Mathematical Problem-solving*, Columbus, OH: ERIC/SMEAR Clearinghouse. (ERIC Documentation Reproduction Service No. ED 304315).

SENUMA, H. (1991) 'An analysis on the results of "Arithmogon" in the Japan–US common survey on mathematical problem-solving', in MIWA, T. (ed.) *Report of the Japan–US Collaborative Research on Mathematical Problem-solving behaviours*, Tokyo: Japan Society For the Promotion of Science.

SENUMA, H. and NOHDA, N. (1989) 'An analysis of Japanese results on "Arithmogon" in common survey'. Paper presented at US–Japan Collaborative Research Meeting on Mathematical Problem-solving, University of Tsukuba (Japan).

SILVER, E.A., LEUNG, S.S. and CAI, J. (1994) 'Generating multiple solutions for a problem: A comparison of the responses of US and Japanese students', *Educational Studies in Mathematics*, **28**(1), pp. 35–54.

STEVENSON, H.W., LEE, S.Y. and STIGLER, J.W. (1986) 'Mathematics achievement of Chinese, Japanese, and American children', *Science*, **231**, pp. 693–9.

STIGLER, J.W., LEE, S.Y. and STEVENSON, H.W. (1990) *Mathematical Knowledge*, Reston, VA: National Council of Teachers of Mathematics.

9   Comparative Studies on Teaching Mathematics in England and Germany

Gabriele Kaiser

Results of qualitative studies of English and German mathematics lessons at the lower secondary level are presented, which show significant differences between mathematics education in the two countries. Differences concerning the following aspects are described — the method and the relevance of introducing new concepts and methods, the relevance of mathematical theory (that is, differences concerning the importance of the mathematical structure or of mathematical proofs), the orientation towards rules, and the emphasis on mathematical precision in speech and in writing. In addition, the investigations show that there are remarkable differences concerning the importance of real-world applications and the interaction in the classroom. Finally, possible consequences for the teaching of mathematics in England and Germany are sketched.

Aims and Conception of the German–English Comparative Study

This chapter describes the results of comparative investigations into mathematics teaching in England and Germany. Empirical research into the teaching and learning within different European school systems is necessary in view of the rising importance of the European Union, which will imply a growing mobility of young people and adults within the different countries of the European Union. This growing mobility within Europe will have the consequence that different school-leaving examinations will have to be accepted across Europe — it will be necessary to know what different qualifications and knowledge the students have, after leaving the school system of one European country, when entering the school system of another country. In order to cope adequately with this difficult situation, it is necessary to develop a mutual understanding of the different educational systems within Europe which surpasses a mere comparison of the different systems and considers the level of teaching and learning within the classroom.

The English and German school systems have been selected as educational systems to be compared in this study because there has been a long tradition of comparing the English with the German school system in pedagogy, and these results have in part influenced the public discussion on reforms of the educational system. Hence, current changes in the English educational system, arising from the Educational Reform Act of 1988, consider characteristics of continental educational systems.

The comparative study of teaching mathematics in England and (Western) Germany has been carried out since the beginning of the 1990s, within the scope of a joint project of the University of Exeter (David Burghes) and the University of Kassel (Werner Blum).

The goals of this study are as follows:

- an examination of the differences in the mathematical achievement of English and German students;
- an analysis of the differences in the ways of teaching and learning mathematics in both countries. Based on this, the teaching methods will be questioned, and ideas gathered on how to improve the different ways of teaching mathematics.

The whole study consists of two parts, which both examine the lower secondary level:

- a quantitative study on the mathematical achievement of German and English students,
- a qualitative study on the differences in teaching and learning mathematics in both countries.

Thus, the whole study combines elements of both quantitative and qualitative methods. Doing this pays respect to a generally demanded plurality of methods in pedagogy.

First, a few remarks on the methodology of research applied will be made. It is not the aim of the quantitative study to measure the representative mathematical achievement of English and German students — it rather aims at finding differences in academic achievement with respect to crucial mathematical topics in both countries. For this reason, informal, non-standardized tests, developed on the basis of an intensive analysis of the curriculum, were used. The qualitative study uses methods of qualitative social sciences, mainly participating classroom observations — about 240 lessons were seen at 17 different schools in England, compared to 100 lessons at 12 German schools. In general, the study aims at generating general knowledge, based on which pedagogical phenomena might be interpreted and explained. Under a narrower perspective, the study aims to generate hypotheses on the differences between teaching mathematics under the educational systems in England and in Germany. For methodological reasons, however, the study cannot make any 'lawlike' statements; in contrast, the study refers to the approach of the 'ideal typus' developed by Max Weber (*Webersche Idealtypen*), and describes idealized types of mathematics teaching reconstructed from the classroom observations in England and Germany. This means that typical aspects of mathematics teaching are reconstructed on the basis of the whole qualitative studies rather than on an existing empirical case.

The research carried out develops hypotheses on the differences between teaching mathematics in England and in Germany concerning the understanding of mathematical theory, the importance of real-world examples, the teaching and learning style, the achievement in mathematics, and more general pedagogical aspects. In the following, I will concentrate mainly on the qualitative analyses and refer only briefly to the results of the quantitative study. For an extended description of the qualitative study see Kaiser (1997, 1998), and for a description of the quantitative study see Kaiser and Blum (1994) and Kaiser, Blum and Wiegand, 1998.

Subject-oriented Versus Pragmatic Understanding of Mathematical Theory

The following general approaches in English and German mathematics education concerning the understanding of mathematical theory can be reconstructed. In German mathematics teaching a subject-oriented understanding of mathematical theory prevails, in contrast to a pragmatic understanding of mathematical theory in England. The different understanding of mathematical theory gets more concrete with the analysis of mathematics teaching in both countries related to different didactical aspects — like the introduction of new mathematical concepts and methods, or the relevance of mathematical theory and rules.

Introduction of New Mathematical Concepts and Methods

In Germany, both the introduction of new concepts and the deduction of new mathematical methods are of high importance for the teaching of mathematics, which are usually either well prepared by the teacher or follow detailed introductions given in the textbooks. New mathematical concepts and methods are often motivated by real-world examples and, in part, they are directed at basic ideas. Furthermore, the introduction of new mathematical concepts and methods usually takes place in a class discussion, during which newly introduced mathematical concepts and methods are formulated in the form of definitions or theorems and written down on the blackboard. That is often followed by exercises, that are supposed to deepen the understanding.

In England, both the introduction of new concepts and the deduction of new mathematical methods are less important and both are done pragmatically. Sometimes, teachers only name the new concepts or methods, often in the style of a 'recipe'. In addition, new mathematical concepts and methods are often introduced by means of experimenting (drawing or measuring), explanations which refer to mnemonics or the calculator, or substitute explanations which refer to the content. In general, the introduction of new concepts takes place implicitly, either during short periods of class discussion or during individual work with the textbook.

Importance of Mathematical Theory and Rules

Generally speaking, mathematics teaching in Germany is characterized by its focus on the subject structure of mathematics and on mathematical theory. This means that theory is made explicit by means of rules and computations. In contrast, in England, the understanding of theory can be called pragmatic — theory is applied practically in an appropriate way. These different basic approaches to teaching mathematics are visible when looking at the following differences.

Organization by Subject Structure versus Spiral-type Curriculum

The focus on theory when teaching mathematics in Germany implies a lesson structure which goes along with the subject structure of mathematics. Thus, in the lessons, large units are taught which are complete in themselves. Mathematical theorems, rules and formulae are therefore of high importance. That varies, though, with the different kinds of school of the three-track system (i.e. differentiation along three achievement levels).

The pragmatic understanding of theory in England is apparent from the curricular structure, which resembles a spiral. As a consequence, smaller units are taught, and they are not necessarily connected with each other. Topics are quickly swapped and, at times, different topics are worked on at the same time. Frequent repetitions of mathematical terms and methods which have already been taught are a feature of this spiral-shaped approach. Mathematical theorems, rules and formulae are of low importance for the teaching of mathematics in England — they are often called *patterns*.

The Role of Proofs

In Germany, proofs of mathematical statements are very important when teaching mathematics at the *Gymnasium* (schools of the higher achievement level), and in some *Realschulen* (schools of the intermediate achievement level). Proofs are considered important to visualize the theoretical frame of mathematics, especially in the context of geometry.

In England, proofs are of low importance, both in selective as well as in non-selective schools. Theorems, found by means of experiments, are often only checked with examples, and proofs and checks with examples are often not distinguished.

Focus on Rules versus Work with Examples

In Germany, the teaching of mathematics is characterized by its focus on rules, and these rules manifest themselves in algorithms. First, the exact and precise processing of arithmetical algorithms is important. Then, in the *Gymnasium*, the processing of algebraic algorithms is essential and, especially at *Hauptschulen* (schools of the lower achievement level), it is considered important to learn the main algorithms by heart. Sticking to exactly prescribed procedures and following certain routines when working with algorithms is also regarded as important. This often leads to rigid and standard solution processes.

General rules are of low importance when teaching mathematics in England. Instead, students work on example-based solutions and first approaches to solutions. This goes along with the fact that approaches and ways to solving problems which the students have posed themselves are often regarded as more important than the acquisition of systematic knowledge and strategies.

The Role of Precise Language and the Use of Formal Notations

Precise language and the use of mathematically correct language are considered very important when teaching mathematics in Germany. This varies, however, with respect to the different levels of achievement. Technical terms are often treated like vocabulary, which has to be learnt by heart. As a consequence, during class discussions, teachers often correct those phrases of the students which are not precise or are slightly incorrect. The use of formal notations is considered very important and is corrected if necessary.

In England, the use of mathematically precise words and phrases is of low importance when teaching mathematics. In addition, for many teachers, correct formal notations are not important — they seldom correct students' notations which are incorrect or imprecise. Some of the incorrect notations show the influence of the early and persistent use of calculators, which is characteristic of the teaching of mathematics in England. Thus, many students write down their exercises in the same way they type them into the calculator.

The Role of Real-world Examples

Real-world examples are only of limited importance for the teaching of mathematics in Germany. Differences can be seen between the three different types of schools, though. They are more important in schools of a lower or a intermediate level of achievement than they are in those of a higher achievement level. Real-world examples are often aimed at the introduction of new mathematical terms and methods or to exercise mathematical methods. As a consequence, many examples used appear artificial or unreal.

Real-world examples are of fairly high importance in England, both with respect to the curriculum and to the lessons themselves. References to the real-world fulfil several didactical purposes, contributing to the ability to apply mathematics to solve non-mathematical problems or to introduce new mathematical terms and methods. Fairly new mathematical topics, such as graph theory or network analysis (which are strongly related to applications) as well as probability, have become more important for the teaching of mathematics in England. Real-world examples are often taught through an activity-oriented method, with students doing research on tasks they set themselves. For the last two years before the students take their GCSE (school leaving exam at the end of the lower-secondary level), this kind of work — so-called coursework — is compulsory. It is often aimed at improving the students' communication skills.

Teaching and Learning Styles

German mathematics lessons are dominated by a teaching and learning style called class discussion — almost all mathematical concepts and methods are introduced during periods of class discussion. Individual work is of fairly low importance, and is used primarily for the working of exercises. Significant differences are apparent between different types of schools and different years. This means that, in the upper years of a *Gymnasium*, class discussion is almost exclusively the teaching and learning style used. In *Hauptschulen*, on the contrary, individual work replaces class discussions and, during periods of class discussion, it is essential that students discuss with each other. Therefore, at least temporarily, students refer to each other. Furthermore, significant differences to the extent a teacher guides a class discussion can be seen, ranging from merely guiding to an authoritative directing of the class discussion. The blackboard is the essential medium of a class discussion, and the students sometimes write their solutions on it. All in all, the students shape the class discussion to an appreciable extent.

In English mathematics lessons, two main teaching styles are currently recognizable. The first one is more traditional, and it focuses on long periods of individual work. During these, the students work on new mathematical topics by using individual work material, or they practise known terms and methods. These periods of individual work alternate with shorter periods of class discussions, rigidly guided by the teacher, during which new topics are introduced or results are compared.

Besides these more traditional teaching and learning methods, another style exists which is more student focused. Its methods consist of several problem-solving activities, during which the students carry out investigations and do coursework, often in the form of projects. Generally speaking, in England, class discussions are dominated by the teachers. All of the communication takes place with the teacher, and the students hardly ever refer to each other. Writing on the blackboard is not important — if something is written down on the blackboard, this is usually done by the teacher. When teaching mathematics in England, an inner differentiation often takes place. This is easily possible, since most of the learning material is designed for individual work.

Differences in Academic Achievement in Mathematics

The differences in academic achievement in mathematics between students is examined in the quantitative longitudinal study. In that, the progress of achievement of Year 8 pupils (in Germany) was compared to that of Year 9 (in England), following those two cohorts until the end of Year 10 (in Germany) or Year 11 (in England). In Germany, the sample consists of approximately 800 students — in England about 1000 students. Three test rounds have been carried out — one in 1993, one in 1994, and the last in 1996 — all focusing on the same cohort of students.

Results of the First Test Round

Three different topic areas were covered: number, algebra and functions/graphs combined with geometry. The results vary, depending on the topic of the test. The German students achieved far better results in number, and their results were also slightly better in algebra. In the functions/graphs/geometry the English students showed far better results. In Figure 9.1 the average scores of both groups for all three tests are displayed (the maximum score has been 50 marks for each test).

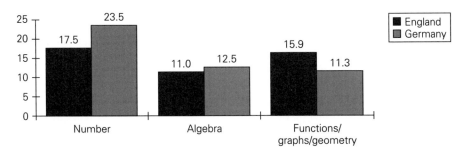

Figure 9.1: Results of the first test round for the English and German students

Results of the Second Test Round

Generally speaking, all students who participated had made progress. The German students, though, improved their results far more than the English students in all three topics. In number, the German students improved more than the English; in algebra the tendency was the same, though less obvious.

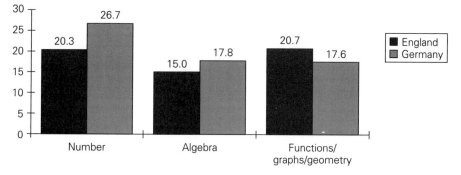

Figure 9.2: Results of the second test round for the English and German students

In functions/graphs/geometry, the English students' margin narrowed. The average scores of both groups are displayed in Figure 9.2 (maximum score 50 marks).

Results of the Third Test Round

At the end of the lower-secondary level the differences between the English and German mathematics students in the different topic areas, already observed in the first and second test round, still existed. The average scores are shown in Figure 9.3 (maximum score 50 marks).

On the whole, the German students had made more progress, especially from the first to the second test round. The samples of both countries show considerable differences in the distribution of the students' achievements. In England, a considerable number of students with very good results, and a relatively moderate number of students with intermediate achievement can be observed. The number of students with poor results is high. In Germany, in contrast, it is noticeable that there are a large number of students in the

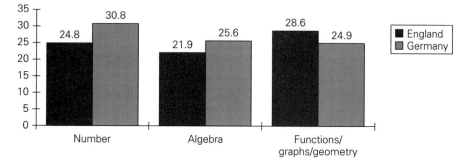

Figure 9.3: Results of the third test round for the English and German students

intermediate area of achievement — there are hardly any extremely good students, and the number of those with low achievement is considerably smaller.

It seems that the differences in the results can largely be explained by the emphases in both the curriculum and the lessons. In German mathematics teaching, number work is far more important than in English mathematics lessons. This holds for all tracks of the German tripartite school system. Additionally, algebra is of higher relevance in German mathematics lessons, but with differences in the different school types. In contrast, geometry is paid more attention in the English mathematics teaching, especially with respect to constructive aspects. Functions are more important in Germany, but the emphasis of the test was on graphs, which are more important in English mathematics lessons.

It also appears that the different progress made can be explained by the different structure of the curricula in both countries. Due to a spiral-shaped curriculum many topics are taught far earlier in English mathematics lessons than in German lessons. That has lead to the strong progress made by the German students, especially from the first to the second test round. The smaller progress of the German students from the second to the third test round is caused by the almost complete lack of repetitive work in German mathematics teaching — many German students had simply forgotten the mathematical topics taught in the earlier grades.

Educational Basis for the Differences in Mathematics Teaching Between the Two Countries

These differences between the English and the German mathematics teaching are based on differences in the school system and the underlying philosophy of education. Approaches developed in comparative education (see McLean, 1990) characterize the English philosophy of education by three principles — morality (the Christian ideal), individualism and specialization. They argue that these principles have given little weight to rational, methodical and systematic knowledge, and have led historically to the low importance attached to mathematics teaching in school.

Mathematics teaching in English schools has little concern for the formal learning of principles and insight into general mathematical rules, but is based on the assumption that children grasp general principles as a result of active discovery and active work through a series of examples. This has led to the wide use of example-based, individualized work in English mathematics teaching. The idea that mathematics can promote general goals such as developing logical thinking has been largely ignored, although the use of mathematics in later life has been emphasized.

The German educational philosophy is characterized by the development of two approaches. First is the humanistic-oriented approach aiming for a general education, developed for the élite (von Humboldt), in which mathematics is as important as the classical language as a means for promoting general abilities like logical thinking. Second is the realistic-oriented approach for the masses, which emphasizes a utility principle and preparation for future life. For mathematics teaching, the first approach places the understanding of structures and general principles in the foreground, and attaches a low importance to active work through examples; the understanding of structures is seen to be more important than deep knowledge in single areas. The second approach emphasizes the connection of school mathematics with everyday life and work, and sees the understanding of structures as less important.

The different approaches developed in England and Germany have a few common points (like the high importance of the individual), but many differences (like the status of mathematics, the relevance of broad knowledge, the status of vocational preparation, the status of folk education in contrast to élite education).

These different approaches have influenced the structure of the school system and the curriculum. The English curriculum is related to the age of the students, allowing a big spread in the achieved goals, while the German curriculum is connected to the year group — the whole class (within the tripartite system) makes progress, with small differences between the individuals. The instrument of the repitition of the class leads to the homogenous classes necessary for such an approach.

Possible Consequences for German and English Mathematics Teaching

Amongst others, it is the aim of empirical comparative studies to recognize strengths and weaknesses of one approach by looking at others. For the German–English comparative study described, this means the characteristics of one educational system should not simply be adopted by the other one. Rather, it is the intention to question and to criticize some characteristics of English and German mathematics teaching which became apparent in the course of the empirical educational studies.

Of high relevance is the different understanding of mathematical theory dominating English and German mathematics teaching, which has strong deficits in both countries and should be changed. This means that the subject-oriented understanding of mathematical theory in German mathematics teaching has to integrate pragmatic elements — in contrast to the English mathematics teaching, which has to consider subject-oriented aspects. This implies detailed changes to mathematics teaching in both countries referring to the introduction of concepts, the relevance of mathematical theory, the orientation towards rules, the relevance of precise language and formal notations, and the importance of real-world examples. Additionally, changes on the level of the teaching and learning styles seem necessary — inclusion of individualized teaching and learning forms in German mathematics teaching and forms of class discussion in English teaching.

To summarize, the study has shown, on the one hand, how strongly both ways of mathematics teaching need to be changed but, on the other hand, how many elements of both ways of teaching should be preserved.

References

KAISER, G. (1997) 'Vergleichende Untersuchungen zum Mathematikunterricht im englischen und deutschen Schulwesen', *Journal für Mathematik-Didaktik*, **18**, 2/3, pp. 127–70.

KAISER, G. (1998) *Vergleichende Untersuchungen zur Unterrichtswirklichkeit in England und Deutschland am Beispiel des Mathematikunterrichts*, Weinheim, Deutscher Studien Verlag.

KAISER, G., BLUM, W. (1994) 'Vergleich mathematischer Leistungen deutscher und englischer Lernender in Klasse 8', *mathematica didactica*, **17**, 2, pp. 17–52.

KAISER, G., BLUM, W. and WIEGAND, B. (1998) 'Vergleich mathematischer Leistungen deutscher und englischer Lernender der Sekundarstufe I', *mathematica didactica*, **21**, 2.

McLEAN, M. (1990) *Britain and a Single Market Europe*, London: Kogan Page.

10 Applications of Arithmetic in US and Chinese Textbooks: A Comparative Study

Lianghuo Fan

This study compares how two series of elementary textbooks — one from the US and the other Chinese — represent the applications of the two basic arithmetic operations of addition and subtraction. By examining the distribution patterns of different types of application problems in the textbooks, the study reveals that the distributions for both operations from Grade 1 to 6 are irregular within the same series and inconsistent across the series. This chapter argues that it is important that we extend our knowledge from knowing 'why' one should emphasize the applications of mathematics to knowing 'how' to emphasize them in curriculum development.

Introduction

Since at least the late 1970s, applications of mathematics have been increasingly emphasized by researchers, reformers and practical developers of mathematics curriculum. Some people have even described their reformed curriculum as 'applications-oriented' (see Wirszup and Streit, 1987). However, the realization of the importance of mathematics applications to the curriculum is not equal to the realization of how to represent well the applications of mathematics in textbooks. The former is a problem of 'why', whereas the latter is a question of 'how'. It seems to me that the former problem has been well attended, attacked and, to some extent, even solved. Yet the latter remains far less well defined and investigated, let alone solved.

This chapter presents a comparative study related to the latter problem. In a general sense, this study was intended to attack one issue only — 'how do textbooks currently represent the applications of mathematics?' — but, specifically, the study chose two series of elementary mathematics textbooks — one American and the other Chinese — and investigated how those two series of textbooks represented the applications of the two basic arithmetic operations of addition and subtraction.

Researchers have pointed out the following aims, amongst others, of comparative educational studies:

- to identify what is happening in different countries that might help improve different educational systems;

- to describe similarities and differences in educational phenomena between systems of education and to interpret why these exist.

Such studies, therefore, can help identify problems in different educational systems and raise doubts about established principles and structures, formulate hypothetical answers and also provide well-founded information and insights concerning educational systems and practices (Postlethwaite, 1988; Robinsohn, 1992). It was mainly with those aims in respect to curriculum and textbooks that I wanted this study to be a comparative one. By examining the United States and Chinese textbooks, I wished to provide empirical evidences about how those textbooks represent the applications of addition and subtraction, explain possible reasons for the differences and similarities, and explore their implications for curriculum development and further research in this area.

Method

Methodologically, there are different elements of the textbooks that one can examine concerning how they represent the applications of mathematics. In this study, I focused particularly on problems presented in the textbooks, since not only are problems at 'the heart of mathematics' and how they are designed a central issue in textbook development, but the essential purpose for students to learn applications is to solve problems.

The study took a quantitative approach, by comparing the distribution patterns of the quantities of problems representing different kinds of applications in the textbooks, because the quantitative patterns, as people have claimed, imply the frequencies with which students are exposed to different kinds of problems and, hence, might have substantial influence on students' learning (see Stigler, Fuson, Han and Kim, 1986).

Textbooks

The series of US textbooks I chose was *Exploring Mathematics*, published by ScottForesman, and the series of Chinese textbooks selected was *The Compulsory Education Six-Year Elementary School Textbooks (Experimental Edition) — Mathematics* hereafter referred to as *Chinese National*, published by the People's Educational Press. Both series' latest versions were used for this study.

Coding Scheme

Numerous researchers have developed coding schemes for categorizing addition and subtraction problems along different dimensions to address issues about addition and subtraction (see Carpenter and Moser, 1987; Fuson, 1992;

Riley, Greeno and Hiller, 1983; Vergnaud, 1982). In this study, all problems of addition and subtraction were first classified into one of two general categories — non-application problems and application problems — so an overall picture could be obtained about how non-application and application problems were distributed in quantity. Problems unrelated to any practical background in everyday life or the real world were defined as non-application problems and, correspondingly, those related to some kind of practical background were defined as application problems.

After the first classification, all application problems were further coded into different types, based mainly on Usiskin and Bell's categorization (1983), which was specifically developed for an analysis of 'application' problems.

According to Usiskin and Bell, all application problems of addition can be classified into three types — *putting together*, *shift* and *addition from subtraction*. The *putting together* problems represent situations that require things physically be placed together, or situations that may only be considered together mentally. The *shift* problems apply to the situations that have the relationship 'initial state + shift = final state'. It differs conceptually from putting together in that the 'shift' need not be a measure of a quantity, but a measure of change. While 'putting together' and 'shift' are two basic use meanings of addition, the *addition from subtraction* type is derived from subtraction. Table 10.1 shows their categorization and examples.

Similarly, they classified subtraction into four types — *take-away*, *comparison*, *subtraction shift*, and *recovering addend*. *Take-away* applies to the situations that have the relationship 'given amount-amount taken away = amount remaining' while *comparison* represents that given numbers or quantities a and b, $a - b$ tells by how much a and b differ. *Take-away* and *comparison* are two basic use meanings of subtraction. In contrast, *subtraction shift* and *recovering addend* are two derived use meanings, with the former derived from addition shift via $a - b = a + -b$, and the latter from addition via related facts, that is, $x = a - b$ is from $x + b = a$ or $b + x = a$. Table 10.2 shows such a categorization and examples.

The reason that this study employed Usiskin and Bell's categorizations outlined above is that not only are their categorizations relatively comprehensive but also, among many other classifications of addition and subtraction problems developed by various researchers, almost none was specially intended for the analysis of application. Nevertheless, I modified Category D in subtraction from *recovering addend* to *recovering addend and subtrahend*, as $x = a - b$

Table 10.1: A categorization of application problems of addition and examples

A: putting together	B: shift	C: addition from subtraction
Jack has 5 marbles, and Frank gives him 3 more. How many marbles does Jack have now?	Susan is 130 cm tall and grows 4 cm. How tall is she now?	After a $50 discount, a TV set is sold for $300. What was the original price?

Table 10.2: A categorization of application problems of subtraction and examples

A: take-away	B: comparison	C: subtraction shift	D: recovering addend
Tod has 15 toys, and he gives 6 of them to Don. How many toys does Tod have now?	Bill has 6 pens, Tom has 11 pens. How many more pens does Tom have than Bill?	Cathy is 15 years old now. How old was she 7 years ago?	After getting $3 from Jin, Kim has $9. How much did she have before getting the $3?

can result from addition $x + b = a$ or $b + x = a$, as well as from subtraction $a - x = b$.

Procedure

Using the above categorizations, I examined and coded all the problems of addition and subtraction in both series across all six grades. The general coding principle was to cover as many problems as possible, including combined addition and subtraction, open-ended, and abacus-using and calculator-using problems. However, I excluded problems that combined with multiplication or division and all estimation problems.

Results and Discussion

Non-application and Application Problems

A detailed tabulation of the presentation frequency of non-application and application addition problems by grades is given in Table 10.3 for *Exploring Mathematics*, and Table 10.4 for *Chinese National*.

Table 10.3: Distribution of non-application and application problems of addition in Exploring Mathematics

	Grade 1	Grade 2	Grade 3	Grade 4	Grade 5	Grade 6	Total
Non-application	1004	834	1088	532	874	555	4887
Application	467	345	192	83	111	76	1274
Ratio	46.5%	41.4%	17.6%	15.6%	2.7%	13.7%	26.1%

Table 10.4: Distribution of non-application and application problems of addition in Chinese National

	Grade 1	Grade 2	Grade 3	Grade 4	Grade 5	Grade 6	Total
Non-application	434	273	121	690	384	120	2022
Application	170	30	68	69	55	24	416
Ratio	39.2%	11.0%	56.2%	10.0%	14.3%	20.0%	20.6%

From the tables, we can find that, overall, *Exploring Mathematics* contains many more addition problems than *Chinese National* (6161 against 2438), with more than twice as many non-application problems and more than three times as many application problems. Though a detailed analysis of this fact is beyond the scope of this article, I think one reason for the difference is that *Exploring Mathematics* contains many more problems reviewing previous topics, as was the case in other American textbooks (see Flanders, 1987).

Within the same textbooks, the ratios of application to non-application problems vary greatly across the six grades in both series. Across the textbooks, the distributions of the ratios over all six grades are inconsistent — for instance, *Exploring Mathematics* has higher ratios than *Chinese National* in Grades 1, 2 and 4, but lower in the other grades; no steady trend can be found by comparison. Nonetheless, the total ratio of all six grades is higher in *Exploring Mathematics* than it is in *Chinese National*: 26.1 per cent against 20.6 per cent. This difference is not very big, but still to a degree consistent with the author's expectation that Chinese textbooks have paid less attention to the application of knowledge (see Fan, 1990). From the perspective of cultural differences, it may partially reflect the fact that American values, as compared to Chinese, are more practical and utilitarian-oriented.

Tables 10.5 and 10.6 present the quantitative distributions of non-application and application subtraction problems in the two series, respectively.

Comparing these two tables, we can easily see that there exist patterns for subtraction problems similar to the two comparative results for addition problems discussed above.

An interesting result that we can find is that, from Tables 10.3 and 10.4 for addition and Tables 10.5 and 10.6 for subtraction, the general patterns of the ratios of application to non-application problems from Grade 1 to 6 are quite consistent across the operations within the same textbooks, but not across the textbooks within the same operations. It seems that the authors of

Table 10.5: Distribution of non-application and application problems of subtraction in Exploring Mathematics

	Grade 1	Grade 2	Grade 3	Grade 4	Grade 5	Grade 6	Total
Non-application	696	663	607	431	710	362	3469
Application	316	310	122	93	93	59	993
Ratio	45.4%	46.8%	20.1%	21.6%	13.1%	16.3%	28.6%

Table 10.6: Distribution of non-application and application problems of subtraction in Chinese National

	Grade 1	Grade 2	Grade 3	Grade 4	Grade 5	Grade 6	Total
Non-application	306	241	132	648	346	109	1782
Application	186	35	61	97	43	14	436
Ratio	60.8%	14.5%	46.2%	15.0%	12.4%	12.8%	24.5%

the textbooks might have had certain general assumptions or preferences, intentionally or unintentionally, about what should be the ratio of application problems to non-application ones, regardless of the different operations.

I once argued that in general the ratio of application problems to non-application problems in schoolbooks should be around 40 to 50 per cent (Fan, 1990). From the fact that all the ratios in the six grades for both addition and subtraction in both series are less than 30 per cent, I would argue that both series did not pay enough attention to application problems.

Different Types of Application Problems

Addition

Figures 10.1 and 10.2 depict the distributions of the percentages of different types of problems in all application problems of addition for both series.

Examining the distributions of the percentages of problems of *putting-together*, *shift* and *addition from subtraction* across each grade, as well as the total percentages in all six grades — 86.3:10.8:2.7 in *Exploring Mathematics*, and 78.8:4.3:14.9 in *Chinese National* — we can see that, for both the American and Chinese series, the *putting together* problems overwhelmingly outnumber

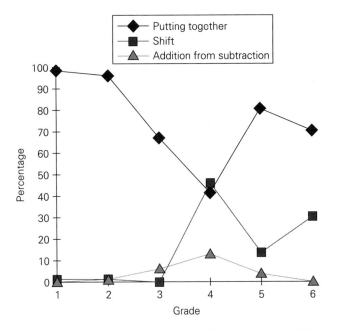

Figure 10.1: The distribution of the percentages of different types of addition application problems in Exploring Mathematics

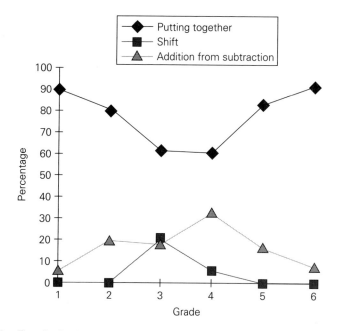

Figure 10.2: *The distribution of the percentages of different types of addition application problems in* Chinese National

the other two types of problems. Except for that similarity, the distributions are rather irregular within the same series and inconsistent across the series.

It is clear, in my view, that the reason there are many fewer application problems of *addition from subtraction* in *Exploring Mathematics* and of *shift* in *Chinese National* is not that it is too difficult to make up these kinds of problems. In fact, before *Exploring Mathematics* introduced the *addition from subtraction* problems in Grade 2, *Chinese National* textbooks had used at least 10 problems of this type in Grade 1. Also, if *Exploring Mathematics* can have a number of *shift* problems in Grades 1 and 2, why can *Chinese National* not have problems of the same type in the same grades — especially since topics are, by and large, the same in both series for these two grades? In terms of the nature of the exercises, many problems (such as age-increasing problems, height-growing problems and moving forward problems) can be easily used to make up addition *shift* problems, and almost all kinds of addition situations can be converted into *addition from subtraction* problems by using the relationship if $a + b = c$ then $c - a = b$.

Subtraction

Figures 10.3 and 10.4 display the distributions of the percentages of the different types of problems in all application problems of subtraction across all grades in these two series.

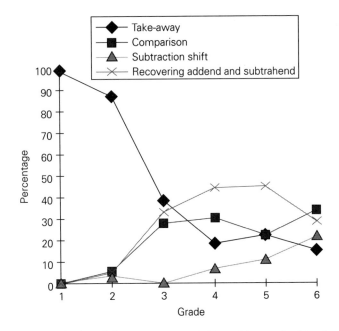

Figure 10.3: The distribution of the percentages of different types of subtraction application problems in Exploring Mathematics

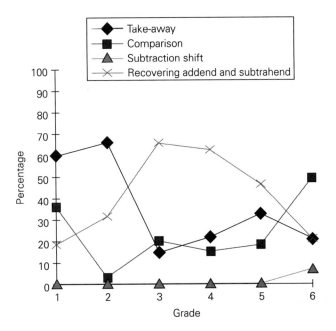

Figure 10.4: The distribution of the percentages of different types of subtraction application problems in Chinese National

Inspecting the distributions of the percentages of problems of *take-away, comparison, subtraction*, and *recovering addend and subtrahend* across each grade, as well as the total percentages in all six grades — 68.2:11.9:4.1:15.6 in *Exploring Mathematics*, and 41.3:18.9:0.2:38.8 in *Chinese National* — reveals two similarities. First, both series overall devoted most attention to the type of *take-away* problems compared to the other types. Second, the orders of the frequency of different types of problems in both series are the same — *take-away, recovering addend and subtrahend, comparison*, and *shift*, from high to low.

The difference is that, overall, *Exploring Mathematics* paid much more attention to *take-away* problems, with the percentage of this kind of problems in all application problems being 68.2 per cent, while *Chinese National* emphasized almost evenly two types — *take-away* (41.3 per cent), and *recovering addend and subtrahend* (38.8 per cent). Again, it is easy to see from the figures that the distributions are very irregular within the same series and inconsistent across the series.

An unexpected result is that there are no *subtraction shift* problems in *Chinese National* for Grade 1 to 5, and only one problem in Grade 6. From the standpoint of students' exposure mentioned above, this fact is not desirable. Also, there are no *comparison* and *recovering addend and subtrahend* problems in Grade 1 of *Exploring Mathematics*. As making up such kinds of problems is not difficult (for example, from the relationship between subtraction and addition, we can find many subtraction *shift* problems from addition *shift* ones, such as counting forward and backward, moving forward and backward, finding previous age, and so on) it seems likely that, as in the application of addition, the authors of the textbooks did not pay enough attention to or were not aware of the different types of subtraction problems in practical situations.

To close this section, I wish to stress that the above analysis is based on the particular coding criteria and classification systems of the problems as well as on the special perspective of this study. Hence, this particular study should not be taken as an overall evaluation of the textbooks, which needs to take into account many other factors.

Conclusions and Implications

In summary, several general conclusions can be drawn according to the results and analysis above about how *Exploring Mathematics* and *Chinese National* textbooks represent the applications of addition and subtraction.

- Overall, both series (especially the Chinese series) paid less than enough attention to application problems, compared to non-application problems.
- Within application problems of addition, both series paid most attention to the *putting together* type of problems in terms of the relative frequency; and to the *shift* and *addition from subtraction* types of problems,

> *Exploring Mathematics* paid more attention to the former type, and *Chinese National* paid more attention to the latter. The distributions of the frequency of different types of application problems over the six grades are irregular within the same series and inconsistent across the series.

- Within application problems of subtraction, both series paid most attention to the *take-away* type of problems and then, in order, to the types of *recovering addend and subtrahend*, *comparison*, and *subtraction shift*. However, the attention *Chinese National* paid to the type of *recovering addend and subtrahend* is very close to that of *take-away*, but this is not the case in *Exploring Mathematics*. Also, the distributions of the frequency of different types of subtraction application problems over the six grades are irregular within the same series and inconsistent across the series.

More generally, taking addition and subtraction together, I think that those two series of textbooks did not represent well the applications of both arithmetic operations. The attention given to different types of applications of addition and subtraction was unbalanced and not well designed.

Considering the fact that, for over a decade, almost no one in the field of mathematics curriculum has denied the importance of the application of mathematics, I would argue that the evidence provided in the study confirms that knowing *why* one should emphasize applications is not equal to knowing *how* to emphasize applications, and it is necessary that we further extend our knowledge from knowing *why* to knowing *how*.

On the other hand, we might say that this study raised more questions than answers. Although, from the results of this study, I do believe that how to represent the applications of mathematics should be well taken into account in curriculum development, this study did not determine the specific criteria for evaluating the representation of applications in textbooks. Also, if we took a different approach or used different categorizations for addition and subtraction problems, what would the pictures of these two series of textbooks be and how should we compare them with the picture revealed in this study? More generally, should we hold different perspectives and, if so, how, to view our theme here?

Another question that appeared in this study is how we should deal with the social and cultural differences to evaluate the representation of the applications, because unlike pure mathematical knowledge and questions, practical background for mathematics application is more often related to some kind of social reality and cultural factors. Taking the mathematical content of probability as an example, in UCSMP *Advanced Algebra* (a US textbook) the knowledge of probability is well applied to explain how lotteries work. Actually, the textbook contains a specific lesson entitled *lotteries*, which includes more than a dozen examples and questions of application. This seems quite reasonable and understandable because lotteries are so popular in the US. However, this kind of application could not be included in Chinese textbooks because, in contrast to the US, games like lotteries were once regarded as a particular part of capitalist culture and strictly prohibited in China, though people's attitudes toward things like lotteries have somehow changed over the last decade because of its reform and open policy. In addition, it seems clear that the dimension of social and cultural differences should be valued with different weight for different topics of mathematical knowledge. In this regard, ethnomathematics can play a certain role in the study of the representation of mathematics applications.

Finally, as researchers have suggested that textbooks represent a kind of instructional environment and, to students, sheer frequency of exposure might have an important impact on the relative difficulty of problems of different types, it would be interesting and valuable, though also more difficult, to know how different textbooks with different characteristics in the representation of applications actually affect students' learning and their performance in solving practical problems.

Acknowledgments

This is an abridged report. A more detailed report can be obtained by contacting the author. The author is grateful to Karen Usiskin of ScottForesman, Jianhua Li of People's Education Press, and David Witonsky of University of Chicago School Mathematics Project, for their help. The author also greatly appreciates valuable comments on early versions of this paper from Professors John Craig, Robert Dreeben and, especially, Zalman Usiskin.

References

CARPENTER, T.P. and MOSER, J.M. (1987) 'Semantic classification of words problems', in ROMBERG, T. and COLLINS, K. (eds) *Learning to add and subtract*, Reston, VA: National Council of Teachers of Mathematics.

Exploring Mathematics (1994–1996) (Grade 1 to 6), Glenview, IL: ScottForesman.

FAN, L. (1990) 'Some comparisons and thoughts on the reform of mathematics curriculum', *Zhejiang Educational Science*, **23**, pp. 22–8; **24**, pp. 25–9, 16.

FLANDERS, J. (1987) 'How much of the content in mathematics textbooks is new?', *Arithmetic Teacher*, **35**(1), pp. 18–23.

FUSON, K.C. (1992) 'Research on whole number addition and subtraction', in GROUWS, D.A. (ed.) *Handbook of Research on Mathematics Teaching and Learning*, New York: Macmillan Publishing Company, pp. 243–75.

PEOPLE'S EDUCATION PRESS ELEMENTARY MATHEMATICS OFFICE (1991–1995) *The Compulsory Education Six-Year Elementary School Textbooks (Experimental Edition) — Mathematics (No. 1–12)*, Beijing: People's Education Press.

POSTLETHWAITE, T.N. (1988) *Encyclopedia of Comparative Education and National Systems of Education*, Oxford: Pergamon, pp. xvii–xxvi.

RILEY, M., GREENO, J. and HILLER, J. (1983) 'Development of children's problem-solving ability in arithmetic', in GINSBURG, H. (ed.) *The Development of Mathematical Thinking*, New York: Academic Press, pp. 153–200.

ROBINSOHN, S.B. (ed.) (1992) *Comparative Education: A Basic Approach*, Jerusalem: The Magnes Press, pp. 31–4.

STIGLER, J.W., FUSON, K.C., HAM, M. and KIM, M.S. (1986) 'An analysis of addition and subtraction word problems in American and Soviet elementary mathematics textbooks', *Cognition and Instruction*, **3**(3), pp. 153–71.

UCSMP Advanced Algebra (1996) Glenview, IL: ScottForesman.

USISKIN, Z. and BELL, M. (1983) *Applying Arithmetic: A Handbook of Applications of Arithmetic*, Chicago, IL: Department of Education, University of Chicago.

VERGNAUD, G.A. (1982) 'A classification of cognitive tasks and operations of thought involved in addition and subtraction problems', in CARPENTER, T.P. (ed.) *Addition and Subtraction: A Cognitive Perspective*, Hillsdale, NJ: Lawrence Erlbraum, pp. 39–59.

WIRSZUP, I. and STREIT, R. (eds) (1987) *Developments in School Mathematics Education Around the World: Applications-oriented Curricula and Technology-supported Learning for all Students*, Reston, VA: National Council of Teachers of Mathematics.

Part II

What Can We Learn from International Comparative Studies in Mathematics Education?

11 The Value of Comparative Studies

Geoffrey Howson

The value of comparative studies is discussed from several different perspectives — the nature of that value, to whom the study has value and how well the intentions are realized. After a biographical interlude to establish the context, several comparative studies are discussed — two small-scale studies, and the large-scale FIMS, SIMS and TIMSS. The efforts of TIMSS to remedy the aspects criticised in SIMS are highlighted — the consideration of the different national curricula, the new focus on classroom reality and textbook analyses. The chapter closes with an outlook into the future.

Beginnings

Alcuin, schoolmaster at the school attached to the great church at York, England, wrote in the eighth century of how his predecessor, Aethelbert, 'More than once went . . . abroad . . . to see if he could find in those lands new books or studies which he could bring home with him' (Sylvester, 1970). The urge to find out what is happening elsewhere, to compare, and to search for ideas which can be usefully imported is, then, far from new.

Interest in comparative education has continued to grow through the centuries and was given added impetus as a result of the spread of state education — the need to ensure that public money was being spent as effectively as possible has proved a great stimulus for comparative studies of all kinds.

There was, therefore, a boom in such studies in the nineteenth century, for industrialization and economic competition made apparent the need for better-educated workforces. Systems of state education at various levels and provisions for teacher training were special fields of interest. Studies were carried out by individuals and government bodies. Certainly, many references to mathematics teaching can be found in the reports which ensued, but the first major mathematics study began in 1908. The early years of the century saw radical changes in both the provision of secondary education and also in mathematics teaching — the latter having an effect akin to that of the 'modern math' reforms of the 1960s. These changes led to a call for an international exchange of views and experiences, and to the establishment of the Commission internationale de l'enseignement mathématique (CIEM, the forerunner of the International Commission on Mathematical Instruction, ICMI). Within the next six or so years, vast numbers of reports were prepared; some assembled by nations described their own systems, curricula, assessment practices, etc., while others gave the results of questionnaires completed by participating countries, and some provided accounts of a country's mathematics teaching written by observers from elsewhere.

What is important to notice is that all the studies to that time were essentially qualitative (although, naturally, they contained data relating to student numbers, timetabled hours, and so on). There was no attempt to compare student attainment by means of any standardized instruments. The spur given to psychometrics by Binet and Simon with their 'intelligence tests' gradually, however, began to exert an influence (along with a growing emphasis on quantitative research methods) and, as has already been described by Gabriele Kaiser in Chapter 1 of this book, this culminated in the establishment of the International Association for the Evaluation of Educational Achievement (IEA) and, in the 1960s, the First International Mathematics Study.

The Value of Comparative Studies: To Whom?

That comparative studies can have great value is undisputed. What must be questioned, however, is the nature of that value, to whom a study has value, and how readily the good intentions, thought and effort, which have gone into its design, convert into 'value for use'. Here it must be emphasized that 'value for use' does not necessarily mean supplying direct answers to questions, but rather in enabling planning and decision-taking to be better informed. National educational systems will not change overnight as a result of any comparative study. Yet a study may well have a significant local effect or, more usually, its effects will gradually permeate through and be absorbed by an educational system.

The nineteenth-century examples mentioned earlier all had clear aims and were intended to answer the questions of, and to provide information and guidance for, those undertaking the study — their purpose and planning were in no way international. For example, Kay-Shuttleworth inspected and compared Swiss and German teacher-training institutions with the sole aim of increasing the effectiveness of the one he planned to establish in England. The design of the study was directly governed by the desired outcomes. The large international study in which CIEM engaged had, however, less well-focused aims. It was driven by the practitioners' desire to compare what they were doing, within the context of their own national educational systems, with what was happening elsewhere. Accordingly, the papers prepared in England were published by the Board of Education essentially to provide English readers with a national overview of mathematics teaching at all levels, and, of course, to enlighten those in other lands.[1] The English, in turn, would read with interest the reports prepared in those countries whose educational systems or economic standing resembled their own, for example, France and Germany. Doubtless, other countries acted in a similar fashion. Essentially the

CIEM study sought to answer the questions of mathematicians, teacher trainers and teachers, and these questions related to practices and aims rather than to the levels of attainment actually achieved by students. Governments shared such interests to the extent that any lessons learned would, it was hoped, eventually enhance the national provision of mathematics education and, with it, the knowledge and ability of the national workforce.

Governments in this period were not, however, seeking any quantitative measures of the success or otherwise of their educational systems. This was not necessarily due to the absence of any competitive/comparative urges. However, secondary education was in its infancy in many countries (e.g. state secondary education did not officially exist in England before 1902) and differed so much between countries in its nature and aims that meaningful comparisons of attainment would have been difficult.

It was only after the Second World War and the coming, within the developed countries, of secondary education for all, that the conditions in which governments could reasonably seek wide-scale comparisons of attainment were created.

We are now in the position that comparative studies can seek to answer the specific questions of governments as well as those of teachers, educators and other interested parties. As a result, tensions arise within today's larger studies which depend upon considerable financial support. Inevitably, there will be a bias towards answering the questions on which the funding agencies place emphasis. Also, because of the vastly increased number of countries which wish to participate in such projects, it becomes increasingly difficult to answer the questions of teachers and educators — or even those of governments — concerning how they should act to counter observed weaknesses in their systems. Well-meaning attempts to cope with diverse systems will founder because of the difficulty of designing procedures and instruments which will have validity in all countries while still providing salient and significant data for those countries which share common aims, educational structures and contexts. We shall return to this problem in later sections, in which we consider in more detail what TIMSS would appear to have to offer and the possible future of such large-scale studies.

Before then we shall consider some examples of various kinds of smaller scale studies and offer some observations on them, on the motivation that may have prompted them, and on the extent and nature of their value.

A Biographical Interlude

Most of the present book is devoted to accounts and critiques of large-scale studies and the use of first-person pronouns is, to say the least, restricted. Yet international studies are carried out by people each of whom has personal reasons for involvement. Some may have little connection with mathematics education *per se* or they may be motivated by desires other than to seek improvements in the teaching and learning of mathematics and in our comprehension of the factors influencing these twin aims. Yet I suspect that personal motives and biases play a much greater role than some of the detached 'objective' accounts may suggest. It is also the case that many authors will have been involved in other types of comparative studies that will undoubtedly have helped form their approaches and viewpoints. I hope it will be useful and illuminative, then, to provide a brief account of my personal involvement in a variety of such studies, leading up to my connections with such current initiatives as TIMSS and the Exeter-Kassel Project.

It is now well over 30 years since I paid the first of many Aethelbert-type visits, on that occasion to schools and universities in what was then East Germany. As the editor-in-chief of the newly established School Mathematics Project (SMP) I was keen to search for new ideas.

Visits to classes in a variety of English schools had already led me to discard notions of there being such a thing as a 'national teaching style', although clearly some methods were more favoured than others. In East Germany, however, although teaching styles still varied, I found a much greater degree of homogeneity, partly in response to the imposition of a single national textbook and a national curriculum — two concepts at that time totally alien to anyone from England. The care with which texts were prepared impressed me, but committee-driven 'care' appeared to be inhibiting 'flair'. I had stumbled on a key issue of curriculum development — one faced by a national administrator, but not by an independent project such as SMP or the individual innovator. *How can one encourage innovation and give freedom to the gifted teacher, without conferring autonomy on the incompetent and risking the creation of a highly diverse system containing large pockets of highly-achieving and low-attaining schools?*

My interest in comparative studies was further fostered by the opportunities to talk with many overseas educators who visited SMP and discussed with me what changes would or would not be possible in their country and why. They helped draw my attention to another major question. *Where within a national system does the power to initiate and guide innovation lie?*

Other aspects of comparative education were revealed as a result of visits in 1965 to four Southern and East African countries. Now the problems of the feasibility and desirability of transferring ideas and practices between countries became much more apparent. *How could one act on the findings of comparative studies?*

Such problems soon became of greater concern to me, for in 1967 I became Assistant Director of the Centre for Curriculum Renewal and Educational Development Overseas (CREDO), a body providing aid to the developing countries. This proved a major personal comparative study for it involved visits to schools, universities and ministries of education in 20 or more countries worldwide.

Now, however, I was asked to work with different criteria. *What was the potential within a country for making worthwhile improvements?* (By now it was becoming clear that 'innovation' and 'improvement' were not synonyms.) *To which sector of an educational system should aid be targeted? How might greater emphasis be placed on the education of those students who could provide the technical foundation on which a country might build and prosper?* Usually the need for changes was well taken in the ministries I visited, but the problems of overcoming old prejudices and actually effecting significant and rapid educational changes were becoming increasingly apparent. Specific attention was focused on these problems in the economically developed countries following the establishment by the Organization for Economic Cooperation and Development (OECD) of a Centre for Educational Research and Innovation (CERI) with which I became involved in the late 1960s. One CERI initiative specifically sought to compare the manner in which educational changes were being effected in its member countries. This crucial area of comparative educational research has received insufficient attention for, although the aim of many comparative studies is to draw attention to desirable changes, it is by no means easy actually to make significant changes in a beneficial way. Many see the value of comparative studies in the way in which they can uncover 'good practice', but good practice in effecting change is as important to exhibit as is good practice in actual teaching. The CERI study has, to some extent, been replicated in recent years and it will be interesting to see how its findings supplement the masterly, if somewhat pessimistic, survey of the first study, Per Dalin's *Limits to Educational Change* (1978).

The fact that Dalin's book appears to be so little known, and that its warnings have been so frequently ignored, raises major issues concerning the reporting of comparative studies, a factor which vitally influences their potential value for non-participants. For example, although my visit to East Germany proved extremely valuable for me and caused me to reappraise much with which I was familiar in England, it did not result in any report, published account or lecture. How then is one to evaluate the various types of study to which I have referred? Some had little impact other than, possibly, on the participants. My work for CREDO and the reports I prepared, but which, because of their critical and sensitive nature, were never made public, did affect the way in which aid was given and consequently education (not only in mathematics) in many countries. The value of the study rested largely upon the way in which it affected the validity of the judgments I made. The study, like the others I have so far described, was highly subjective.

Yet, I believe it is far too easy to dismiss studies as 'subjective' without perhaps realizing the degree of subjectivity governing the scene setting and structure of so-called 'objective quantitative studies'. We shall return to this point later. Perhaps it suffices here briefly to describe a few further studies in which I have been involved.

Taking its cue from the earlier 1908 CIEM study, ICMI, in the 1970s, invited selected authors from various countries to describe the aims of the changes which had taken place in their countries in the 1960s and the extent to which these had been realized. The resulting papers, published in *Educational Studies in Mathematics* (1978, vol. 9) provided much of interest but, as so frequently in comparative education, there seemed to be little attempt actually to analyse, synthesize and derive possible implications from the data generated. For all the perceptive insights to be found in the various contributions, I believe that the study had little influence on the thought of, or policies followed by, any of the participating countries.

This need to attempt to analyse and synthesize data, observed practices and experiences provided the motivation for *Curriculum Development in Mathematics* (1981), a book I wrote with Christine Keitel and Jeremy Kilpatrick. This was, in effect, a subjective comparative study, drawing on the three authors' varied knowledge and experiences. Its value was intended to lie in providing frameworks within which readers might view curriculum development and also providing information that we hoped would help improve the level of planning and decision-making whatever the context within which these took place.

A second book, *National Curricula in Mathematics* (1991), had a totally different genesis. I was asked to chair a committee to produce a report describing mathematics education in the countries of the European Union. This would then enable teachers to gain a quick and reasonably accurate idea of the mathematical background of any students temporarily joining their classes. Such an information-gathering exercise, however, had no great appeal to me. Here, again, we have to draw a distinction between data gathering, which might still have considerable value, and an actual study based on the analysis and interpretation of such data. What particularly concerned me at that time (1989) was the National Mathematics Curriculum recently imposed on English schools, for I believed that to have serious educational, mathematical and pedagogical deficiencies. As a result, the report was not merely a description of the mathematics curricula and educational systems of other countries. Rather, it was a personal attempt to illustrate the many ways in which mathematics curricula are presented, the different cognitive, mathematical and educational structures to be observed, and the wide variety of expectations instanced concerning students' mathematical attainments. The value of the book was, I hoped, in providing decision-makers with a greater knowledge of possibilities and a clearer notion of the criteria to be met when constructing a curriculum. It was, however, an idiosyncratic publication which illustrated the value of such reports and also showed the need for other types of study that were not so subjective.

This need for both subjective, personal reports and, in addition, seemingly objective ones led to the last of the personal projects to which I wish to refer in this section. This was a study undertaken for the Third International Maths and Science Study (TIMSS) and published in 1995 with the title *Mathematics Textbooks: A Comparative Study of Grade 8 Texts*.

A major feature of TIMSS was an attempt to analyse and compare national curricula and, in particular, textbooks. We shall consider this further below. Here it suffices to say that I believed that the methods used could throw only limited light upon a very difficult to describe, yet enormously important, factor in mathematics education — the textbook. My own study, then, was meant to complement the major piece of work by looking in more detail at specimen texts drawn from eight countries and attempting to indicate, using examples and descriptions rather than numbers and percentages, their qualities and the great diversity which they displayed. The value of my work, as I viewed it, was the way in which it illustrated ideas drawn from textbooks in different countries and indicated features that might with benefit be adopted elsewhere. The objects of comparison were textbooks, drawn from different countries and traditions, rather than the national educational systems, for these might be only weakly characterized by the textbooks chosen for study.

This distinction is significant, since so often international comparative studies are automatically linked with rankings of countries. This need not necessarily be the purpose of such studies. Thus, for example, the 'best' textbooks will not necessarily come from those countries which lead the rankings, and the books from those countries which 'perform badly' might contain many valuable ideas and examples which 'higher attaining' countries could, with benefit, adopt. It is, to say the least, unfortunate if major studies time the release of their data and findings in such a way that overmuch attention is laid on rankings.

Two Small Studies

In this section I wish to comment briefly on two recent studies in which I have been peripherally involved. One was carried out under the aegis of the National Institute of Economic and Social Research, based in London (NIESR); the other, the Exeter-Kassel Project, has been described in Chapter 9 of this book. These illustrate different ways in which international studies can have 'value'.

The NIESR Project is of particular interest because of the way in which it moved from being an international comparative study of industrial productivity and its determinants to one specifically concerned with curriculum development in English schools. It owes much to the driving force of Professor Sig Prais, an economist and mathematical statistician rather than a professional mathematician or mathematics educator. During a decade of factory management, he found that his company, along with others from England, had difficulty competing technologically with foreign rivals. Returning to academic research, he organized study visits to matched samples of German and English factories which led him to attribute a substantial part of English deficiencies to the poor vocational training which the English workforce as a whole had received. This prompted what developed into a series of national studies of vocational training and education (involving France, Germany, Japan, the

Netherlands and Switzerland) comparing the qualification processes of those likely to be employed in jobs requiring both technical skills and also the ability rapidly to acquire new ones. What appeared significant was the degree of proficiency in mathematics which school-leavers were expected to attain. In particular, it was inferred that in England relatively little was expected of (and consequently achieved by) average and below-average students — a state of affairs confirmed by the studies undertaken by the International Association for the Evaluation of Educational Achievement (IEA) and the International Assessment of Educational Progress (IAEP).

The next move was to try to improve mathematics education in English primary schools in an attempt to ensure that many children did not already at an early age feel left behind and unable to cope with mathematics. The project was not unique in seeking that objective, but what qualifies it for mention here is that the project retained, indeed built on, its 'comparative' beginnings. Links were formed between Zurich in Switzerland and a local education authority (school district) in London having a high proportion of low-attaining children. Study visits were then arranged for NIESR researchers, senior teachers from the London schools and their school inspectors, in order to focus attention on Swiss teaching methods and the standards attained by Swiss students. As a consequence of these visits, a pilot project was established in London seeking to incorporate those features of Swiss classroom practice that had impressed the visiting teams. A much fuller account of the project and its genesis can be found in Prais (1996) from which we quote the following paragraph because of its especial relevance.

> The new features and changes introduced so far . . . were decided upon after repeated systematic observation of Continental practice by our teams of teachers and researchers; but these features are rarely described and analysed with adequate clarity and requisite detail in academic international research, such as the IEA or IAEP studies; the same holds for the organisational aspects . . . What success the present project may claim is very much the result of experienced practising English teachers and inspectors forming the core of our observation teams . . . Earlier international research undoubtedly provided background and starting points: but the drawing of relevant empirical conclusions, and the setting of priorities, depended on their experienced eyes (1996:7).

This project, then, had similarities with the Kay-Shuttleworth approach — the study of other systems with the specific intention of seeing what could be done to improve the education of average and below-average attaining students in England. However, what was important was its recognition of the fact that views are changed by seeing and experiencing and not merely by being told how to do better. Teachers and inspectors were not given edited accounts of what happened in Swiss classrooms or descriptions of typical lessons there, but they were allowed to visit the classrooms and to judge whether, and in what ways, to adopt the teaching methods they observed.

Here, one or two points spring immediately to mind. One concerns the choice of Switzerland for the study. The teachers might well have found equal inspiration elsewhere, but the cost of visiting a wide range of countries would have been exorbitant (although, in fact, some teacher visits were also arranged to France, Germany and the Netherlands). The decision to focus attention on Switzerland (and to some extent Southern Germany) was taken based on the IEAP results and the preliminary studies. In so deciding, the team opted not to search for the chimera of 'best practice', but settled for what they saw as 'better practice'. The second point is that the cost of such team visits might seem excessively high, yet the travel and maintenance costs amounted to less than half the salary of a research assistant. A personal view, based on many years of curriculum development, is that such an investment could prove extremely rewarding — shared observation and group curriculum development form an excellent motivation and foundation for progress. The subsequent pilot development project (which also built on the findings of a detailed study of English, German and Swiss primary school texts (Bierhoff, 1996)) has attracted much attention from politicians and the media. Of course, once the number of schools involved in the project increases then the international comparative element of the project may acquire less importance. An attempt has been made to keep this element through the use of videos of Swiss classrooms, together with videos of these methods being applied in British classrooms. Videos of foreign classrooms have, of course, been produced by other projects (as described in Chapter 6) and have considerable value. This lies, however, more in their ability to initiate valuable discussion (which will need to be well led, preferably by someone who has actually observed such teaching) about what the viewers saw, approved or disapproved of, and were surprised or puzzled by, than in actually conveying a full sense of the flow of mathematics teaching and learning in that particular class or in providing direct models for emulation.[2]

To sum up, the value of the NIESR project appears to have arisen from the way in which it was so strongly focused and directly linked with practical curriculum development. It was seen and planned as a preliminary to what was considered to be desirable action, and it involved those who would be called upon to act. There will be great interest in seeing how the project develops and to what extent, and in what form, Swiss practices are absorbed into the English educational system.

The Exeter-Kassel Project, too, had its genesis in a similarly well-focused attempt to explore, in three countries, a problem relating to the curriculum (again, taken in its widest sense — including teaching and assessment methods and not merely syllabus content). The initial concern was not simply comparative attainment — for that had been, and was being, attempted by others, but the way in which students' learning progressed. It was a study driven by pedagogical considerations and, although supported financially by the same charitable foundation as the NIESR Project, it had to rely to a considerable extent upon the goodwill, enthusiasm and support of its participants. Thus, although the limited funding led to some administrative problems and constraints, the project enjoyed considerable commitment from those involved. However, schools and teachers willing to provide time, support and encouragement for such a project are unlikely to be representative of a country's schools as a whole. In addition, the Exeter-Kassel project differed substantially from, say, TIMSS or IAEP in the degree of commitment it asked of participating schools. Since 'progress' was to be measured, attempts had to be made to find starting points and to assess the 'potential' of students. In addition, the schools were asked to devote a considerable amount of time for several years to the testing of pupils. Since so few schools were involved and attention was directed at the progress of individual classes, it was necessary to test every pupil every year on the whole range of mathematics. That is, pupils were expected to take three or four test papers annually, whereas TIMSS tested a much larger sample of pupils once only, each student taking only a subset of its bank of items, and then drew on its technical statistical expertise to arrive at 'country' scores.

Enthusiasts will attract enthusiasts from elsewhere and they will clearly benefit from meeting and exchanging views and experiences. Not surprisingly, then, there was soon pressure to expand the activities of the Exeter-Kassel Project to other countries. This appears to have had both positive and negative effects on the value of the project.

In a positive sense, it brought more people from different countries into contact and allowed for a more widespread comparison of levels of attainment. The results of this were still of interest. Although one could argue that the choice of schools in the Exeter-Kassel Project was far from random, that the test items were constructed with the curricula of the three original countries in mind, and that there was little uniformity in times of testing or actually in the number of test papers taken by pupils, the ranking of the countries by student attainment — despite all these factors — showed few or no significant differences from that of TIMSS. On the other hand it would appear that the international growth of the project has lessened the emphasis on its really distinctive feature — its longitudinal nature in which progression was studied both quantitatively and through classroom observation.

The findings of the Exeter-Kassel project cannot claim to satisfy the rigorous research and statistical criteria of, say, TIMSS. Yet this is not to discount their value. Findings that are firmly based on collected data, including those arising from subjective classroom observations, may well prove of more value than answers, based on the most reliable quantitative data, to questions which no educator would ever ask.

We see, however, that in contrast to the NIESR Project, which became ever more focused and goal-driven, the Exeter-Kassel Project, by increasing the number of countries involved, significantly changed the type of value that it could offer.

FIMS and SIMS

It is impossible to consider TIMSS without first paying some attention to the two IEA mathematics studies which preceded it. In retrospect the most interesting feature about the First International Mathematics Study (FIMS) to me was the lack of interest which was shown in it at the time. I can recall a colleague who had been asked to review the FIMS report fulminating about its inadequacies and what to him were the unjustifiable assumptions drawn in it, but it was not until Freudenthal (1975) published a scathing criticism that most educators became aware of the study's existence. Looking back, the most valuable aspect of FIMS was probably the way in which it provided guidance on what worked and also on what required to be rethought. Moreover, FIMS took place at a time of general economic and educational expansion. Education systems were undergoing rapid and in many cases important structural changes. In England, for example, between the FIMS testing and the publication of its report, the move to comprehensive schools had gathered pace and a new 16+ national examination had been introduced for students between the 40th and 80th percentiles, and so the 1964 data referred to a system which had been substantially overhauled. Perhaps most significantly of all, the FIMS results could not be compared with any others — no country had got 'better' or 'worse' and the data supplied provided neither governments nor their critics with obvious ammunition.

The Second International Mathematics Study (SIMS) was carried out in a different climate. The oil crisis had left its mark on the economies of many countries and, in the early 1980s, governments had become much more interested in whether educational systems were providing value for money. In addition, the educational changes of the preceding 15 years had often become the subject of criticism, and there was interest in seeing to what extent these had affected student attainment.

Those responsible for SIMS, and here I am basing my remarks on my somewhat marginal role as a consultant, had realized the dangers that were associated with any study that was seen as simply ranking countries by student attainment on a bank of items which did not fairly reflect the different curricula followed in the participating countries (a charge levelled by Freudenthal) and using only a very limited form of assessment, the multiple choice question. Nothing was done about the latter point, but steps were taken to ensure a better fit between item banks and curricula. This, of course, necessitated more careful consideration of the mathematical content studied in the various countries — no one believed that syllabus content was the sole, or even the most important, variable. Accordingly, more was done to tease out differences in teaching styles and also to investigate such obvious factors as school organization, teachers' experience and training, and students' motivation, social background and out-of-school support, both from their families and in the form of extra tuition.

Essentially, the problem was that educators possessed a rough and ready way of assessing and comparing the output of school systems by means of tests, the reliability and validity of which were still open to question. On the other hand, a knowledge of output means little unless one also has information about the context in which schooling is taking place, the general aims of the system and the inputs to their system, financial, human and in kind. No one would think of comparing the outputs of the Skoda and BMW works in isolation — why, then, rank educational systems in such a simplistic way?

Yet the complexity of the educational inputs is truly enormous. What is the country's investment in education?[3] How is this divided between capital investment (including that on teacher training — the most important form of capital investment) and recurrent expenditure. Here we must think, for example, about teacher salaries (and how these compare with national norms), classroom materials (textbooks and apparatus — including the new technology), assessment procedures (for example, in England more is spent on assessing students than on providing them with textbooks and apparatus) and on provision for research. What can be said about the support which society provides, through the status it grants to education and, in particular, to teachers? How does one assess student effort (the hours spent at school, the proportion of that time devoted to the learning of mathematics, on homework and tutorials) and student motivation (the extent to which students have been persuaded that mathematics is worth learning)? Similar questions can be asked about teachers: what are their timetabled hours for teaching and what other duties are they expected to perform; what are the provisions for, and their expectations regarding, in-service training?

Other questions, so far unexplored, relate to the 'drop out' from mathematics once it becomes optional, and the numbers (and percentages) who opt to study mathematics and those subjects relying greatly upon it (such as physics and engineering) at university. Such data would have to be treated with caution, for many factors influence career choices, but one cannot measure successful mathematics teaching simply by attainment at 13 or even 17 — one must also ask to what extent the teaching is encouraging students to continue with the study of mathematics.

SIMS attempted to deal with many of these questions as best it could through the use of a variety of questionnaires directed at schools, teachers and pupils. Unfortunately, though, it lacked the funds to ensure that it could analyse the data it collected and produce its reports within a reasonable time span. There was too long a gap between data collection and the appearance of the international reports, and even then it was the volume on student attainment that claimed most attention.

Yet SIMS represented an advance on FIMS and, in particular, it tried hard to meet some of the criticisms made of the earlier study. It had value in providing countries not only with a measure of how their educational systems were performing (even if there were those who would decry the measure as too simplistic), but it also indicated what, in some countries, it was possible for students of a particular age group to achieve (and gave strong hints about what the majority of students could not). It may be useful to elaborate on these last remarks. There is a tendency within educational research to concentrate on learning within one's own country and to move from observed results to hypotheses about what children of a particular age can and cannot be reasonably expected to do. The outcomes of comparative tests will often (rightly) lead to the questioning of such assumptions.

SIMS also permitted comparisons over time. In some countries it had a longitudinal aspect — students were tested at the beginning and end of a year. The results of this testing have not become widely known, but for me held much of interest and value. For example, at a first glance the data for Japan showed varying degrees of improvement by the cohort over the year. However, when the data were disaggregated to show how individuals had answered items on the two occasions they were tested, then interesting questions about the 'stability' of an individual's attainment were raised. Thus, for instance, one item on percentage was answered correctly by 59 per cent of Japanese students at the beginning of the year and by 60 per cent at the end. Yet only 38.5 per cent answered the question correctly on both occasions — over 80 per cent answered correctly on at least one occasion. What does this tell us about the percentage of Japanese students who knew how to solve such a problem? Such instability has been observed in other studies since then, but this is but one example of the value of comparative studies in raising important questions. However, was the effect in this case exacerbated by the use of only multiple choice items?

Comparisons with FIMS were now possible but raised many questions, particularly concerning references to the items used in both studies. Emphases in mathematics education change with the years and some items would not have been given the same emphasis in the classroom in 1981 as in 1964. Yet merely comparing the results obtained on the same items in FIMS and SIMS can have enormous value since it can cause one to re-assess the desirability of shifts in emphasis. For example, 'arithmetical standards' appeared to have dropped in all countries between FIMS and SIMS, probably as a result of the impact of new technology on society's perceived needs for arithmetical competence, but how does poorer arithmetical understanding and technical ability (such as on fractions) affect the learning of other mathematical topics? Nevertheless, the data resulting from repeated testing at long intervals can, if not properly interpreted and because of the publicity the results generate, act as a constraint on sensible curriculum development.

The general value of SIMS, then, in providing information not only on student attainment but also on the educational systems of the participating countries, and of drawing attention to questions which warranted further examination is fairly obvious. SIMS, however, also offered value, in a way largely hidden from those not closely connected with it. For example, it led to the development and elaboration of statistical techniques needed for dealing with such large-scale studies and, in particular, vastly expanded the research and technical expertise of a number of educators and administrators from second and third world countries.

TIMSS

The Third International Mathematics and Science Study (TIMSS) was an enormous undertaking. It surpassed any predecessor not only in the number of countries involved but also in covering two subjects, its range of populations tested, and its ambition in delving more deeply than before into a variety of aspects of teaching and learning. Not surprisingly, some goals were not attained as successfully as others. The relative failures, due on occasion to over-ambition coupled with a lack of experience, should not be allowed to detract from the study's achievements. These latter, however, tell us little about the study's 'value' — indeed, there is no objective measure of this. In some countries the findings of TIMSS will have little 'value for use'. In others, although potentially of value, they may well be 'swept under the carpet'. Either countries may not wish to heed the messages in the findings or, possibly more likely, ministries of education will believe that there is little that they can actually do to effect desired changes. It is necessary, then, to consider the value the study might have for a specific country — again, for obvious reasons, I have chosen England.

First, however, let us look at two defining features of TIMSS. What are the benefits and disadvantages of its being mounted under the auspices of the IEA? The benefits are clear: IEA has a pedigree and so TIMSS could build not only upon preceding mathematics studies but also on those undertaken in other subjects. TIMSS could call, therefore, upon a great range of technical expertise. Only this vast bank of knowledge and experience allowed TIMSS to achieve so much in so short a time: to design and trial five item banks, oversee translation problems, organize quality control of the testing procedures, collect, weight and analyse the test results and questionnaires and prepare reports approved by the participating countries (Beaton et al., 1996a and b). The drawback is that IEA has many national members which wished to participate in a key study involving what were thought of as the two most important academic disciplines to be found in their shared curricula. Yet with every additional country the problem of matching test items to national curricula became greater, as did the more complex tasks of, for example, analysing curricula and textbooks, and making sense of the mountain of data generated by the various questionnaires, to say nothing of the extra problems of communication and liaison which were created. This problem of increasing multinational complexity will not go away and we shall consider how this might lead to studies being established outside the orbit of the IEA.

The second determining factor of TIMSS was also two-edged. Unlike its predecessors, TIMSS was generously financed — in particular, it received very large sums from US and Canadian sources. The resulting benefits were great — it made it possible to administer the project efficiently and to carry out its manifold activities. Also, the generous funding facilitated the participation of several countries, including several mathematically high-attaining ones from Eastern Europe, which might otherwise not have been possible. On the other hand, certain *a priori* conditions were imposed, for example, that the study should cover both mathematics and science. It also gave the study a strong North American bias, particularly in the crucial planning stages, which appeared to inhibit fundamental thought regarding problems to be addressed and possible modes of action.

TIMSS, like SIMS, made great efforts to meet criticisms made of its predecessor. In this respect the most obvious development was the inclusion of open and extended response items in the main item banks and the provision of separate performance assessment tests (although the latter were taken by a minority of countries). Both of these initiatives built upon the work of the IAEP studies carried out in the years between SIMS and TIMSS. A less well appreciated, but extremely valuable, addition to the range of tests was that intended for final year secondary school students (not necessarily mathematics students/specialists) which tested what might be called 'advanced mathematical numeracy' — the mathematical (and, indeed scientific) knowledge needed by today's informed adult. Since this requirement is independent of national curricula, the item bank could be constructed unhindered by questions of whether or not a topic had been taught, and neither was it constrained to follow patterns established in previous studies. I believe that the resulting item bank offers great value both for present use and also as a starting point for discussion on what might constitute 'mathematics for all'. Regrettably, few countries participated in this aspect of TIMSS and I hope this will not mean that its results and existence will attract little attention in countries, such as England, which even though they did not participate could still find much of value in it.

The provision of videos of classroom practice has already been described in this book as has TIMSS's work on textbook and curriculum analysis. This latter aspect deserves further consideration. As I wrote earlier, 'value' is a subjective concept and I have opted to concretize this by concentrating on England. Here, then, it must be reported that England opted not to participate in the TIMSS textbook and curriculum analysis, on the grounds that its curriculum was in a state of flux. The problem of how one actually describes the curriculum raises important questions. There is no doubt that the authorities in England would have welcomed information on the curricula followed in what they regarded as important 'competitor' countries, but how is such information to be obtained? In Japan, the national curriculum is set out in considerable detail, year by year, and is followed by all students. Elsewhere, reporting is not always so easy. In Germany, every Land has its own curriculum, and for most secondary school systems there will be different curricula according to whether or not a student attends a *Gymnasium*, a *Realschule* or a *Hauptschule*. Also, in many German Lands and in some other countries, the curriculum is not given by year but by 'stage' — for example for students between 11 and 14. In some countries, such as England and France, the national curriculum is statutory; in others, such as Scotland and the Netherlands, it has an advisory role. In England and New Zealand, for example, students work through a common curriculum at their own pace — thus, of three 13-year-olds, the high-attainer might be already studying work which the average student will not reach before 16, while the low-attainer will be doing work done by the high-attainer at 10. How does one make sense of such complexity? Averaging things out tells us very little about the curriculum followed by any student. Moreover, attempts to quantify inevitably lead to frameworks which prove too fine to use for widespread collection and coding purposes, or too coarse to result in anything of value to curriculum planners. Similar considerations apply to textbook analyses. Now, however, the relation between the intended curriculum and that implemented becomes even more perplexing. For, to take an example, the encyclopedic US grade texts could never be taught in their entirety in one year. However, teaching is not solely a matter of time on task, relative emphasis given to topics and so on — it concerns the quality of exposition, and the quality and nature of the activities and exercises to which students are exposed. Howson (1995 and forthcoming) report on TIMSS-sponsored work which, in particular, contrasts treatments of operations on the integers to be found in textbooks drawn from eight TIMSS countries. The mathematical and pedagogical approaches vary enormously, as does the manner in which the exercises are compiled — a variation in aims and quality entirely concealed in any quantitative approach.

Certainly, TIMSS had to take national curricula into account when constructing its item banks, and again the influence of textbooks on student performance is a subject well worthy of study. However, the *ad hoc* procedure TIMSS eventually had to adopt — namely, the test-curriculum matching analysis — was probably the best solution then available to a very difficult problem. In this, countries were asked whether or not items matched the curriculum likely to be followed by the average student — a process not without its difficulty and, one imagines, occasional arbitrariness of decision taking. What must be realized, however, is that in many countries 'average students' were not tested on everything contained in their curriculum (for example, Japanese students would have covered far more formal algebra than was tested). Also, high-attaining students in countries with multi-partite, multi-lateral, or multi-streamed systems (such as those in Germany, the Netherlands and England) were frequently not tested on the curriculum they were following, but on that followed by the 'average' student. Such effects are difficult to evaluate. I suspect that the gaps in attainment between the higher and lower ranking countries may be even greater than is demonstrated by the TIMSS findings. Students in some countries have not always been given the chance to show how much mathematics they know and can do. What TIMSS has done is to allow students to demonstrate what they do not know or cannot do. (This criticism applies to most, if not all, examinations, but usually their local nature permits a better match between the curriculum and what is tested.) Nevertheless, even if TIMSS appears only to test a core of mathematics largely common to all countries, this more-or-less universally agreed core forms an essential foundation on which further mathematics learning is built. If a country finds that this core is not contained in its national curriculum, or that its students do not match international levels of achievement on that core, then there would seem to be a strong case for reconsidering that curriculum and investigating whether or not there are valid reasons for under performance. Yet one must again emphasize that no such core could expect to stand absolutely unchanged for any long period of time. Curricula will evolve for many reasons — mathematical, social and technological — and it is important that comparative studies recognize this and adjust item banks accordingly.

So far as textbook analysis is concerned, I can think of no practicable way in which textbooks, used in over 40 different educational systems and written in over 30 languages, could usefully and reliably be compared — either quantitatively or qualitatively — and their influences on teaching and learning in the classroom assessed. The analysis offered by TIMSS will certainly throw some light on certain issues, but I cannot imagine that it will prove useful as an aid to decision-taking in the way in which, for example, the much more focused analysis by Bierhoff (1996, see Section 4) has.

Nevertheless, the Survey of Science and Mathematics Opportunities (SMSO) report (Schmidt et al., 1996) offers much of value in its qualitative descriptions of the various lessons observed in the six SMSO countries and in its general (essentially subjective) summaries. Even then, after studying the textbooks concerned, I should treat with suspicion a table (Schmidt et al.: 55) which tells me that, for example, Grade 8 US textbooks devote about 5 per cent of their emphasis to 'mathematical reasoning', whereas in Spain this percentage rises to 35. To be fair, I find less to quibble about in the data referring to content coverage, than in those on the ill-defined 'performance expectations'. Yet, perhaps misguidedly, I still feel that the exact proportions of time allocated to teaching integers in Spain and the US, even if this could be inferred from the study of textbooks, is less significant than exactly what is taught, and what students are expected to know and be able to do as a result.

What, though, is the 'value', as I see it, of the TIMSS findings to date for England? First, considerable value arises from the dual nature of the study. Here I must confess that, when a member of the TIMSS Steering Committee, I believed that the added complexity of studying two disciplines in tandem was to TIMSS's detriment. This may well have proved the case for countries that showed similar levels of attainment in both subjects (for example, at Grades 7/8, Singapore, Czech Republic, Canada and Kuwait). However, other countries (such as Hong Kong, England, France and Switzerland) have been posed interesting questions concerning their varying levels of 'success', the relative emphasis placed on these two subjects and, in some cases, the very different weight students attach to success in them. In England's case, relatively pleasing performances in science were offset by weaker ones in mathematics — the vital factor being that the tests were taken by exactly the same students on the same day. Refuge for the poor mathematics results could not be sought in sampling effects or sociological causes, and attention had to be directed at what happened in mathematics classrooms — the quality of the national curriculum, of textbooks, of national assessment procedures, and of teachers and their teaching.

The weakness of the mathematics results came as no surprise to those who for years had been issuing warnings, but one hopes they have had the value of removing all the grounds for the complacency previously displayed. No sooner had the first results been published, however, than 'remedies' for England's problems began to appear in the press. Here again, though, the TIMSS international reports (not, then, available to those who offered solutions) demonstrate that far too frequently changes were being demanded to practices which in other countries proved successful. The problem, TIMSS suggests, often lay not in the practices, but in the manner and appropriateness with which they were being executed in England. It is essential, if true value is to be obtained from TIMSS, that as much attention is paid to the data generated by the various questionnaires as to the different country ranking lists by attainment.[4] Yet it must be admitted that the data on teaching methods (and much else) provide little guidance on how countries might improve their performances. There are weaknesses in the questionnaires, for these fail to take sufficient account of the differences between the structures of the various educational systems. More importantly however, it would seem beyond the powers of any short questionnaire to supply worthwhile information relating to the quality of a teacher's teaching, the effectiveness with which he or she makes use of alternative teaching practices and, of course, the teacher's levels of expectations. These would seem the critical variables, rather than the percentages of time spent on particular tasks.

Some of the data generated by the questionnaires raise great problems for mathematics educators. For example, pp. 117–20 of Beaton et al. (1996a) describe 'How do students perceive success in mathematics?'. The majority of 13+ students in Hong Kong (62 per cent), Japan (55 per cent) and Korea (62 per cent), three high-attaining countries, felt they were not doing well. On the other hand, 93 per cent of 8th graders in England felt that they usually did well in mathematics (a view shared by their low-attaining peers in, for example, Colombia, Denmark, Greece, Iran, Kuwait, Scotland and the USA). This, I believe, tells us much about teacher expectations and the way in which these are transmitted to students. It would appear, therefore, that in many of the low-attaining countries expectations are too low — but what are the consequences for further recruitment to mathematics of the feelings reported from these high-attaining countries? Itaka et al. (1995) suggests that Japan has great problems. Here, then, there is a nice balance to be observed between setting goals which are too low and those which result in too many students becoming discouraged even though, in international terms, they are perform-ing at a high standard.

Other data, for example the emphasis which teachers place on 'real-life' mathematics and its apparent effects, would repay further study. Unfortu-nately, this brings us to a decision taken by TIMSS which, in my view, seriously diminishes its value to the mathematical community — the decision to release data on only a selection of items (including that most vital piece of information — what the items actually were). One can understand the reasons for this, in that TIMSS was originally planned as a two-part study with the tests to be repeated in four years' time. Thus it was a longitudinal study not of a group of particular students (as in the Exeter-Kassel Project) but of an educational system. Clearly problems concerning the confidentiality of items could arise; the Exeter-Kassel Project dealt with this by the use of similar items in which only the numbers or the contexts occurring in the items were changed. I believe, however, that TIMSS' fear that countries would spend the intervening four years coaching pupils to answer the 1995 items was mis-placed. Moreover, this problem could have been circumvented by the replace-ment of a quarter or so of the items — a sufficient proportion to display any suspicious differences in performance on the old and new items. Perhaps more to the point, however, is the value such a repeat test might have for the countries involved. It could throw doubt on the accuracy of the 1995 data, but any response made to these findings, such as in changes to curricula or teaching practices, would not have had time to make their effect by 1999. Certainly, I find it hard to imagine that England would find any great value in taking part in the planned second series of tests. Here, it is essential to empha-size that value is not only subjective, but also relative — could one obtain better value by spending the money in a different way? To take another example, the results of TIMSS demonstrated large differences in attainment between the different Lands of Germany. However, it would seem much more sensible to carry out a national investigation into these differences, using instruments specially devised to match the German curricula, than to repeat an international test, employing relative blunt instruments, on larger samples of students.

We are left, then, in the totally unsatisfactory situation of having research data published based on items which are not open to public inspection and validation. This, alas, is frequently the case within educational research and is to the latter's detriment. Problems might have been alleviated had TIMSS provided more information in its first report. Thus, for example, I should have wished to see the following:

(a) Scores on multiple-choice and non-multiple-choice items disaggreg-ated. TIMSS introduced the latter for the first time in an IEA mathematics study, but what new information did they give us? In particular (and see Chapter 14 in this volume), were there differences in the results between the two sexes?

(b) Past studies have attempted to classify items by cognitive level. One does not have to be a fanatical follower of Bloom to realize that

> If m represents a positive number, which of these is equivalent to $m + m + m + m$? ($m + 4$, $4m$, m^4, $4(m + 1)$)

tests 'know that', while

> Peter bought 70 items and Sue bought 90 items. Each item cost the same and the items cost $800 altogether. How much did Sue pay?

tests 'know how'.

Of course, questions arise in classifying the cognitive complexity of items, but similar problems also occur when items are classified by content. There is no reason, for example, why a student should use proportionality concepts to solve the latter question, although TIMSS defines it to be a 'proportionality' item.

In England, one response to the publication of poor results has been that '. . . our children are good at problem-solving'. It is important to be able to see to what extent the TIMSS data justify such claims. The TIMSS International Report (Beaton et al., 1996a) does, in fact, attach performance category labels to the selection of items it contains, but it provides no analyses by category. Of course, if all the items and international data were freely available, then such problems could be investigated and the result laid open for general inspection within participating countries.

(c) One of the striking features of previous studies has been the ability of students to answer items not contained in either the country's intended or its implemented curricula — they have gained the requisite knowledge outside the mathematics classroom. The TIMSS test-curriculum-matching analysis demonstrates this particularly well — see Appendix B of Beaton et al. (1996a) and the corresponding Appendix in the science report (1996b). Some of the knowledge displayed may well have been acquired in other lessons or may now constitute common sense or local knowledge amongst adolescents in developed countries — certain aspects of data handling and probability, for instance. Again such matters could be readily investigated if full data on all the items were available, together with an indication of whether or not they were considered to be included in a country's curriculum.

It has been argued, that educational research draws heavily on two traditions which are linked with the names of Galton (1822–1911) and Fisher (1890–1962). The former sought to generate hypotheses inductively on the bases of analyses of natural situations, whereas Fisher was concerned with the deductive testing of hypotheses through controlled experimentation. Essentially, TIMSS is in the Galton tradition: it collects data and using statistical techniques akin to those employed by Galton (ranking, percentiles, correlation) and hopes to generate hypotheses which will illuminate our understanding. It did not commence by setting out hypotheses that it wanted to test and devising item banks with these in mind. This does not detract from the value of TIMSS, since one could not have tested any significant hypothesis in a serious manner on so vast a scale. Moreover, as I have indicated, even the TIMSS data that are freely available pose many interesting and serious problems worthy of more focused investigation. However, viewed in this light it would seem more important than ever that all data are made available for study.

To revert to a specific example, there is probably considerably more value for England in realizing that after over eight years of formal education fewer than half our students gave the correct response to

A person's heart is beating 72 times a minute. At this rate, about how many times would it beat in one hour?
(a) 420000, (b) 42000, (c) 4200, (d) 420,

than in knowing that on the 51 Fractions and Number Sense items (the nature, relevance and importance of which are concealed from us), English students scored on average X per cent points fewer than students of country Y — which probably has quite different curricular emphases and even policies on the promotion of pupils (for instance, in England 99 per cent and in Japan 100 per cent of all 13-year-olds were in Grades 7 or 8, compared with 78 per cent in France and 73 per cent in Germany).

It would, I believe, be helpful if TIMSS reconsidered its earlier decision not to release data on all the items and, in so doing, emphasized the fact that its main concerns are to provide educational guidance, rather than merely to produce rankings of countries.

The Future

What is the future for international comparative studies? Will there be a Fourth International Study involving 70 or more countries and generating more and more volumes of data on attainment, curricula and textbooks, and responses to questionnaires on attitudes, experiences, values; etc.? I suspect not. However, more focused regional or economically-linked studies will surely take place and will build upon the very valuable foundations which the IEA studies have laid.

In a recent review of international surveys of educational achievement involving England (Reynolds and Farrell, 1996), the authors recommend 'Future studies of the IEA and similar organizations should attempt to describe cross cultural differences rather less and analyse the reasons for their existence rather more'. One sympathizes with this desire for greater analysis provided, as I have made clear already, that analyses are always accompanied by full descriptions of data.

However, is IEA seriously to be expected to analyse the reasons for cross-cultural differences between Singapore, Japan, England, Iceland, Iran and Colombia? The demand for more analysis is, I am sure, a correct one, but this can only be profitably undertaken if the study is more focused. The OECD is now known to be planning its own studies of mathematics and science attainment to be repeated at fixed intervals. Such an initiative would appear to make good sense, and would facilitate both the improved design of the international study and also more serious analysis of its results. It should, however, be noted that there are now 25 OECD countries (and even more educational systems) and that those involved in TIMSS ranged over 35 places in the mathematics Grade 8 rankings (the top country and the bottom four were not members of OECD). Moreover, of the 10 comparator countries especially selected by England to feature in its TIMSS National Report (Keys et al., 1996), two are not members of OECD. By restricting the study to OECD countries, therefore, one would still be left with considerable complexity and variety, but there would be associated losses. Such a move would also probably sound the death knell for future IEA mathematics studies, for no OECD country would be likely to want to involve itself in two such largely similar studies, and this could deny non-OECD countries the opportunity to participate in future large-scale international mathematics studies.

Whatever eventually happens, I believe that comparative studies will continue in some form, for they have demonstrated that they have much of value to offer. However, I hope that the value of smaller-scale projects will not be overlooked, and that there is a move from what I have called the Galton model of comparative research to one which will offer more guidance on how perceived deficiencies might be corrected. For, to revert to England as a test case, TIMSS has clearly demonstrated the need for action on mathematics teaching, but so far it has proved of little value in indicating what form that action might most profitably take. If, however, we are to move to the Fisher model, then it is imperative that subject specialists play a much more active role in the planning of the studies and, equally, that the technical expertise acquired through the IEA studies is properly tapped. For example, it may be that certain of the 'rotating forms' (subsets of items) used in TIMSS are designed in future specifically to test particular hypotheses or to examine advanced mathematical topics to be found in the curricula of only a few of the participating countries (such forms would then be offered as national options). Not only would the resulting findings prove of general value, but also they would lessen the apparent 'horse race' emphasis, which diminishes the status of international comparative studies in the eyes of so many educators. For, although comparative studies can be of value because of what they tell us about relative attainment, the great worth of such studies, viewed in the wider sense that I have indicated, would appear to be in causing us to look again at what might be termed 'national educational axioms', and thus making us realize that what are regarded as universal self-evident truths may be little more than local traditions urgently in need of re-examination and re-appraisal.

Notes

1   Throughout this chapter I shall tend to take examples from England to illustrate the more general points I wish to make. To attempt to provide examples from other countries would probably be too foolhardy!

2   A specific example will illuminate the last sentence and also illustrate some problems concerning the choice of lessons to film. It concerns a video I recently saw which had been prepared by one comparative project (not TIMSS) showing 'good teaching' of 6-year-olds. There was much to admire in the way in which the teacher handled the class (which teachers in many countries would have found unusually small in number). The classroom atmosphere seemed excellent, the children interested, well behaved and intelligent. All were involved in the various activities and I believe all were invited to respond to questions. It was very impressive. Yet there was no teacher exposition and only one child supplied a 'wrong' answer to a question. In fact, it was an interesting response — the teacher wanted 'opposites' and on asking one child for the opposite of 'wide' immediately rejected 'long'. She appeared to react not so much to the actual response, but to the fact that it was not 'narrow'. Once the next child supplied this answer, she continued through her list. Of course, away from the classroom, watching the video, I could take a more detached view and think of how often in mathematics, particularly in the early years, one contrasts 'width' with 'length'. How was the little boy to sort out in his mind why in one lesson the two words were opposites and in the next lesson they were not? Many of the word pairs were far from easy and the knowledge of the children and the speed with which they produced the answers was most impressive. Had the previous lesson been devoted to learning lists of such pairs written on the blackboard? Was the teacher testing what the children had learned out of school? In fact, the video showed little in the way of 'teaching' taking place and told us nothing of where and how the children had 'learned'. It would have been extremely useful as a starting point for discussion and there were many valuable lessons to be observed about the art of handling a class (which is, of course, 'good teaching' in a rather different sense). Yet how much more valuable would it have been actually to have been present at that lesson (and the preceding and following ones) and have seen, for example, if and how the teacher worked with children on a one-to-one basis. The video adds much to the descriptive case study to be found in, say, Schmidt et al. (1996), but it cannot replace actual observation and participation.

3   The TIMSS report (Beaton et al., 1996a, 1996b) gives the public expenditure on primary and secondary education as a proportion of the GNP and also GNP per capita. However, even this information by itself can be misleading. The percentages of the population in primary and secondary education varies greatly between countries (as does the relative financing of the two sectors of education), while in some countries there is considerable non-public expenditure on education, for example, private schools in England and evening tutorial schools in Japan.

4   Keys, Harris and Fernandez (1997) contains several findings amongst the English TIMSS questionnaire data that merit further investigation. For example, although many English school inspectors and educators have for years accused teachers of being too tied to commercially produced materials, it appears that the students of those teachers who placed most reliance on textbooks performed most highly.

Other data on how the perceived effectiveness of English secondary school mathematics teachers varies with age and experience raise interesting questions.

References

BEATON, A.E., MULLIS, I.V.S., MARTIN, M.O., GONZALEZ, E.J., KELLY, D.L. and SMITH, T.A. (1996a) *Mathematics Achievement in the Middle School Years*, Boston, MA: Center for the Study of Testing, Evaluation and Educational Policy, Boston College.

BEATON, A.E., MARTIN, M.O., MULLIS, I.V.S., GONZALEZ, E.J., KELLY, D.L. and SMITH, T.A. (1996b) *Science Achievement in the Middle School Years*, Boston, MA: Center for the Study of Testing, Evaluation and Educational Policy, Boston College.

BIERHOFF, H. (1996) *Laying the Foundations of Numeracy*, National Institute Discussion Paper no. 90, NIESR, London.

DALIN, P. (1978) *Limits to Educational Change*, London: Macmillan.

FREUDENTHAL, H. (1975) 'Pupils' achievement internationally compared — the IEA', *Educational Studies in Mathematics*, **6**, pp. 127–86.

HOWSON, A.G. (1991) *National Curricula in Mathematics*, Leicester: The Mathematical Association.

HOWSON, A.G. (1995) *Mathematics Textbooks: A Comparative Study of Grade 8 Texts*, Vancouver, Canada: Pacific Educational Press.

HOWSON, A.G. (forthcoming) *Meaning in School Mathematics*.

HOWSON, A.G., KEITEL, C. and KILPATRICK, J. (1981) *Curriculum Development in Mathematics*, Cambridge: University Press.

ITAKA, S., UETAKE, T., FUJITA, H. and YOKOCHI, K. (1995) 'Mathematics education at risk', in FUJITA, H. and ITAKA, S. (eds) *Toward a Revison of Mathematics Curriculum in Japan*, Tokyo: Science Counsel of Japan.

KEYS, W., HARRIS, S. and FERNANDEZ, C. (1996, 1997) *Third International Mathematics and Science Study — First and Second National Reports (Parts 1 and 2)*, NFER, Slough.

PRAIS, S.J. (1996) 'Reform of mathematical education in primary schools', *National Institute Economic Review*, London: NIESR.

REYNOLDS, D. and FARRELL, S. (1996) *Worlds Apart?*, London: OFSTED.

SCHMIDT, W.H., JORDE, D., COGAN, L.S., BARRIER, E., GONZALO, I., MOSER, U., SHIMIZU, Y., SAWADA, T., VALVERDE, G., McKNIGHT, C., PRAWAT, R., WILEY, D.E., RAIZEN, S., BRITTON, E.D. and WOLFE, R.G. (1996) *Characterizing Pedagogical Flow*, Dordrecht: Kluwer Academic Publishers.

SYLVESTER, D.W. (1970) Educational Documents 800–1816, London: Methuen, pp. 2–4.

12   School Mathematics: The Impact of International Comparisons on National Policy

Thomas A. Romberg

In any country, educational policy involves establishing overall, high level plans for the nation's educational system. Such plans include specification of general goals for the system and a listing of the acceptable procedures for reaching those goals. Comparative studies are important for policymakers, if the information derived from such studies have clear implications either for rethinking the goals or modifying the procedures of the nation's current educational system. My contention is that in the United States we are currently in a reform movement in school mathematics. Recently, policymakers have established new national goals and are now searching for suggestions about how to reach those goals. Comparative studies have contributed to these policy considerations in many ways.

Comparative Studies Make What One Takes for Granted Problematic

For many years American educators who have attended conferences at which mathematics programs of other countries were described, or who have examined textbooks used in other countries, or who have visited schools and mathematics classes in other countries, have been struck by the differences in the mathematical content covered, the concepts/content emphasized and the methods of instruction utilized compared with common practice in the United States. However, the policy implications of such differences were not apparent until reports were published indicating that American students rank poorly on mathematical tests in contrast to students in other industrial countries.

For example, in 1964 when 10 nations administered a common achievement test in mathematics for 13-year-olds, the mean for American students ranked ninth among the ten countries. To prepare the tests, the international committee drafted an outline of topics that might be covered in a mathematics curriculum. This topic outline was sent to the national centers with instructions to judge whether the topic was covered in that country. The results made it very clear that topic coverage varied dramatically across countries (Husén, 1967). This fact surprised many Americans and led to a number of visits and exchanges among scholars attempting to understand the differences in content coverage and pedagogy. Unfortunately, these exchanges failed to lead to careful analyses of differences. For example, one finding was that the Japanese, who ranked the highest on the achievement test, attributed success in mathematics to hard work, whereas Americans attributed it to ability. The inference, falsely interpreted, was that 'hard work' meant 'more drill and practice'. Thus, the inference was that American children needed more drill on basic skills. This interpretation was used to justify the 'back to the basics' movement in the United States during the 1970s.

Another example comes from the second international study of mathematics achievement, conducted in 1981 and 1982 in 20 countries (14 industrialized and 6 emerging nations). American student performance again ranked poorly, and content coverage information was collected, with respect to each item from each country, both from experts at the national centers (as an indication of the intended curriculum) and from teachers (as an indication of the implemented curriculum). Once more the conclusion was that there were big differences among national curricula (Travers and Westbury, 1989). Awareness of both the performance and curricular differences contributed to the calls for reform by policymakers in the 1980s, as reported in *Nation at Risk* (National Commission on Excellence in Education, 1983) and *Educating Americans for the 21st Century* (National Science Board Commission, 1983). The authors of those documents claimed that competing in today's global economic environment depends on a workforce knowledgeable about the mathematical, scientific and technological aspects of the emerging information age. Furthermore, they argued that our schools were not adequately preparing very many of our students to participate meaningfully in the real world of work, personal life, higher education and in the country's social and political institutions. In particular, in our increasingly multicultural society, both the participation and achievement of women and minorities in mathematics and science lags behind that of white males.

One consequence in the United States has been the development of new bipartisan National Education Goals (US Department of Education, 1991). In particular, two of the new national goals explicitly refer to mathematics — 'All students will leave grades 4, 8, and 12 having demonstrated competency in challenging subject matter including . . . mathematics' and 'US students will be first in the world in mathematics and science achievement'. In addition, three other goals implicitly refer to the need for reform in school mathematics — the increase in high school graduation rate, adult literacy (including quantitative and scientific literacy), and professional development of the nation's teaching force. Although these proposed goals are couched in terms of the US social situation, they have been influenced by information about what other countries are doing.

Recently published reports from the Third International Mathematics and Science Study (TIMSS) again show that the overall mean for American students in mathematics is below the international mean. However, this time the inference is that the reform efforts of the previous decade have yet to be implemented in most US classrooms (Peak, 1996).

In summary, over the past quarter century, because of the American students' poor performance in mathematics, many policymakers have questioned the organization of our curriculum, the way it is taught in our schools and the way performance is assessed. To understand these concerns, one must be aware of the system of education that has developed over the last century and that Americans take for granted. It is a system that we now know is unlike any other in the world, with features as follows. First, in the United States educational policy is *not* national — since the US Constitution omits any reference to education, decisions about education are left to the states. The states, in varying degrees, have turned over the control of schools to local communities with locally elected school boards. These district boards in turn hire administrators and teachers, and approve programs. Today, there are nearly 16,000 school districts in the United States. As a consequence of shared state and local control, there are vast differences in the quality of programs, facilities, staff and teachers both across and within states. There in no national curriculum, no national set of standards for the licensing or retention of teachers, no common policies for student assessment of progress, nor common admission practices to universities, and so forth. The reasons for this diversity are historic, economic and political.

Second, the mathematical content in American schools is a large collection of concepts and skills that are hierarchically arranged. The goal for students is that they sequentially master one concept or skill after another. Furthermore, the student's task is to get correct answers to well-defined problems or exercises. The emphasis in both elementary and middle school (Grades K–8) is on arithmetic computational proficiency. The standard topics include addition, subtraction, multiplication and division of whole numbers, fractions and decimals. At the secondary school level (Grades 9–12), the picture is quite different. First, for the math/science student who is intending to proceed to college, there is a four-year mathematics sequence. The 'layer-cake' sequence includes a year of algebra, followed by a year of Euclidean geometry, followed by another year of algebra, and completed with a year of precalculus mathematics. Students who are planning to go to college, but not planning to study mathematics or the sciences, are expected to take two or three years of the same sequence of courses. Then, for students who are not college bound, another year of arithmetic (general math) is usually required. Finally, a few students are accelerated by having them start algebra in middle school, taking a calculus course in the final year.

Third, the job of the teacher is often perceived to be to transmit knowledge — and the job of the student is to receive it, regurgitating it on demand. The result is that the traditional classroom focuses on competition, management and group aptitudes taught under the assumption that learners absorb what has been covered.

Finally, the technology of traditional instruction includes a basal text, which is a repository of problem lists, a mass of paper-and-pencil worksheets and a set of performance tests. Although a few of the books include things to read, very little of it is interesting to students. Thus, workbook mathematics gives students little reason to connect ideas in today's lesson with those of past lessons or with the real world. The tests currently used ask for answers that are judged right or wrong, but the strategies and reasoning used to derive answers are not evaluated.

This system of school mathematics that evolved over the past century is a coherent educational system. The underlying problem with the current system is that it is based on an industrial metaphor. Schooling is viewed as being analogous to an assembly line — students are the raw material input to the system, teachers are workers passing on a fixed body of mathematical knowledge by telling students what they must remember and do, and the output of the system is judged by scores from tests that assess knowledge of facts and procedures. This metaphor is based on the need to prepare the majority of students efficiently and smoothly to fit into a mass-production economy. According to the model devised to meet this need, knowledge is construed as objective, learning as absorption and teaching as transmission and control. Policymakers are now aware that each of these assumptions has changed. Today our society needs individuals who will continue to learn and adapt to changing circumstances and who will produce new knowledge. Today, knowledge is seen as constructive, learning as occurring through active participation and teaching as guiding. Furthermore, many Americans in the past have assumed that the rest of the world organized and taught mathematics in a similar system; we now realize that ours is a unique and outdated system that needs to be changed. One of the starting points for reform was to consider what and how mathematics was taught in other countries.

Comparative Studies can Illuminate Procedures Used by Different Systems to Solve the Same Problems

If the new US education goals are to be reached, high expectations of achievement in school mathematics for all students need to be set and every student must be provided the means and the opportunity to achieve those expectations. To initiate procedures to reach these goals, curriculum, teaching, assessment and evaluation standards for school mathematics were proposed by the National Council of Teachers of Mathematics (NCTM, 1989, 1991, 1995). To summarize the influence of work in other countries on the proposed procedures for changing the system, I have chosen to use five key notions from the *Curriculum and Evaluation Standards for School Mathematics*. The document's authors reached the conclusion '. . . that all students need to learn more, and often different, mathematics and that instruction in mathematics must be significantly revised' (NCTM, 1989:1).

First, teaching mathematics to 'all students' emphasizes the fact that all need to be mathematically literate if they are to be productive citizens in the twenty-first century. In the United States, mathematics courses, more than most other curricular offerings in schools, have become a filter in our society that restricts access to knowledge (Mathematical Sciences Education Board, 1989). Women and most minority students are too often encouraged to quit taking mathematics or denied any opportunity to study more mathematics. This denial has major consequences for employment and citizenship. The school mathematics curriculum still reflects the industrial needs of the 1920s, not the workplace needs of the 1990s. Most other countries expect all of their students to study mathematics every year they are in school. Furthermore, the way we have organized mathematics courses for most students (eight years of arithmetic, a year of algebra, a year of Euclidean geometry, another year of algebra, and so forth) is not the way courses have ever been organized in other nations. Maths (not math) has been emphasized in an integrated manner throughout the curriculum in many countries. The current American 'layer-cake' curriculum focuses on mathematics divided into subjects for study and taught independently. Furthermore, within each subject area it is assumed that knowledge can be broken down into clearly defined, self-sustaining parts, that there is a logical sequence of development in which each part builds on a preceding foundation, and that, if knowledge were acquired in this manner, students would be able to use and apply their mathematical knowledge as needed.

Second, 'more mathematics' implies that all students need to learn more than how to manipulate arithmetic routines. The mathematics that we have taught all students in the past, arithmetic procedures, was an artifact of the industrial age, but is no longer sufficient for a technological age. Other countries have not only stressed an integrated curriculum, but have placed different emphases on arithmetic computations. For example, 23 American arithmetic textbooks were compared with 36 books from 21 European countries by Schutter and Spreckelmeyer (1959). The authors found that European schools gave students a wider variety of problem types, stressed mental computation, gave more challenging tasks and began instruction on various topics as much as two years earlier.

Another example involved comparisons of tests given to graduating high-school students in European countries (Shafroth, 1993). Her examination made it clear that counting correct answers to multiple-choice test items is an American tradition not followed in other countries. Other countries tend to judge performance in terms of strategies and answers to complex problems. This practice is now being advocated for American schools (NCTM, 1995).

Third, 'often different mathematics' refers to the fact that the mathematics all students need to learn includes concepts from algebra, geometry, trigonometry, statistics, probability, discrete mathematics and even calculus. In the past quarter of a century, significant changes have occurred in the nature of mathematics and in the way it is used. Not only has much new mathematics been discovered, but the types and variety of problems to which mathematics is applied have grown at an unprecedented rate. One of the most visible aspects of this phenomenon, of course, has been the development of computers and the explosive growth of computer applications. Many of these applications of mathematics, not feasible prior to the advent of computers, have required the development of new mathematics (Howson and Kahane, 1986). In many countries, students are expected to study the mathematics used in such applications in order to grasp the power of mathematics, to solve real-world problems, and to reflect on the consequences of such uses. Of particular interest is the realistic curriculum developed over the past two decades in The Netherlands (Freudenthal, 1987).

Fourth, 'to learn' means more than to be shown or to memorize and repeat. Learning involves investigating, formulating, representing, reasoning and using strategies to solve problems, and then reflecting on how mathematics is being used. Today, virtually all cognitive theorists share the fundamental assumption that an individual's knowledge structures and mental representations of the world play a central role in the capacity to perceive, comprehend and act (see Calfee, 1981; Greeno, 1987; Pea, 1987; Resnick, 1987). An individual's perception of the environment and his or her actions are mediated through cognitive structures that are actively constructed and modified as a result of experience. To know and understand mathematics from this perspective requires having acquired or constructed appropriate knowledge structures. These notions have their roots in European psychology, led by contemporary followers of Piaget and Vygotsky.

Fifth, 'revised' instruction implies that classrooms need to become discourse communities where conjectures are made, arguments presented, strategies discussed, and so forth. Since an individual student constructs his or her knowledge in a social context, and this context helps to shape the constructed understanding, instruction must reflect this perception. Activities should encourage interactions between students as they try to understand the mathematics being studied. Students need experience in a range of prototypical situations so that they can analyze their structure, finding essential features and the ways in which aspects are related. In this context, prototypical is meant in two ways — the situation should be representative of the kind of cultural context that has traditionally given rise to mathematics (Freudenthal, 1987), and the situation should be familiar in the context in which it is presented to the student. Students need to be able to pose a question, see the next question, evaluate a strategy, and construct and discuss alternative methods. Having done so, they need to examine assumptions and arguments and make efficient choices. This instructional approach is evident in many countries.

In summary, what is being suggested in NCTM's statement is not simply a requirement that all students take more courses of the same mathematics, or that the number of days of instruction be increased, and so forth. The reform documents argue for a reduced emphasis on mastery of paper-and-pencil algorithms; they advocate a shift in focus to meaning and the appropriate use of operations, to judging the reasonableness of results, and to choosing appropriate procedures. Mathematical topics that are considered increasingly important, but are seriously under-represented in current curricula, include geometry and measurement, probability and statistics, algebra, patterns, relationships, functions and discrete mathematics. This change in content emphasis reflects what is being taught in other countries and is supported in several recent documents that describe mathematics in these terms: (see Jaffe, 1984; MSEB, 1990a; MSEB, 1990b; Romberg, 1992; Steen, 1988).[1]

Comparative Studies Reinforce One's Understanding of Common Contemporary Problems in Education

The current reform movement in school mathematics is international and began more than a decade ago in many industrialized nations. The need for reform is an outgrowth of the shift from an 'industrial society' to an 'information society'. Several authors (Naisbitt, 1982; Shane and Tabler, 1981; Toffler, 1985; Yevennes, 1985) have described some of the attributes of the 'information age'. It is based on a new technology that replaces the traditional human and mechanical means of communication — the printed page, letters — with electronic means, by which information can be shared almost instantly with persons anywhere; information is the new capital and the new raw material, and communication is the new means of production. The impact of technology is an economic reality, not merely an intellectual abstraction. As a result, the pace of change will be accelerated by continued innovation in communications and computer technology. Also, although the new technologies were originally applied to old industrial tasks, they are now generating new processes and products. Finally, basic communication skills are more important than ever before, necessitating a literacy-intensive society. To illustrate, because the computer is a fast idiot that can carry out prodigious calculation feats, its impact on mathematics is similar to the impact of the printing press on writing and reading. The printing press, which made certain skills (calligraphy) obsolete, also made texts universally available and vastly increased the need for people to write and read. Similarly, today's technology has made a certain range of skills (from simple to intricate paper-and-pencil calculations) obsolete, thus making it possible for people to model complex problem situations, make predictions, and so on. Television, satellites, robots, our financial empire and high tech corporations, all would be impossible without these changes in mathematics.

This shift has immediate consequences for schooling and, in particular, for the teaching and learning of mathematics. Many countries are now attempting to deal with the following problems. First, the content and structure of the curriculum should not operate to indoctrinate students with past values, but should be derived from visions of the future (Shane and Tabler, 1981). All students should be taught to reason, to design models, and to create and solve problems. The most important attribute of the information economy is that it represents a switch from physical energy to brain power as the driving force, and from concrete products to abstractions as the primary outcomes. Over the ages, people have invented and used mathematics to count, measure, locate, design, play, conjecture and explain. They have also examined its generalized abstractions and developed out of them further mathematics — explanations, designs, proofs or new theorems — that may or may not have had practical application (Bishop, 1988). People are continuing to do all of these, but in a rapidly increasing variety of contexts, in increasingly complex situations, and with shorter and shorter time spans for development.

Second, all children must be taught critical thinking skills. Although creative intelligence is the driving force, innovation and appropriate uses of innovation depend on communal intellectual effort rather than on the activity of a small cadre of elite thinkers. A critical problem brought about by these shifts has been expressed by the Norwegian scholar, Ole Skovsmose. He referred to the pressing need for all citizens to become 'mathematically literate' as 'the problem of democracy in a highly technological society' (1990:109). The conviction that democratic ideals will prevail cannot be taken for granted in this highly technological information age. Arthur Jaffe made the following claim.

> In the past quarter century, mathematics and mathematical techniques have become an integral, pervasive, and essential component of science, technology, and business. In our technically-oriented society, 'innumeracy' has replaced illiteracy as our principal educational gap . . . In fact, we could say that we live in an age of *mathematics* — the culture has been *'mathematized'* (1984:117).

The German scholar Christine Keitel pointed out that the process of mathematization involves specialists and experts 'outside ordinary democratic control and outside the competent discourse in society' (1993:27). The danger is that democracy could be replaced by an expertocracy. She went on to argue as follows:

> How is it possible to combine democracy with the necessity of selecting a small group of experts to actually advise or do the ruling? How is it possible to control the 'people in charge?' While the ruling-competence of the people in charge is of special nature, the judging-competence is of common nature: we could call it a democratic competence. In other words, democratic competence should be a common capacity of human beings and has to be produced by education. Democratic competence does not only mean a certain system of knowledge or abilities, but a certain attitude: to be willing to stress the importance of a democratic way of social control and acting (1993:27f).

Thus, democratic competence in a highly technological society includes both the technical knowledge of mathematics and its uses and the reflective knowledge necessary to analyze and evaluate technological developments. To meet this challenge of preparing all students to be democratically competent, Philip Davis (1989) called for changing mathematics education from teaching 'grammar' to teaching 'literature', that is, focusing on alternative modelling activities that should lead to critically analysing and judging the applications of mathematics. The point is that discussing and criticizing a mathematical model does not depend simply on technical knowledge of the modelling process. Instead, it also must be based on reflective knowledge about the criteria used in the constructions, applications and evaluations of mathematical models for social problems.

It is because of the pervasiveness of these technological advances that reflective knowledge about the power of mathematics has become so important for every citizen in a democratic society. The argument is that, to be mathematically powerful in a mathematical and technical culture, students should learn to explore, conjecture, reason logically, and integrate a variety of mathematical methods effectively to solve non-routine problems. In becoming mathematical problem solvers, they need to value mathematics, to reason and communicate mathematically, and to become confident in their power to use mathematics coherently in the effort to make sense of problematic situations in the world around them. Note the differences between this vision and the mathematics encountered in the current system — a collection of fixed concepts and skills to be taught and mastered in a certain strict order.

Ian Westbury (1980) argued that the problem all nations currently face involves the difference between the intellectual structure of a discipline and its institutional structure in schools, where it can readily become, as it is currently, an administrative framework for routine tasks. The consequence is that administrative stability impedes intellectual change.

Conclusion

Current school mathematics in the United States is a coherent system that has evolved in response to the pressures of the industrial revolution, it is a product of our society. However, it differs in significant ways from the mathematics programmes in other countries. During the past decade, as we have become aware of both the relatively poor performance of our students and the different ways mathematics is organized and taught in other countries, there has been a growing demand to reform school mathematics. The American mathematics education community has responded to these demands for reform: standards for the content, teaching, and assessment of school mathematics have been prepared; new state and district curricular frameworks based on those standards have been or are being developed; a variety of new curricular and assessment materials have been or are being created and tested; and research studies have been directed toward student learning, teaching, and assessment as schools and teachers struggle with the explicit changes advocated by the leaders of the reform movement. All of this activity has been strongly influenced by what other countries do.

Note

1 For an examination of curricular expectations across eight countries, compared with those presented in the NCTM's *Standards*, see Romberg, Allison, Clarke, Clarke, Pedro and Spence (1991).

References

BISHOP, A.J. (1988) *Mathematical Enculturation: A Cultural Perspective of Mathematics Education*, Dordrecht, The Netherlands: Kluwer.

CALFEE, R. (1981) 'Cognitive psychology and educational practice', in BERLINER, D.C. (ed.) *Review of Research in Education*, Washington, DC: American Educational Research Association, pp. 3–74.

DAVIS, P.J. (1989) 'Applied mathematics as social contract', in KEITEL, C., DAMEROW, P., BISHOP, A., GERDES, P. (eds) *Mathematics, Education, and Society*, Paris: UNESCO Document Series No. 35, pp. 24–7.

FREUDENTHAL, H. (1987) 'Mathematics starting and staying in reality', in WIRSZUP, I. and STREIT, R. (eds) *Proceedings of the USCMP International Conference on Mathematics Education of Development in School Mathematics Education Around the World: Applications-oriented Curricula and Technology-supported Learning for all Students*, Reston, VA: National Council of Teachers of Mathematics, pp. 279–95.

GREENO, J.G. (1987) 'Mathematical cognition: Accomplishments and challenges in research', in ROMBERG, T.A. and STEWART, D.M. (eds) *The Monitoring of School Mathematics: Background Papers, Vol. 2, Implications from Psychology: Outcomes of Instruction*, Madison, WI: Wisconsin Center for Education Research, pp. 3–26.

HOWSON, G. and KAHANE, J.P. (eds) (1986) *The Influence of Computers and Informatics on Mathematics and its Teaching*, International Commission on Mathematical Instruction Study Series, Cambridge: Cambridge University Press.

HUSÉN, T. (1967) *International Study of Achievement in Mathematics: A Comparison of Twelve Countries*, **1**, New York: Wiley.

JAFFE, A. (1984) 'Ordering the universe: The role of mathematics', in National Research Council, the Commission on Physical Sciences, Mathematics, and Research (eds) *Renewing US Mathematics: Critical Resource for the Future, Report of the ad hoc Committee on Resources for the Mathematical Sciences*, Washington, DC: National Academy Press, pp. 117–62.

KEITEL, C. (1993) 'Implicit mathematical models in social practice and explicit mathematics teaching by applications', in DE LANGE, J., KEITEL, C., HUNTLEY, I. and NISS, M. (eds) *Innovation in Maths Education by Modelling and Applications*, New York: Ellis Horwood, pp. 19–30.

MATHEMATICAL SCIENCES EDUCATION BOARD (1989) *Everybody Counts*, Washington, DC: National Academy Press.

MATHEMATICAL SCIENCES EDUCATION BOARD (1990a) *Reshaping School Mathematics*, Washington, DC: National Academy Press.

MATHEMATICAL SCIENCES Education BOARD (1990b) *On the Shoulders of Giants*, Washington, DC: National Academy Press.

NAISBITT, J. (1982) *Megatrends: Ten New Directions Transforming our Lives*, New York: Warner Books.

NATIONAL COMMISSION ON EXCELLENCE IN EDUCATION (1983) *A Nation at Risk: The Imperative for Educational Reform*, Washington, DC: US Government Printing Office.

NATIONAL COUNCIL OF TEACHERS OF MATHEMATICS (1989) *Curriculum and Evaluation Standards for School Mathematics*, Reston, VA: Author.

NATIONAL COUNCIL OF TEACHERS OF MATHEMATICS (1991) *Professional Standards for Teaching Mathematics*, Reston, VA: Author.

NATIONAL COUNCIL OF TEACHERS OF MATHEMATICS (1995) *Assessment Standards for School Mathematics*, Reston, VA: Author.

NATIONAL SCIENCE BOARD COMMISSION ON PRECOLLEGE EDUCATION IN MATHEMATICS, SCIENCE AND TECHNOLOGY (1983) *Educating Americans for the Twenty-first Century: A Plan of Action for Improving the Mathematics, Science, and Technology Education for all American Elementary and Secondary Students so that their Achievement is the Best in the World by 1995*, Washington, DC: US Government Printing Office.

PEA, R.D. (1987) 'Cognitive technologies for mathematics education', in SCHOENFELD, A.H. (ed.) *Cognitive Science and Mathematics Education*, Hillsdale, NJ: Erlbaum, pp. 89–122.

PEAK, L. (1996) *Pursuing Excellence*, Washington, DC: US Department of Education.

RESNICK, L.B. (1987) *Education and Learning to Think*, Washington, DC: National Academy Press.

ROMBERG, T.A. (1992) 'Problematic features of the school mathematics curriculum', in JACKSON, P.W. (ed.) *Handbook of Research on Curriculum*. New York: Macmillan, pp. 749–88.

ROMBERG, T.A., ALLISON, J., CLARKE, B., CLARKE, D., PEDRO, J. and SPENCE, M. (1991) *School Mathematics Expectations: A Comparison of Curricular Documents of Eight Countries with the NCTM Standards of the US*, Madison, WI: National Center for Research in Mathematical Sciences Education.

SCHUTTER, C.H. and SPRECKELMEYER, R.L. (1959) *Teaching the Third R: A Comparative Study of American and European Textbooks in Arithmetic*, Washington, DC: Council for Basic Education.

SHAFROTH, C. (1993) 'A comparison of university entrance examinations in the United States and in Europe'. *Focus* [The newsletter of the Mathematical Association of America], **13**(3) 1, pp. 11–14.

SHANE, H.I. and TABLER, M.B. (1981) *Educating for a new millennium: Views of 132 international scholars*, Bloomington, IN: Phi Delta Kappa Educational Foundation.

SKOVSMOSE, O. (1990) 'Mathematical education and democracy', *Educational Studies in Mathematics*, **21**, pp. 109–28.

STEEN, L.A. (1988) 'The science of patterns', *Science*, **240**, pp. 611–16.

TOFFLER, A. (1985) *Adaptive Corporation*, New York: McGraw-Hill.

TRAVERS, K.J. and WESTBURY, I. (1989) *The IEA Study of Mathematics I: Analysis of Mathematics Curricula*, New York: Pergamon Press.

US DEPARTMENT OF EDUCATION (1991) *America 2000: An Education Strategy*, Washington, DC: Author.

WESTBURY, I. (1980) 'Change and stability in the curriculum: An overview of the questions', in *Comparative Studies of Mathematics Curricula: Change and Stability 1960–1980*, Proceedings of a conference jointly organized by the Institute for the Didactics of Mathematics (IDM) and the International Mathematics Committee of the Second International Mathematics Study of the International Association for the Evaluation of Educational Achievement (IEA), Bielefeld, FRG, Institut für Didaktik der Mathematik der Universität Bielefeld, pp. 12–36.

YEVENNES, M. (1985) 'The world political economy and the future of the US labor market', *World Futures*, **21**, pp. 147–57.

13 International Benchmarking as a Way to Improve School Mathematics Achievement in the Era of Globalization

Bienvenido F. Nebres

In a world where quality improvement has become a dominant concern, for business and industry as well as for education, one methodology — benchmarking — offers itself as a tool for schools and school systems seeking to continually improve themselves. Benchmarking can be simply defined as the search for best practices that lead to superior performance. In the world of mathematics and science education, TIMSS and the studies deriving from TIMSS provide a rich resource for identifying areas (so-called critical success factors) where the search for best practices is likely to lead to significant improvement. Schools can begin by looking at best practices in their own institution or their school system, called internal benchmarking. From here they can move on to looking for external benchmark partners. Successful benchmarking has heavy prerequisites, notably support from top management, process owner involvement, detailed planning and benchmarking skills. However, for schools willing to invest in the effort, it can provide a systematic methodology for focused and continuing quality improvement.

Introduction

The release in the last year of the results of the Third International Mathematics and Science Study (TIMSS) for the population of 13-year-olds and 9-year-olds has focused a lot of attention and concern on school mathematics and science in countries all over the world. In the Philippines the Department of Science and Technology has asked for a detailed presentation of the Philippine performance and has asked the various institutions responsible for school science and mathematics to develop strategies and plans to improve our performance. A massive in-service teacher training program for elementary and secondary mathematics and science teachers is being initiated this year. This is not the first time, of course, that national leaders have reacted strongly to the need for educational reform. What is important to note is the change in strategies and response, and how those of us in mathematics education may best cooperate with these national concerns to seek improvement in school mathematics in our countries.

I have two specific school systems in mind as I write about the new responses and new ways of using international cooperation needed to make better progress on school mathematics achievement in the Philippines. The first is the network of Jesuit schools in the country, for which I have some direct responsibility. We are now actively seeking partner schools abroad with whom we might cooperate towards strengthening the quality of our programs. The second are clusters of public schools with whom I work in different capacities. Owing to the recent release of TIMSS results, we are being asked to prepare a project for our Department of Science and Technology on how we might work with partner schools, especially in the East and Southeast Asian region, towards improving the quality of science and mathematics education in the system.

Changing Paradigms of International Cooperation

In a paper I gave at Monash University, Australia, in April 1995, I noted that over the years, the structure of international collaboration in mathematics education followed socio-political structures (Nebres, 1995). First, there was the colonial period — where mathematics education was divided into colonial blocs, namely those influenced by different colonizing nations, and cooperation and exchange was almost exclusively within these blocs. For example, in the Philippines of the 1960s the new mathematics was introduced into the schools by Peace Corps Volunteers from the United States (Nebres, 1981). Subsequently, we went into the period of development aid — development of mathematics and science education came to us in large part through loan packages from the World Bank and through development aid from various donor countries. These loan or aid packages came with consultants and specialists from developed countries, working with local experts from tertiary institutions, within school reform frameworks developed by the donor country or the international financing organization. There were programs involving the development of curricula, textbooks and teacher-training funded by the World Bank and the Asian Development Bank. There have been and there are continuing programmes for science and mathematics in the schools supported by Australian aid.

From Aid to Trade

The shift today is stated in the slogan *From aid to trade*. Today the dominant framework for worldwide collaboration comes no longer from colonial powers or from the power blocs of the cold war period, but from the globalizing impact of business and technology. In my Monash paper I noted that the forces seen to be behind the phenomenon of globalization — the rise of the global consumer, a changing workforce, technology and culture — are paralleled, in the world of mathematics education, in a more universal and more differentiated group of students, in the changing role and centrality of teachers, in the opportunities coming from computers and communications technology, and the challenge and barriers of culture. In this shift of framework from aid to trade, there is a dominant concern for quality and competitiveness. These have developed first within the business and technology world, but the concern for quality and competitiveness is also emerging more strongly in universities and schools.

The Timeliness of TIMSS

The TIMSS report notes that

> . . . as the 21st century approaches . . . countries will need citizens prepared to participate in 'brain-power' industries such as micro-electronics, computers and telecommunications. The young adolescents of today will be seeking jobs in a global economy requiring levels of technical competence and flexible thinking that were required by only a few workers in the past. To make sensible decisions and participate effectively in a world transformed by the ability to exchange all types of information almost instantly, these students will need to be well educated in a number of core areas, especially mathematics and science.
>
> The fact that skills in mathematics and science are so critical to economic progress in a technologically-based society has led countries to seek information about what their school-age populations know and can do in mathematics and science (Beaton, Mullis, Martin, Gonzalez, Kelly and Smith, 1996:7).

The Third International Mathematics and Science Study (TIMSS) provides a vehicle for countries to find and assess information about their own students and schools, and to compare them with information about students and schools in other countries. In this assessment and comparison, the concern is for levels of achievement and quality, and how a school or a school system might use the given information to strengthen or improve the mathematics education of its students.

Benchmarking as a Mode of International Cooperation

As noted earlier, this concern for achievement and quality has been the dominant concern of the world of business and industry in this period of globalization. Thus we might ask what we can learn from this world on how information and cooperation might lead to the goal of improvement in quality. There are many quality improvement techniques that have evolved over the years, for example Total Quality Management (TQM). Given the wealth of information that is emerging from TIMSS, which allows us to look at and compare schools and school systems on a broad range of issues and concerns, I would like to focus on one major methodology, which depends very much on information and competitive comparisons — benchmarking. It may offer detailed directions for seeking improvement based on national or international cooperation for those schools or school systems that are willing to work continuously and systematically at improving the quality of their instruction and achievement.

What is Benchmarking?

Webster's Ninth Collegiate Dictionary defines 'benchmark' as '. . . a point of reference from which measurements can be made . . . something that serves as a standard by which others may be measured'. Sue Tucker quotes Robert Camp, benchmarking pioneer and author: 'Benchmarking is the search for best practices that lead to superior performance' (Tucker, 1996:1). Michael Spendolini defines benchmarking as '. . . a continuous, systematic process for evaluating the products, services and work processes of organizations that are recognized as representing best practices for the purpose of organizational improvement' (Spendolini, 1992:9). In our case, it would mean that a school or school system would identify certain areas where better practices would lead to significant improvement in performance, and look for partner schools or school systems whose best practices in these areas will be studied and used to help the school's own efforts at quality improvement. It is important to note that benchmarking '. . . is not a general measurement of your school against another school. Instead, it is the study and transfer of specific exemplary practices, measures, and processes from another school or organization to your school' (Tucker, 1996:2).

There are many levels of detail and specificity in the use of the benchmarking process. In terms of goals, one could aim to use it simply to find ways to improve on present practices and performance. On a higher level, one can aim actually to incorporate best practices from other schools. At the top level, one can aim at actual world-class or best-in-class practices and achievement (Spendolini, 1992:113). Since schools are more complex and multi-dimensional than businesses, it would be better to begin with more modest goals. I propose that we begin simply with the goal of improving current practices and using best practices learned from other schools and school systems to find ways to improve on present practices. Later on we can aim at actually incorporating best practices from other schools. Only much later should we aim at best-in-class or best-in-the-region or world-class. From this more modest point of view, many aspects of benchmarking are not new. We have always had studies of other educational systems and practices. The difference is that benchmarking asks us to do it on a continuing and systematic basis — information gathering towards quality improvement is not something one looks into every 10 years, when FIMS or SIMS or TIMSS results come out, but it must be an ongoing concern. Second, we should not only look at outcomes such as the performance of our students in the achievement examinations, but we must also look into process issues — school variables, teacher variables, student variables. TIMSS provides initial information on and methodologies for studying some of these process issues. Finally, Spendolini points out that benchmarking became a tool used by more and more companies towards quality improvement because it featured in the selection process for a major award in the American business world, the Baldrige awards for excellence. The Malcolm Baldrige National Quality Improvement Act of 1987 was signed by President Reagan on August 1987 and is an award intended '. . . to promote quality awareness, to recognize quality achievements in US companies and to publicize successful quality strategies' (Spendolini, 1992:5). The submission papers for these awards included an item asking for '. . . the company's approach to selecting quality-related competitive comparisons and world-class benchmarks to support quality planning, evaluation and improvement' (p. 5). This formalized the inclusion of comparison with other institutions and benchmarking with them as an important measure of the company's commitment to excellence. Tucker notes that, in 1995, after two years of research and input by educators and educational organizations, a Baldrige Quality Award for Education is to be instituted. 'Many leaders expect that it will radically change the way we assess school effectiveness. Schools that are pioneers in benchmarking will be on the leading edge of the Baldrige quality assessment process' (Tucker, 1996:6).

Beginning with Internal Benchmarking

How do we begin? *The Benchmarking Book* recommends that we begin with internal benchmarking (Spendolini, 1992:16). For a school system this means looking at its own members and sectors (within an individual school and across schools in the system) and identifying so-called 'best practices' in the system. Ateneo de Manila University did something like this in a study done for the Philippine Department of Education a couple of years ago. We looked at best-performing (and worst-performing) schools and sought out variables that might account for their performance. Among the key variables were the leadership of the principal and the support from the local community. We then went on to take a closer look at the 'best schools' and to document characteristics of the effective principals and of the strong community support. Similar results have been obtained by many national studies of effective schools and these studies can be of great help for school systems beginning their internal benchmarking efforts.

Learning from Best Practices Found through Internal Benchmarking

Internal benchmarking asks that the information obtained be used by the school system to introduce such best practices into the rest of the system. This process of working to introduce best practices identified within the system into other schools in the system is a crucial and not easy first step. For example, for our Department of Education to use what we learned about effective principals, and introduce reforms on this basis across the system, would require reforms in the selection, training and continuing support of principals. This is obviously difficult, but it measures the commitment of the system to quality improvement and measures the readiness of the system actually to profit from external comparisons. This internal benchmarking establishes a '. . . baseline for all subsequent investigation and measurement involving external benchmark partners' (Spendolini, 1992:18). It bridges gaps within the system '. . . by encouraging internal communications and joint problem solving' (p. 18). Successful internal benchmarking thus lays the groundwork for the competitive and generic benchmarking to be done with schools from outside the system.

Benchmarking has Heavy Prerequisites and can Easily Fail

When several organizations were asked what were the main causes of failure in benchmarking, four causes stood out from the rest (Tucker, 1996:13):

- no top management support;
- no process owner involvement (the people most affected by potential changes were not included in the project);
- poor planning;
- insufficient benchmarking skills.

Another way of looking at the problems and dangers is to list the prerequisites for success (Tucker, 1996:13–15).

- Top administrators and leaders in the school and school system have an understanding of and commitment to benchmarking and continuous improvement.
- The school has a clear mission and has identified specific improvement goals through strategic or long-range planning. It is expected that there is shared knowledge and agreement on these goals, as well as on the strengths and weaknesses of the school.
- The school has developed a culture of teamwork.
- The school has some experience in problem solving and process management — instead of always blaming people, the school looks for improvement opportunities.
- Training and professional development must be highly valued in the school by both administrators and staff.
- School-based management and decision-making has progressed to the degree necessary for school teams to implement changes.

Tucker realizes that these are formidable requirements, and thus says that these prerequisites '. . . are not intended to discourage benchmarking but rather to provide guidance on factors that are likely to affect your success with the process' (Tucker, 1996:13). Such guidance can be obtained by beginning with internal benchmarking. Internal benchmarking can check whether there is commitment from top administrators, whether the school can agree on specific improvements to be pursued, and so forth. In other words, internal benchmarking provides a school or school system with a process to see whether it has the internal readiness to profit from external benchmarking.

What is New about Benchmarking as a Mode of International Cooperation?

How does this mode of seeking quality improvement and cooperation across national or international systems differ from those in the past? First and foremost is that the initiative and locus for quality improvement rests with the school or school system itself, rather than with project aid consultants or a group of outside experts. The school or school system must want to improve. If this desire is not there, then the first step needed is to bring in the needed motivation and changes in leadership and management. If one is dealing with a large system, then the first step would be to identify the schools or school clusters that have the needed desire to improve.

External Benchmarking — Critical Success Factors

What do we benchmark? For benchmarking to work, there is need to be specific in terms of areas to be studied. The process is very demanding in terms of resources of time and money, and thus there is need to choose carefully those factors that will have most impact on the improvement of quality in the school. The term used in the literature for these factors is 'critical success factors' (CSFs).

The study we made of effective schools identified the leadership of the principal and the support of the community as two such critical factors. As they were studied further, it turned out that the two factors were quite closely related. Sometimes support came from the community because of the leadership qualities of the principal. At other times the intervention of the community was important to support the leadership of the principal. In the Philippines principals normally rise through the ranks, but the process for selection is not precise and there is little systematic training given them in management. A World Bank project on improving elementary education in the country invited some leaders of our school system for a visit to France, and we spent time looking into and discussing the system for selecting and training school administrators in France. In the summer of 1996, I spent a session with leaders of elementary schools from around the country and outlined for them the system for selection and training of principals and other administrators in French schools — a selection process based on competitive examinations, then a two-year training program including coursework and apprenticeship. We then divided into workshop groups that tried to work out in some detail recommendations for improving the process of selection, training before entering the job, and continuing support while they are on the job. The results of the workshop showed much experience and insight and can be used to begin to identify benchmark partners for this area of administration. At an Asia-Pacific School Principals Forum held in Manila in February 1997, the Director of the Institute for School Administrators in Malaysia gave a talk about the present system in Malaysia for selecting and training school principals, and we could look to them as benchmark partners.

In terms of community support, our visit to France also noted that the local communities are responsible for taking care of school buildings and other facilities for the elementary schools, and this elicited much interest from our authorities as a model and benchmark for our efforts to devolve some of the responsibility for schools to the local level.

Critical Success Factors for Achievement in School Mathematics

These are examples of initial comparisons with other systems on critical success factors on the overall school level. How about now on the more specific area of mathematics education? A starting point for identifying CSFs in school mathematics achievement may be the results of TIMSS, and the long-term studies that have been made by Stevenson and his colleagues at the University of Michigan comparing school mathematics education in the United States, Japan and China (Stevenson and Stigler, 1992).

Effort Model versus the Ability Model

Stevenson and Stigler note the importance of beliefs and values in supporting school mathematics achievement. Among these beliefs and values is whether we believe that success in mathematics learning comes primarily from ability or primarily from effort. They study in detail the impact of the effort model in East Asian schools, and note important practices arising from this model. Thus we can study critical success factors arising from the effort model. That is, we can study schools among the top performing Asian countries (Singapore, Japan, Korea, Hong Kong) and look into practices that are consequences of and supportive of the belief that achievement in mathematics comes mainly from perseverance and hard work. Among the examples given by Stevenson and Stigler are the provision of study desks at home, the encouragement of slower students to keep on trying, and the organization of school time to encourage maximal effort during class time (Stevenson and Stigler, 1992:94).

Curricular Coverage and Textbooks

One of the noteworthy pieces of data from TIMSS is that coverage of mathematics topics, both in terms of prescribed curriculum and in terms of textbooks in the high-achieving countries in East and Southeast Asia, is more focused than in the United States. The East Asian countries focus on fewer topics, and their approach appears to lead to better mastery than the broader sweep of the American curriculum and American textbooks.

One can go into much greater detail from a study of the TIMSS results. Two of the most interesting tables in the TIMSS results for mathematics are Tables B1 and B2, the Test-Curriculum Matching Analysis for Grades 8 and 7 respectively (Beaton et al., 1996, Appendix B pp. B–3 and B–4). The tables allow a country to see how it compares with other countries in the group of items which it identified as part of its national curriculum. The results are quite interesting, showing that the relative performance of countries does not change depending on the selection of items. The top performing countries remained on top, whether one used the full set of items or any of the different sets of item selections. We can use these TIMSS data to look into the coverage of our curriculum and decide on future directions to strengthen coverage.

Beyond coverage we have to be concerned about mastery. To achieve best results it is important to focus on specific areas. For example, the published TIMSS results look into performance in the areas of fractions and number sense, geometry, algebra, data representation, analysis and probability, and measurement and proportionality. We can choose some or all of these areas and compare coverage and depth in our curriculum with that in the countries or school systems chosen for comparison. I understand that although Japan did excellently in the overall mathematics test, they are looking into overcoming weaknesses in certain topic areas that were identified in the TIMSS results.

Finally, we can set actual performance goals and see how our students would compare with students in the other countries or school systems in achievement on the specific areas we have chosen for comparison. This detailed comparison allows us to measure gaps more precisely and to measure improvement over time.

Teachers

TIMSS includes data on the pre-service preparation of teachers and also on the allocation of their time between classroom teaching and other school-related activities. Stevenson and Stigler have some very useful cross-cultural comparisons regarding the preparation of mathematics teachers. They note, for example, the amount of on-the-job training given to teachers in Japan. They also note that Japanese teachers spend less time in front of a class, but teach larger classes. The gain is that they have more time for preparation of lessons and for regular meetings with colleagues to discuss and develop materials and for professional growth. They also note that master teachers spend most of their time no longer teaching regular classes but in being mentors of younger teachers. They also note the priorities in terms of the attributes of an ideal teacher. American teachers emphasized sensitivity and patience. Chinese teachers emphasized the ability to explain things clearly and to be enthusiastic. We can look at these practices and choose some as critical success factors and study them in greater detail (Stevenson and Stigler, 1992:156).

Organization of Schooling

Many comparisons have been made regarding the length of the school year, the number of hours given to mathematics, the actual use of class time, the use of breaks and recesses, the size of classes and the impact that these school variables have on mathematics achievement.

Thus the results of comparative studies on national and international levels provide us with initial information which can help schools and school systems identify critical success factors towards their goal of improving mathematics achievement.

Examples of Initial Efforts at Benchmarking

Where Do We Start?

The United States Office of Educational Research and Improvement (OERI) and the National Center for Educational Statistics (NCES) have taken the initiative of producing a set of materials called *Attaining Excellence: A TIMSS Resource Kit*. It contains information and resources from TIMSS that schools and school systems can use in their own effort at ongoing educational improvement. There are five modules in the resource kit:

- overview module (TIMSS as a starting point to examine US education);
- achievement module (TIMSS as a starting point to examine student achievement);
- teaching module (TIMSS as a starting point to examine teaching);
- curricula module (TIMSS as a starting point to examine curricula);
- assessment module (TIMSS as a starting point to examine assessment frameworks).

The TIMSS website (*www.ed.gov/NCES/timss*) announced that the first four modules could be purchased by the middle of September 1997 and will be available online sometime in 1998. The kit includes videotape classroom studies — a video survey of eighth-grade mathematics lessons in Germany, Japan and the United States — which were conducted in a total of 231 classrooms. Together with the videotapes are analyses of cross-cultural differences covering the way lessons are structured and delivered, the kind of mathematics that is taught, the kind of thinking students engage in during the lessons and the way teachers view reform. They provide video materials which the United States intends to use for initial benchmarking with schools in Germany and Japan.

The TIMSS Resource Kit provides an excellent starting point for schools or school systems interested in benchmarking. It has been designed

> . . . as a catalyst for careful contemplation, open discussion and considered action. The kit is designed to be . . . shared in groups — among the education community, public decision-makers, community leaders, and the general public — to enlighten, explain and stimulate. It does not tell schools and districts what they should or should not do. It does help schools, districts, parents, and the business community think about improving mathematics and science education (quote from the TIMSS website).

Initial Efforts in the US and the Philippines

A call has been issued in the United States for school districts who wish to participate in a national benchmarking effort using the materials from the TIMSS Resource Kit as a starting point. This is expected to be carried out beginning in 1998.

In the Philippines the Department of Science and Technology (DOST) has asked a group of mathematics and science education specialists to help in initiating some benchmarking efforts. We are beginning with two clusters — one group composed of private schools and a second group composed of public schools. We are obtaining the US TIMSS Resource Kit and will be using it for the initial discussions with the two clusters. From these discussions we expect to move forward along the steps as outlined by benchmarking books such as Tucker (1996):

- plan our study — identify what to benchmark and select our team;
- study and document our own practices, success measures, and problems.

We expect that we will be spending the first year on these two steps. This is the phase of internal benchmarking.

Identifying a Network of Benchmark Partners

The third step is for us to look for benchmark partners and identify best practices among them. The two groups of schools that will begin the benchmarking effort mentioned above will be chosen from among the stronger schools. We will then go on to look for benchmark partners for them within the East and Southeast Asian region. New clusters of schools which may wish to join the benchmarking effort may either benchmark within the East or Southeast Asian region or with the schools that have started earlier.

How do we proceed systematically in this selection of regional bench-mark partners? TIMSS is coming out with international publications, and individual countries are also coming out with more detailed national studies and reports; there will also be more focused studies on specific areas, such as textbooks. These publications should be of immense help in knowing more about other countries and school systems. We are looking to establish a library of these materials from TIMSS and other comparative studies. We can use them to help in our internal benchmarking and then to seek out potential partner schools or school systems for external benchmarking. We also have a regional mathematics organization, the Southeast Asian Mathematical Society (SEAMS), which regularly organizes Mathematics Education congresses. The SEAMS and these congresses can help us to identify potential partners.

Studying and Documenting Best Practices

We then go into the core of the work — to collect and analyse benchmarking information. This task assumes that we have worked seriously on the first task, namely deciding on the critical success factors to be benchmarked and on the level of specific detail required of each factor. For example, we can speak of principals needing training in financial management and management of personnel, but each of these areas will also have detailed subfactors. In particular, there is a need at some point of precise metrics for us to measure the quality gaps and to develop strategies for narrowing these gaps.

It is important to note here that aside from obtaining data about best practices for the use of a particular cluster of schools, it is hoped that we will be able to start building a benchmarking information network to which we can return in the future as new challenges arise and new questions come up. Thus an important consideration for the selection of benchmark partners is the possibility of a long-term relationship.

Improving Other Parts of the Educational System

We have focused mainly on quality improvement on the level of the schools. What one observes in looking at these variables is that we have to compare and improve not just the schools themselves but also the tertiary institutions involved in the training of administrators and the preparation of teachers. In the Philippines efforts are beginning to strengthen the system for the training of principals. I noted earlier that we can work closely with the systems in Malaysia and in France to help us make more rapid progress in this effort.

Centers of Excellence and Centers of Development for Teacher Training have also been designated by the Philippine Commission on Higher Education. There are now initial efforts to look for international partners who can help in strengthening these centers.

Taking Action

The opening sentences of the last chapter of *The Benchmarking Book* are 'The primary objective of benchmarking is to take action. Although benchmarking is a process of investigation, the motivation for initiating an investigation in the first place is to stimulate and support change' (Spendolini, 1992:181). If the process of change has already started from the results of the internal benchmarking, and if the earlier steps were undertaken with seriousness, then the institution should be ready actually to move to implementation of actions that will lead to the much desired improvement.

For schools, as for the business institutions where benchmarking originated, the use of comparative investigations and competitive comparisons with chosen partners for benchmarking purposes is a long and demanding process. It will only make sense if the school or school system truly believes that improving the quality of school mathematics and science achievement is a high priority goal and that this is a long-term and continuing process. For this effort to be sustained, leaders on the national level and on the school level have to continually look into the link between the quality of its citizens' education in mathematics and science and its competitiveness in the larger economic and political world. At no stage of history has there been greater awareness of this link, and thus we may have the opportunity to move forward in a systematic and continuous way towards the strengthening of mathematics and science achievement in a large number of schools and school systems in different parts of the world.

References

BEATON, A.E., MULLIS, I.V.S., MARTIN, M.O., GONZALEZ, E.J., KELLY, D.L. and SMITH, T.A. (1996) *Mathematics Achievement in the Middle School Years: IEA's Third International Mathematics and Science Study (TIMSS)*, Boston, MA: Center for the Study of Testing, Evaluation and Educational Policy, Boston College.

NEBRES, B. (1981) 'Major trends from ICME IV: A Southeast Asian perspective', in STEEN, A.S. and ALBERS, D.J. (eds) *Teaching Teachers, Teaching Students: Reflections on Mathematical Education*, Boston, MA: Birkhauser, pp. 56–67.

NEBRES, B. (1995) 'Mathematics education in an era of globalisation: Linking education, society, and culture in our region', *International Conference on Regional Collaboration in Mathematics Education*, Monash University, Australia.

SPENDOLINI, M.J. (1992) *The Benchmarking Book*, New York: The American Management Association.

STEVENSON, H.W. and STIGLER, J.W. (1992) *The Learning Gap, A Touchstone Book*, New York: Simon & Schuster.

TUCKER, S. (1996) *Benchmarking: A Guide for Educators*, Thousand Oaks, California: Corwin Press.

14 Gender Differences in Mathematics Achievement — Here Today and Gone Tomorrow?

Gilah C. Leder, Christine Brew and Glenn Rowley

In this chapter we draw on data from the Victorian Certificate of Education (VCE), an innovative curriculum and assessment system fully introduced in 1992 to all schools in Victoria, Australia. Here we examine whether student performance in mathematics is affected by the format of assessment tasks and, in particular, whether the nature of assessment contributes to apparent gender differences in mathematics performance, as is suggested in some research. The findings from the large data base have implications for other large-scale, high-stake, examinations.

Introduction

Gender differences in performance on mathematical tasks and participation in optional mathematics courses and activities have attracted much attention over the past two decades. A careful reading of the literature reveals that there is considerable overlap in the performance of males and females. Yet some differences in above average performance, most often in favour of males, continue to be reported on selected mathematical tasks assessed through standardized or large-scale testing. However, when achievement is reported in terms of (usually low-stake) classroom grades, females are often rated slightly higher than males (Kimball, 1989).

Participation

Internationally, mathematics and related occupations have been identified as a male domain. Statistics in the USA (Central Statistical Office, 1994) and elsewhere reveal that women and minorities are under-represented in the most advanced mathematics courses and in related professions. Even at the high-school level, the most demanding mathematics subjects are more likely to be taken by males. Despite their increasing participation in mathematics education, females remain under-represented in the most rigorous mathematics courses. For example, in their historical survey of gender outcomes in Australian education Teese, Davies, Charlton, and Polesel (1995) noted '. . . despite a nearly-universal availability . . . [subjects such as] calculus and physics, in particular, remain largely male academic fiefs . . .' (p. 11). Perusal of recent statistics confirmed that '. . . in the traditional areas of mathematics, gender differences are still quite pronounced, especially in specialist preparatory maths' (Teese et al., 1995:28). Such statements are also relevant in other industrialized countries, despite the removal of formal barriers preventing women from pursuing an education in mathematics (Leder, 1992). As a rule, patterns of gender differences in participation in education in general, and in mathematics and related areas in particular, are exaggerated further in less-developed countries. For example, in the mid-1980s, it was estimated that seven males were enroled for every female in African universities, and that women were grossly underrepresented in natural science and engineering courses (Graham-Brown, 1991).

Performance

A number of studies have attempted to assess more systematically the effect of the nature and format of the assessment instrument on performance in mathematics. Anderson (1989) compared the achievement of first-year female and male mathematics students enroled in specialized mathematics degree courses at several universities in the UK on a range of objective tests — multiple-choice items, analysis questions, and two sets of true-false questions, one with and one without a penalty for incorrect answers. The female students, he reported, on average scored somewhat lower than did the males on each of the four types of questions asked. Earlier work by Murphy (1981) reported findings consistent with those of Anderson (1989). Using a sample 15-year-old Irish school students, Bolger and Kellaghan (1990) compared students' school performance on multiple-choice and free-response test items in mathematics, Irish and English tests. Only slight differences, generally in favour of males, were found on both the multiple-choice and free-response language measures. Gender differences, again in favour of males, were more pronounced on the mathematics tests and 'Males score[d] one third of a standard deviation higher than females on the free-response test and almost one half of a standard deviation higher on the multiple-choice test' (p. 170). Johnson (1984) used American college students to trace gender differences in problem solving over time. Nine different experiments were carried out. He concluded that

> . . . the male advantage seems to extend broadly through the domain of word problems . . . and to be independent of prior exposure to the particular problem used . . . However, when the same subjects are given more formally deductive problem-solving tasks to perform, the male advantage evaporates into insignificance . . . suggesting that the male advantage may have something to do with translating a verbally expressed situation into a representation that can be attacked analytically or mathematically. A facility for bringing relevant real-world knowledge to bear on the problem may also be involved (pp. 1368–9).

More recent English data (Goulding, 1992) are also noteworthy. Goulding compared student performance on mathematics examinations with different weightings for the traditional final examination and coursework assessment component. Males seemed to perform slightly better than females — a somewhat higher percentage were awarded a grade of C or above when the final examination component was 80 per cent or 66 per cent, but females, on the other hand, achieved slightly higher than males when the exam component dropped to 50 per cent.

The results from two other studies, concerned with performance in science, are also relevant. Harding (1981) found that boys excelled in multiple-choice papers, that no generalization about gender differences in performance could be made about science tests consisting of essay-type papers, and that structured questions appeared to show least bias. Harding's findings seem to be supported by Victorian examination data. Short-answer questions were introduced to the physics paper in 1988, in what was then called the Higher School Certificate. The paper contained 65 questions worth one mark each. Many of these were multiple-choice items — others required some mathematical calculations, but needed only the answer to be recorded. The remaining items on the paper were short-answer questions which required a written explanation of the relevant physics principles. Drawing on Victorian Curriculum and Assessment Board data from 1989, 1990, and 1991 Forgasz and Leder (1991) reported that females performed less well than males, on average, in physics overall and on the one-mark questions, with no difference in the performance of the two groups on the short-answer questions. Thus females performed relatively better on the items requiring a short answer than on the one-mark questions.

Collectively the work reviewed suggests that the format of assessment may affect apparent gender differences in mathematics achievement. On average, males seem to do better than females on multiple-choice items, but not necessarily on unstructured items or those which require an essay-type response.

The Victorian Certificate of Education (VCE)

Changes in the format of a state-side examination in Victoria, Australia, presented a unique opportunity for a more detailed exploration of the affect on performance of different types of assessments. Briefly, under the new examination structure put in place, the same group of students was required to sit for four distinct examination tasks during the school year. Thus, for this large group of students, performance on different high-stake assessment tasks could be compared. The findings from this large data source are readily generalizable to other large-scale examinations which are attempted by large regional or state-wide populations.

The data used in this chapter are based on the 1992 Victorian Certificate of Education (VCE). As is described in more detail in the next section, that year students enroled in mathematics subjects were required to complete four different assessment tasks which focused on different mathematical skills and required substantially different responses. A brief description of the aims and structure of the VCE, also included in the next section, serves as an important context for the findings which follow.

Background to the VCE

The VCE was introduced for English and mathematics in 1991 at grade 11 in all Victorian schools, after 10 pilot schools had trialed the new curricula in the previous year. By 1992 the VCE was fully implemented into schools across the state. The data from that year are thus of particular interest for investigating performance trends for the new examination structure.

From its inception, the VCE was envisaged as a two-year course which spanned grades 11 and 12, and served as a common credential for completing secondary school. Its assessment format symbolized and reinforced real structural changes in the delivery and format of post-compulsory education in Victoria. Two of its fundamental aims were to encourage innovative teaching practice, through a broadening of the assessment tasks, and to provide a broad curriculum to allow all students, not just those intending to go on to tertiary education, an opportunity to remain within the mainstream school and examination structure.

The VCE examination has two quite different components: work requirements and common assessment tasks (CATs). All work requirements in a particular subject need to be completed and rated as satisfactory or unsatisfactory by school staff, whose decisions are informed by centrally set guidelines. Entrance to tertiary institutions and courses is based on performance on the CATs. While all CATs are centrally set, in some cases they are initially marked by the school and external moderation and verification processes are used to maximize consistency of teacher marking across the state. Other CATs are externally marked from the outset. Student achievement on the common assessment tasks are the focus of this paper. Keen competition for university places ensures that far more importance is attached to marks obtained for the CATs, since these serve as an important filter for entry to university and individual courses, than to the pass/fail ratings assigned to the work requirements.

Since its introduction, the assessment structure of the VCE has attracted much attention, both praise and criticism. Over the years various changes have been made to the mathematics subjects (also known as studies) — in nomenclature, in the grouping of the subjects, and in the number of CATs set. Details of these changes are beyond the scope of this chapter. Suffice it to say that, with time, assessment of the VCE mathematics subjects has gradually returned to being more examination-oriented, less school-based, and more centrally-controlled.

The VCE in 1992

In 1992 there were six mathematics studies. Each of these studies had four prescribed CATs, described as follows.

- *CAT 1 — Investigative project:* a written report (of 1500 words) based on an independent mathematical investigation. Set annually, on a theme devised centrally, the total time spent on the task was expected to be between 15 and 20 hours — some in class, the bulk outside school hours. However, determined to do well, many students exceeded this suggested time. Initial grades were decided within each school according to centrally-specified guidelines and were then subjected to verification procedures.

- *CAT 2 — Challenging problem:* a problem selected from four set centrally each year. This task required students to undertake a problem-solving or modelling activity and to submit a report of their work which contained details of the methods and procedures used, as well as of the solution obtained. In an attempt to maximize their marks, many students again exceeded the six to eight hours recommended for this CAT.

- *CAT 3 — Facts and skills task:* a set of 49 multiple-choice questions, completed under test conditions in school, and designed to assess mathematical concepts and skills in standard ways.

- *CAT 4 — Analysis task:* a traditionally-administered, strictly-timed, examination of four to six questions of increasing complexity, designed to test interpretive and analytical skills.

Thus there were several important differences between CATs 1/2 and CATs 3/4. The former were longer-term projects, and initial solution attempts were expected to be redrafted after some teacher input. Further, CATs 1/2 were attempted primarily outside school hours, required considerable explanations of the methods used and solution steps taken, had a strong language component in the presentation of the final product, and were initially teacher-marked. These CATs are consistent with the innovative, more open-ended assessment tasks advocated by, for example, the *National Council of Teachers of Mathematics* (NCTM) who argue for

> . . . investigating, formulating, representing, reasoning, and applying a variety of strategies to the solution of problems — then reflecting on these uses of mathematics — and away from being shown or told, memorizing and repeating (NCTM, 1995:2).

Silver and Lane (1993) similarly called for the use of assessment tasks which involve

> ... understanding and representing problems, discerning mathematical relationships, organizing information, using procedures, strategies and heuristic processes, formulating conjectures, evaluating the reasonableness of answers, generalizing results, and justifying answers or procedures (p. 63).

CATs 3/4, on the other hand, were rigidly-timed assessment tasks, done in school under examination conditions, had a much lower language component, and were marked externally. These latter CATs conform to the traditional examination requirements.

The Investigation

Students wishing to take mathematics in grade 12 were able to select from different blocks. These were Space and Number (S&N) — concerned with the study of algebra, geometry and trigonometry; Change and Approximation (C&A) — dealing with calculus and polynomials; Reasoning and Data (R&D) — which focused on probability and statistics; and Extension blocks (Ext) for each of these — to allow specialized study and more in-depth treatment of work covered in the three basic blocks. Six different mathematics studies or subjects were thus available in the 1992 VCE; C&A (Ext) was recognized as the most demanding of the six mathematics subject.

This variety of subjects allowed students to study mathematics at different levels of difficulty. Of particular significance for the purposes of this chapter is the opportunity also presented for repeated exploration of the effect on performance of different types of assessment.

Questions Addressed

The following related questions were asked in this investigation.

- Do females and males participate equally in mathematics?
- Are there any differences in the performance of females and males on the different CATs, using data from the innovative 1992 examinations?
- Do any differences identified suggest that particular groups of students (females/males) are advantaged/disadvantaged by certain modes of assessment?
- Is there evidence to support the view that the innovatory assessment tasks (CATs 1/2) assessed something different and distinctive compared with the traditional examination-type tasks (CATs 3/4)?

The Results

Participation in Mathematics in the 1992 VCE

The number of students who studied at least one mathematics subject was 34,500. Of these, 49.5 per cent were female. The uptake of the six mathematical studies in 1992 varied considerably, as can be seen in Table 14.1. The large sample sizes for all but one of the studies are noteworthy, and strengthen our confidence in the significance of consistencies in identified patterns of achievement.

The lower number of females who studied C&A (Ext), 38.6 per cent of enrolments, is consistent with females opting out of the higher-level mathematics more frequently than males. More generally, females represented 42 per cent of enrolments in the Extension subjects, compared to 48.2 per cent of enrolments in the three basic mathematics blocks.

Table 14.1: Details of the 1992 sample

Study	Total enrolment	per cent Female	per cent Male
Space & Number	7,181	49.5	50.5
Space & Number (Ext)	4,653	50.5	49.5
Change & Approximation	5,951	56.2	43.8
Change & Approximation (Ext)	10,385	38.6	61.4
Reasoning & Data	13,655	44.5	55.5
Reasoning & Data (Ext)	152	44.1	55.9

Performance Trends

Significant gender differences were found for 19 of 24 CATs. While some of these mean differences were quite small, in 11 CATs the differences represented at least half a grade — at least 5 marks out of 100. This difference is highly significant in the context of strong competition for tertiary places. The data summarized in Table 14.2 for C&A and C&A (Ext) are representative of the findings for all six subjects. A distinct pattern clearly emerged across the studies, with females generally outperforming males in CATs 1 and 2, while males outperformed females on CATs 3 and 4.

Table 14.2: Relative performance on the 1992 CATs by gender, for C&A and C&A (Ext)

	CAT 1		CAT 2		CAT 3		CAT 4	
Study	Female	Male	Female	Male	Female	Male	Female	Male
Change & Approximation	**6.4**	5.9	**6.6**	6.4	5.3	**5.6**	6.1	6.3
Change & Approximation (Ext)	**6.7**	6.2	**6.8**	6.7	5.8	**6.0**	5.6	**6.1**

Bold type denotes statistically significant difference at least at the $p < 0.01$ level.

Who is (Dis)advantaged?

It is worth recalling that, for each mathematics subject, the same group of students sat for the four assessment tasks (the CATs) during the year. The data in Table 14.2 clearly illustrate that there were substantial group differences in performance. On average, the females performed better on the two innovative CATs which were part of the overall assessment in C&A and C&A (Ext). While still having time constraints, these tasks were longer-term, open-ended, required a sustained commitment particularly out of school hours, had a much stronger verbal component for their presentation and were initially assessed by the school. Males, on the other hand, did better on average on the rigidly-timed, traditional assessment tasks done under strictly supervised examination conditions. While CATs 1 and 2 were initially teacher-marked, external authentication and verification procedures ultimately minimized teacher effects.

As can be seen from Table 14.2, seven of the eight differences were statistically significant at the 1 per cent level. The pattern of differences for the other mathematics studies mirrored those shown for C&A and C&A (Ext).

A Further Comment

The introduction of the new styles of assessment in CAT 1 and CAT 2 arose from a wish to assess skills that had not been previously assessed by traditional assessment methods, represented in this case by CATs 3 and 4. Their format is consistent with new assessment guidelines now widely advocated (NCTM, 1995). The results summarized to date suggest that the innovative assessment tasks (CATs 1 and 2) assess different skills from those assessed by traditional examinations tasks (CATs 3 and 4). This was further investigated statistically by examining the intercorrelations among the CAT scores and through the use of factor analytic techniques.

The Common Assessment Tasks — Does the Assessment Format Make a Difference?

The results of the intercorrelations between the CAT scores and the factor analysis produced a clear pattern.

- For each mathematics study, the highest correlations were found between the two examination CATs 3 and 4 (range 0.70 to 0.84, average 0.79).
- The next highest correlations were between the two innovative CATs 1 and 2 (range 0.64 to 0.72, average 0.67).

- The lowest correlations occurred when CAT 1 or CAT 2 was correlated with CAT 3 or CAT 4 (range 0.44 to 0.66, average 0.56).
- A simple principal components analysis on each set of study scores suggested strongly that a one-factor solution was defensible. Each study yielded a single eigenvalue greater than one (range 2.68 to 3.06), and the next well below one (range 0.50 to 0.72). We take this to indicate that the single composite score used for tertiary selection is not put in doubt by our data.
- Nevertheless, when forced into a two-factor solution, the data yielded interesting and very consistent patterns. For each of the six studies, the same pattern emerged — the two-factor solution consistently identified CATs 1 and 2 as a single factor, and CATs 3 and 4 as a second (orthogonal) factor.

The consistency of this pattern across all six studies suggests most strongly that method of measurement is an important factor. In simple terms, the results support the assertion that what CATs 1 and 2 measured was different, at least in part, from what CATs 3 and 4 measured, and that the differences are strongly gender-related.

A Comment and Possible Explanation

There are several properties that distinguish between the two pairs of CATs — CATs 1 and 2 are largely completed in the students' own time, are internally assessed, and involve extended written work in which there is (in the case of CAT 1) no correct answer and (in the case of CAT 2) no single correct way of solving the problem. Various drafts are generally completed before the final assignment is submitted. CATs 3 and 4, on the other hand, are completed under examination conditions, with the pressure of time and temperament that this involves, and are externally marked. They involve less writing than CATs 1 and 2 (none, in the case of CAT 3), and there are 'correct' and 'incorrect' answers, although CAT 4 allows for different paths to the same solution and for the recognition of degrees of merit in incorrect responses. As already indicated, careful verification strategies have been put in place to ensure that possible variations in marking introduced for tasks initially evaluated at the school level are minimized.

For CATs 1 and 2, on which females generally do better than males, it is widely believed that presentation skills are important, and there is some fear that students may put as much effort into the presentation and packaging of their work as into the mathematics content. As there is a long history of evidence for the greater language skills of girls at this age, the question immediately arises as to whether the pattern of results is attributable to the greater language component of CATs 1 and 2 compared to CATs 3 and 4, on which males typically did better (see Table 14.2).

The Role of English

English is the one compulsory subject which all students who sit for the VCE have in common. Females typically outperform males by a significant margin in this subject. As for mathematics, the 1992 VCE English examination consisted of four common assessment tasks (CATs).

For each cohort of students doing a mathematics subject, we were able to look at the interrelationships between the four English CATs and the four mathematics CATs. Similar patterns were identified within all six mathematics subjects.

- An English factor and a Mathematics factor emerged, as would be expected.
- Mathematics CAT 1 and 2 were found to have higher English loadings (range 0.29 to 0.53, average 0.38) than did Mathematics CATs 3 and 4 (range 0.16 to 0.26, average 0.22).
- Mathematics CATs 1 and 2 had lower loadings on the Mathematics factor (range 0.60 to 0.76, average 0.70) than did CATs 3 and 4 (range 0.85 to 0.87, average 0.86).

It seems clear that the skills assessed by CATs 1 and 2 have more in common with the skills required to do well in English than do those assessed by CATs 3 and 4. This accounts to some degree for the gender differences observed, given the higher performance by females on the English examination. Thus the 1992 results revealed some important gender differences in achievement, which were related to the types of assessment tasks and the skills required for solving and reporting those tasks.

Conclusions

Much effort has been spent over the past two decades exploring gender differences in mathematics learning. Small, subtle, but consistent gender differences continue to be reported.

> Despite the considerable overlap in the participation patterns in mathematics of females and males, somewhat more males than females enrol in intensive, high-level mathematics courses. Similarly, there is much overlap in the mathematics achievement of females and males. Yet some performance differences in favour of males continue to be found, particularly on mathematical tasks that require high cognitive level skills. Reference to cross-cultural data confirms the pervasiveness of these findings (Leder, 1992:616).

For many years, gender differences in mathematics performance have primarily been inferred from student achievement on traditional assessment tasks. The prevalence of such tasks for measuring student achievement perpetuates and reinforces perceptions of gender differences and male superiority in mathematics. The data reported in this chapter show convincingly that, given a different assessment process and format, previous assumptions about superior performance in mathematics by males are challenged. On more open-ended tasks, which require sustained effort in and outside school, on which early attempts are expected to be perfected through redrafting and further work, and for which presentation and verbal explanations form an integral part of the solution process, females on average out-perform males.

This study has shown very clearly that the introduction of new assessment modes in mathematics did have an impact on the fundamental nature of the assessment. CATs 1 and 2 did measure something quite different from CATs 3 and 4 — something that is more language-based, and something that enables females to gain more success. CATs 1 and 2 may well have served to make the study of mathematics at senior levels more attractive to girls. Use of more innovative assessment tasks similar to CATs 1 and 2 in other large-scale examinations may extend these benefits to females in other countries. Yet traditions change slowly.

In the years following 1992, the number of common assessment tasks in mathematics was reduced from four to three CATs, with the corresponding increase in the examination component of assessment from 50 per cent to 67 per cent. The discontinuance of CAT 2 seems to have negated some of the advantage that was gained by female students with the introduction of the new assessment modes in mathematics. The return to a more hierarchical structure of mathematical studies has coincided with a reduction, since 1992, in the proportion of females enroled in the higher-level mathematical studies.

Yet the lessons to be learnt from the 1992 VCE data set remain. As a group, males and females performed differently on inherently different assessment tasks. The traditional assessment tasks appeared to favour males. More innovative but still demanding assessment tasks, with a focus on the solution process as well as the answer, which required sustained and independent efforts over a longer period of time, and which had a stronger verbal component, seemed to favour females.

The evidence is clear that tasks such as those represented by CATs 1 and 2 measure aspects of mathematics achievement which differ, at least partly, from the assessment demands represented by CATs 3 and 4. The inclusion of these tasks in high-stake examinations not only achieves a more comprehensive assessment of skills needed for sound performance in mathematics, but also leads to a more equitable assessment of mathematics performance.

Note

We gratefully acknowledge the financial assistance of the Australian Research Council for this project and the Victorian Board of Studies for generously providing us with the raw data file.

Gilah C. Leder, Christine Brew and Glenn Rowley

References

ANDERSON, J. (1989) 'Sex-related differences on objective tests among undergraduates', *Educational Studies in Mathematics*, **20**(2), pp. 165–77.

BOLGER, N. and KELLAGHAN, T. (1990) 'Method of measurement and gender differences in scholastic achievement', *Journal of Educational Measurement*, **27**(2), pp. 165–74.

CENTRAL STATISTICAL OFFICE (1994) *Annual Abstract of Statistics 1994*, HMSO, London.

FORGASZ, H.J. and LEDER, G.C. (1991) 'To guess or not to guess: A question of risk', *Mathematics Competitions*, **4**(2), 58–69.

GOULDING, M. (1992) 'Let's hear about it for the girls', *Times Educational Supplement*, February 2, pp. 38–40.

GRAHAM-BROWN, S. (1991) *Education in the Developing World*, New York: Longman Publishing.

HARDING, J. (1981) 'Sex differences in science examination' in KELLY, A. (ed.) *The missing half: Girls and Science Education*, Manchester, England: Manchester University Press, pp. 192–204.

JOHNSON, E.S. (1984) 'Sex differences in problem solving', *Journal of Educational Psychology*, **76**(6), pp. 1359–71.

KIMBALL, M.M. (1989) 'A new perspective on women's maths achievement', *Psychological Bulletin*, **105**, pp. 198–214.

LEDER, G.C. (1992) 'Mathematics and gender: changing perspectives' in GROUWS, D.A. (ed.) *Handbook of Research on Mathematics Teaching and Learning*, New York: Mac-Millan, pp. 597–622.

MURPHY, N.K. (1981) 'The effects of a calculator treatment on achievement and attitude toward problem solving in seventh grade mathematics', *Dissertation Abstracts International*, **42**, 2008A (University Microfilms No. 81–21, 439).

NATIONAL COUNCIL OF TEACHERS OF MATHEMATICS (1995) *Assessment Standards for School Mathematics*, Reston, VA: Author.

SILVER, E.A. and LANE, S. (1993) 'Assessment in the context of mathematics instruction reform: The design of assessment in the QUASAR project', in NISS, M. (ed.) *Cases of Assessment in Mathematics Education. An ICMI Study*. Dordrecht, The Netherlands: Kluwer Academic Publishers, pp. 59–69.

TEESE, R., DAVIES, M., CHARLTON, M. and POLESEL, J. (1995) *Who Wins at School? Boys and Girls in Australian Secondary Education*, Canberra: Australian Government Publishing Service.

VICTORIAN CURRICULUM AND ASSESSMENT BOARD (1990, September) *Mathematics Study Design*, Melbourne: Victorian Department of Education.

15 Measurement Obstacles to International Comparisons and the Need for Regional Design and Analysis in Mathematics Surveys

Richard G. Wolfe

International surveys in mathematics have always provided rankings of countries on overall achievement. However, in addition, country rankings can be produced for different mathematics topics and even test items, and the overall average can be replaced with a profile (vector) of topic and item means. These profiles lead to distinct and often discrepant comparisons, depending on which items are considered or how the topics are formed and weighted — a country's performance may rank relatively high for some topics or items and relatively low for others. Such variability may be the consequence of different curricular intentions (or opportunities), or it may simply be unexplained measurement error; consequently, overall international comparisons are often difficult to interpret; when the profiles of opportunity or achievement are too discrepant, the overall comparisons are either fundamentally unfair or essentially random. In this chapter, a framework is developed for looking at country achievement and opportunity profiles, and examples are given from recent and older surveys in mathematics. In the conclusion, it is suggested that regionalization of educational surveys might lead to more interpretable inter-country comparisons.

Introduction

With the release of each successive international survey of educational achievement, in mathematics and in other topics, the cries of the researchers and survey designers — that their motives are pure, that the international league tables are irrelevant, and that the real importance of the surveys is in the correlational findings and the knowledge that is gained about the structure of the teaching and learning process — are drowned in the enormous wave of public and political attention given to those league tables.

This inevitable social and political reality suggests that the survey analysts and reporters should develop and employ the best possible methodology for preparing, interpreting and presenting international comparisons. My view is that this methodology has to deal not with overall average achievement but rather with profiles of achievement. For example, in a given mathematics topic area we may have a dozen test items, and the profile of item-specific achievement for a country consists of the vector of a dozen item means (per cents of correct response). These profiles will vary between countries in general level (average of the item means) but also in detail. There are item-by-country interactions, in which items that are relatively easy in one country may be relatively hard in another. If we compare countries on the topic total, we need to worry about the measurement error implicit in the item selection: What would the comparison be if we took a different dozen items?

Consider then what happens when a test contains several topics — say arithmetic, geometry and algebra. The topic-specific achievement profile for a country consists of the vector of topic means (average for arithmetic, average for geometry, average for algebra). The topic profiles will vary between countries in general level (average over the topics) but also in pattern — one topic may be relatively easy in one country and relatively hard in another. For example, if algebra is a major part of a country's curriculum we would expect the scores on the algebra subtest to be relatively high; if, in another country, there is emphasis on geometry we would expect its scores on the geometry test to be relatively high. A comparison between these countries that is based on overall performance masks the difference in curricular intentions and depends on the perhaps arbitrary weighting of the topic areas in the test. What would the comparison show if the algebra subtest were twice the size of the geometry subtest?

My view is that the methodology for international comparisons should begin with the country by item or topic tables of achievement averages — that is, with tables of profiles. The row (country) averages of such a table are effectively what is used for gross international comparisons, but the elements of the rows considered as profiles of achievement provide essential information for understanding the comparisons and knowing their real accuracy.

There are two fundamental interpretations of these profiles. If we regard the columns (items or topics) as meaningful subunits of the content domain, then profile patterns represent substantive differences in the learning, and presumably the teaching, of the domain. If we regard the columns to be essentially random replications or samples from the content domain, then profile variability reveals interactions that represent measurement error in comparing countries.

What I have found in various international surveys is that, when we regard the achievement profiles as descriptive of content subunits and compare them with profiles of curricular intention (opportunity to learn), we learn that country differences in achievement may be partly consequences of intentionally-different treatments of the content domain. On the other hand, when profiles are regarded as random interactions, the marginal accuracy of the average achievement is seen to be overrated and country comparisons are less precise than conventional reporting would lead us to believe.

Measurement Framework

In matters of public opinion polling, we are used to dealing with single items as the units of tabulation and reporting. If we were asking about support for a particular policy, we would want to know exactly how a question was worded and what per cent of people responded in exactly which way. We would be unsatisfied with a report of an average per cent of agreement over several different and undisclosed questions. The interpretation of the tabulation depends on the face (visible) validity of the question. The statistical accuracy of the response tabulation for a single item depends on the size of the respondent sample. Population (such as country or stratum) comparisons are carried out as cross-tabulations, and the percentaged response distributions are compared.

The original substantive and technical posture of the US National Assessment of Educational Progress (NAEP), as discussed by Womer (1970), proposed item-by-item reporting that looked very much like the output of opinion polls. Achievement items, many of which were supposed to elicit complex student performance such as problem solution and communication, were to be printed together with statistical distributions of student response. There has since been a drift away from single-item reporting in NAEP, partly for a very practical reason — it is difficult to maintain a large pool of items, some secure and some released, for building a time series of achievement results. The methodological emphasis has shifted to producing averages and scaled scores that summarize, presumably in a consistent manner, the achievements as measured by item collections that can be linked over time. Individual items are publicly exposed only for exemplifying the performances expected at different scale points.

In international comparative surveys, starting with the IEA International Study of Mathematics (Husén, 1967), the tradition has been to report and compare average test scores, where the averaging (or totaling or scaling, which are equivalent to averaging) is over items from a more or less general content domain, which might be, for example, all of the mathematics relevant to a given grade level or to a major topic (or other classification) within the mathematics domain, such as geometry, algebra or computation. Many, but not all, international volumes also provide items and item statistics. For example, in Husén (1967) all the test items appear in an appendix with their average difficulty over all countries and with indications of which countries found each item particularly hard or easy. Such publication is apparently considered problematic in later studies, such as the Third International Mathematics and Science Study (TIMSS), where there is the intention of replicating the survey after a short period (four years), and so half of the items are being kept secure.

The conceptual and statistical basis of reporting and comparing student populations between countries using average test score statistics rather than individual item statistics can be based on the following two interpretations about test items.

Richard G. Wolfe

Fixed Effects between Content Sub-domains

In the Third International Mathematics and Science Study (TIMSS), for example, there is separate reporting of results, at each grade level, for mathematics and science. There are further distinctions made in the test design and item allocation among the different topics within mathematics and science. In theory and in practice there is, for each country, an underlying profile of achievement across these topics. Some will do better in algebra, some will do better in geometry, some will do better in everything. Statistically, these are fixed effects and interactions. When a composite or aggregate score or scale is calculated across these topics, the relative importance of different topics to that composite is (unless special weighting is used) essentially proportional to the number of items that that were devoted to them. That test design or weighting then combines with the fixed effects and interactions to determine the country comparisons. For example, if the test design or weighting favours the geometry topic, then countries with relatively high geometry performance will rank higher overall — an example of international measurement bias.

Random Effects within Content Sub-domains

For a given content or topic, there are many items that satisfy our specifications of what belongs to the topic and that could be used to represent the topic in a test. If there is any breadth to a particular topic, then some test items from the topic will be easy and some will be hard. Unless there is exactly parallel structure of knowledge, learning and language in different student populations, some items will be relatively harder in some populations than in others. The random (unexplained) variation within a content sub-domain for which a score is to be developed must be regarded as error because, once we have formed the score, we are not interested in the particular set of items that were used but rather in generalizing to a larger set of items that might have been used. This is the basic argument of generalizability theory (Cronbach, Gleser, Nanda, and Rajaratnam, 1972), with the specific twist that item-by-country interactions or error variances determine the accuracy of measurements of differences between countries. For example, if we have a small number of items in a topic, and the items vary differently in difficulty from country to country, the overall ranking of the countries in the topic will have lots of international measurement error.

A Re-evaluation

From this conceptual basis we can re-examine the comparative results from international achievement surveys, and our conclusion often is that the comparisons are substantively biased due to mis-alignment of the content profiles (fixed-effect differences) or the accuracy of the comparisons as presented in international reports is considerably overstated (random-effect differences).

The conventionally-reported standard errors take into account only the survey sampling errors in each country or stratum. It can be assumed that those errors are independent between countries or strata. The crucial mistake is that the standard errors contain only one of the two major sources of variance in making international comparisons. That is, they reflect the between-student variance (and the related school variance) but they do not reflect the country by item and country by topic interactions. If we had taken different items within topic, then the between-country results would have been different and the rankings would have been different — this is international measurement error. If we had chosen different topics or weighted the topics differently, the between-country results and rankings would shift — this is international measurement bias.

Some Examples

The left panel of Figure 15.1 shows an analysis of achievement percentages for 32 algebra items in eight countries (systems) from the IEA Second International Mathematics Study (SIMS), Longitudinal Component, Population A (grade 8), the right panel analyses the opportunity to learn. A median-based two-way analysis has separated the original table of percentage data (achievement or opportunity to learn) into grand centers (49 and 81), column averages deviated around the centers, row averages deviated around the centers, and the residual matrices of row by column interactions. These components add to give the original percentages. For example, the original percent of achievement in Japan on Item 20 was 72 per cent. In this analysis, this is broken down into: a general center (49), an amount by which Japan is generally higher (11), an amount by which Item 20 is generally lower (−3), and an interaction (15) corresponding to the amount by which the achievement in Japan on this particular item exceeds these averages.

The interpretation of the row effects is presumably technical — some items within the algebra domain are easier, some are harder, on the average, for these countries. The column effects are important country differences and show which countries, when their results are averaged over all these items, did better or worse.

Computationally, the residuals are the original percentages with the overall, the row effects, and the column effects subtracted out. They are interpreted in one of the two ways mentioned above.

- Each column of residuals can be thought of as defining how the specific achievement profile for a country differs from the average profile for all countries, further to how the general achievement for the country differs from the average general achievement. For example, Japan does

	Achievement (per cent correct)									Opportunity to Learn								
	Belgium (Flemish)	British Columbia (Canadian provinces)	Ontario (Canadian provinces)	France	Japan	New Zealand	Thailand	USA	average	Belgium (Flemish)	British Columbia (Canadian provinces)	Ontario (Canadian provinces)	France	Japan	New Zealand	Thailand	USA	average
1	19	-8	-8	9	24	-3	0	0	-25	10	-5	-7	5	11	-12	8	-14	-1
2	-13	1	7	9	-1	-3	-4	3	22	-12	-3	5	-1	-5	6	1	4	11
3	-1	1	-3	1	6	-14	2	-9	19	-1	1	0	0	-4	15	0	7	15
4	-11	6	7	-3	-10	6	-5	3	1	0	-1	4	-5	0	3	3	-5	11
5	9	5	1	-8	-1	10	-21	-2	2	0	-1	6	0	-3	14	-20	7	13
6	5	0	-2	13	-1	0	12	-4	15	2	9	-11	-2	30	-6	30	-5	-21
7	4	-10	0	-9	10	2	-6	0	-6	-26	3	-7	9	22	-3	-16	3	-31
8	-7	3	0	-14		1	7	-3	15	-5	3	18	-8		-5	15	0	-4
9	3	-1	3	0	0	3	-4	-2	-26	2	-6	10	-2	8	-2	-5	2	4
10	5	0	2	0		-7	-21	-1	4	0	0	6	-4		-16	8	-13	1
11	-1	1	1	2	6	-9	-8	-5	-1	-2	-1	0	0	-1	15	1	0	12
12	0	6	16	-3	0	-2	-5	10	4	0	0	13	0	1	2	-4	-2	6
13	-11	2	9	8	-3	-2	-5	3	-16	-29	16	-1	11	-58	-29	1	20	-16
14	1	-1	-2	-22	5	6	-6	7	2	4	-1	-5	-6	1	18	-2	4	11
15	-7	-1	-1	1	10	7	-4	2	-21	-13	10	-2	0	3	12	-28	0	-32
16	9	-5	-3	4	20	-4	3	-3	-3	3	1	-2	1	6	-17	-1	-4	6
17	-5	6	1	4	-26	0	11	-3	-24	-2	23	2	17	-63	-11	-11	16	-20
18	31	-3	-12	35	29	2	-7	-2	-15	13	-8	-1	20	1	23	-7	-11	-8
19	9	-2	-2	17	2	-13	1	-1	8	-3	-10	4	-1	0	0	0	2	12
20	0	0	2	16	15	-10	-6	-3	-3	1	-1	3	-1	-4	17	-3	7	15
21	-10	0	-1	-31	7	0	12	5	2	-4	8	8	-13	23	-8	-2	2	-13
22	-1	6	1	-16	-24	-5	2	8	6	5	4	7	-9	15	-13	13	-4	-5
23	2	0	1	0	-5	-1	-1	2	-8	0	-2	0	5	-4	7	1	-10	5
24	0	0	-6	11	5	-5	3	-2	-7	8	1	-18	18	-26	-6	11	-1	-4
25	-12	1	-4	-10	0	0	2	3	25	-32	-3	-12	11	6	3	-24	8	-2
26	7	-18	-11	6	15	-6	9	-11	-7	11	-36	-23	18	4	-4	13	-29	-3
27	-8	10	8	-3	-8	12	-5	3	3	-8	2	6	0	-5	15	-3	0	12
28	23	-8	-1	-1	-2	14	3	1	-22	38	-2	-8	32	-10	42	-50	2	-24
29	-11	5	-1	-2	-8	7	4	1	23	3	1	-9	8	-2	0	0	-4	1
30	-4	-3	3	-21	-3	3	14	9	-10	5	9	1	-3	-54	-1	26	-2	-14
31	14	-2	-5	-4	16	2	1	-1	-14	0	0	-17	2	37	-8	22	-9	-28
32	-5	5	2	-1	-1	1	0	0	19	-3	1	0	0	-2	11	-1	4	14
average	10	3	-4	9	11	-7	-8	-3	49	-3	3	-7	3	8	-17	5	-10	81
Standard error of international measurement	1.8	1.0	1.0	2.2	2.1	1.2	1.4	.8		2.2	1.7	1.6	1.7	4.0	2.5	2.8	1.6	

Figure 15.1: Median-based two-way analyses of achievement and opportunity by country and algebra item in SIMS

15 per cent even better on Item 20 than we would expect given that it does 11 per cent better on the average.
- The matrix of residuals is conceived as a random-error outcome due to item sampling and item by country interactions. Each value represents a specific and random (unexplained) fluctuation in how students in the country do better or worse on a particular item, given the general difficulty of the test, their country's relative performance on the test, the relative difficulty over countries of the item.

In this latter interpretation, the standard deviations of the columns of residuals, divided by the square root of the number of items, can be used as standard errors for the country effects that take into account the international component of measurement error. These errors need to be added to the conventional survey errors in making comparisons among countries. It may be noted that the standard error for France is the largest in this set, not because it had a small student sample (in fact it had the largest sample) but because its profile of achievement in algebra is not the same as the average profile. The international measurement errors in SIMS are about as large as the survey sampling errors, which demonstrates the importance of this analysis.

Analytic Framework and Opportunity to Learn

While it is important to get the standard errors right, and adding measurement error to survey error is a needed correction, we would like from an educational perspective to go further and to understand the nature and origin of the profile differences.

At the very beginning of the IEA studies it was recognized that item selections might prejudice the international comparisons, and as early as the IEA Feasibility Study of 1959 there was an attempt to systematize the measurement of opportunity to learn (Walker, 1962). Generally, this has involved asking teachers in each classroom in each country to judge the questions in the student test and to estimate whether the students have had the opportunity to learn the content necessary to answer the question.

The exact form of the opportunity to learn (OTL) question or questions has varied across the different IEA and other international studies. It is conceptually difficult to define the precise skill requirements of a given test item, or what constitutes opportunity to learn those skills. Teachers may not be the best respondents — they may not have much information about curriculum in prior years, they may not know much about testing, and they may find difficulty in translating their subject area expertise into the specific opportunity question. In the Study of Mathematics and Science Opportunities (SMSO), a research project affiliated with TIMSS, various rigorous methodologies were developed for analyzing curricula and textbooks, and providing linkages with test items through an elaborate coding system.

For the SIMS data reported in the right panel of Figure 15.1, a simple opportunity to learn questions was asked of the teachers — did the students in their classrooms have the opportunity to learn the content necessary to answer the item, either before the testing year or during the testing year. These alternatives were added and then averaged over all teachers to get the percentage of opportunity to learn. A median-based, two-way analysis was applied to the item-by-country table. The column effects are important county differences and show which countries, averaging over all these items, offered more or less opportunity to learn algebra. At this time in the development of mathematics education in these countries (1982–83), there were some substantial differences in how much emphasis was placed on algebra in grade 8 — more in France, less in New Zealand and the USA, and so on.

Of particular interest from the perspective of possible fixed-effect content differences between countries is whether the differential opportunities are related to differential achievements. This question is answered in Figure 15.2. In each scatterplot is shown the relationship of average opportunity and average achievement. In the first case, this is over countries and in the second it is over items. In both cases there is a strong regression effect, indicating that opportunity tends to lead to achievement. There is also a considerable error of regression, suggesting that there are many other determinants of the achievement levels. For example, items can be generally easier or harder examples within a given sub-content domain for which opportunity is offered, or can have specific content that is more or less difficult to learn.

Figure 15.3 provides more detail about the connection of achievement and opportunity. For each of the eight countries there is given a scatterplot of the relationship of opportunity and achievement over the 39 algebra items. The regressions are all positive, showing within-country dependencies of achievement on opportunity, although the structures of the regressions seem to vary somewhat. The dotted lines show the country averages for achievement and opportunity. Only a few items show low opportunity and high achievement (upper left quadrants).

A final analysis from the SIMS data is given in Figure 15.4. This is a scatterplot array for item difficulties, country by country. For each pair of countries the scatterplot of item difficulties is given, each point corresponding to an item's difficulty in one country compared to its difficulty in the other country. The critical observation here is that the correlations are systematically higher among the English-speaking countries — USA, Ontario, British Columbia and New Zealand. Of course these countries (actually three countries with one represented by two provinces) share a common language and considerably-common educational culture. Perhaps an algebra average score would be meaningfully compared among these countries. However, when we look at the possibility of comparison between these countries and the others, or comparisons among the others, it is clear that the magnitudes and even the directions of the comparisons are very much a function of the item sample.

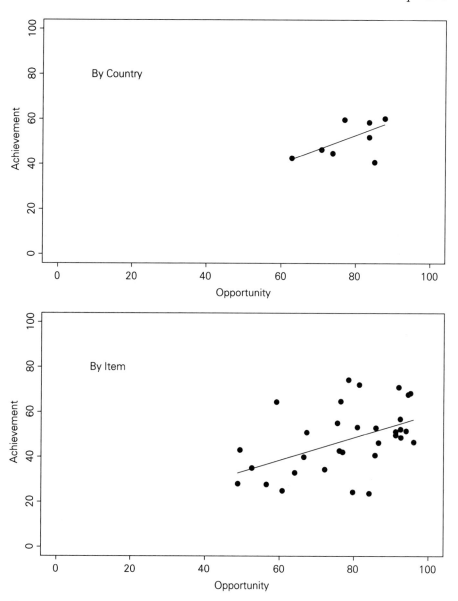

Figure 15.2: Plots of achievement and opportunity, averages by country and by item for algebra in SIMS

Further Examples

The same general data structure for achievement and opportunity results, with countries crossed with topics and items within topics, appears in other international achievement surveys, and we can apply our re-analysis.

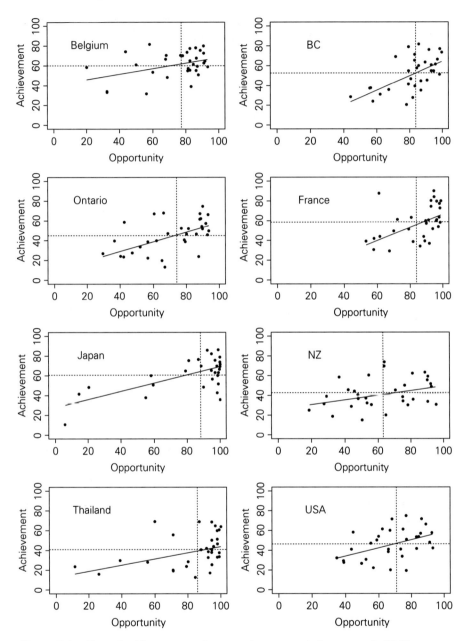

Figure 15.3: Plots of achievement and opportunity, separately by country in SIMS

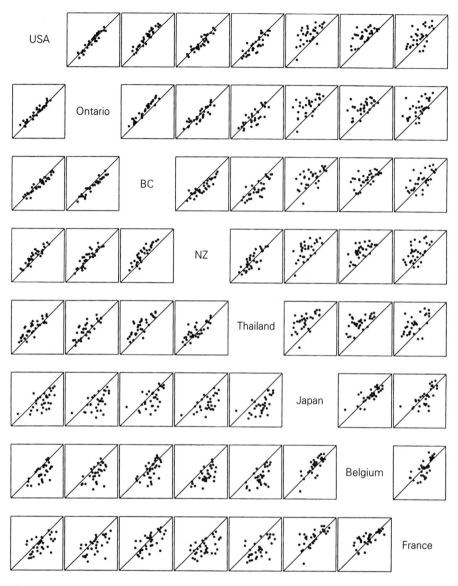

Figure 15.4: Scatterplot array for item difficulties, country by country in SIMS

Figures 15.5, 15.6 and 15.7 give results from the IAEP World of Differences report on mathematics achievement among 13-year-olds (Lapointe, Mead, and Phillips, 1989). Unfortunately item-level statistics were not available, so we cannot assess directly the international measurement error due to item interactions. (This is also going to be true in TIMSS because, as noted above, half of the test is being secured for a second round of testing.) However, we

	Numbers and operations	Relations, functions, etc.	Measurement	Geometry	Data organization	Logic and problem-solving	
Achievement							
British Columbia	1	−4	−2	−1	1	1	3.7
Ireland	−1	1	2	−2	−9	2	−2.8
Korea	−3	−1	5	1	5	−9	10.1
New Brunswick (Eng)	1	0	0	4	0	0	0.8
New Brunswick (Fr)	4	2	−2	2	−4	−3	−3.1
Ontario (Eng)	0	−2	0	0	2	2	−1.5
Ontario (Fr)	0	7	−1	1	0	−4	−9.2
Quebec (Eng)	2	−1	0	0	0	−1	2.3
Quebec (Fr)	2	1	−1	1	−2	−3	4.2
Spain	−2	1	6	0	−2	0	−0.8
United Kingdom	−13	0	3	−5	0	2	2.9
United States	0	−1	2	−6	5	0	−10.2
Average	6.3	5.3	−8.1	−5.3	−5.9	7.6	65.5
Number of items	24	6	10	8	6	8	62
Opportunity							
British Columbia	4	1	−4	−1	−2	3	−10.6
Ireland	2	4	−10	−2	−6	7	−12.1
Korea	−10	2	19	2	−2	−5	3.8
New Brunswick (Eng)	−5	−2	2	10	5	−10	−10
New Brunswick (Fr)	1	−1	8	5	−12	−4	5.6
Ontario (Eng)	0	0	−4	2	4	−3	−0.5
Ontario (Fr)	−1	−2	0	0	4	1	1.4
Quebec (Eng)	6	0	−8	−3	2	0	−5.6
Quebec (Fr)	3	−1	1	−6	−2	2	5.3
Spain	−6	1	8	−1	−6	2	13.9
United Kingdom	−16	−3	1	3	−1	6	0.5
United States	3	1	−2	−1	17	−3	−7.5
Average	11.3	6.9	−16.6	5.6	−5.6	−9.3	62

Figure 15.5: Median-based two-way analyses of achievement and opportunity by country and topic in IAEP World of Differences

can operate our analysis on the published table of country (system) by topic area average percentages. In Figure 15.5 are given the median-based two-way analyses of achievement and opportunity; also of interest is the number of items composing each topic scale. There are some large residuals, indicating achievement below or above the amount expected from the system and topic averages.

Figure 15.6 shows that the residuals in achievement are positively correlated with the residuals in opportunity; the more a topic is especially taught in a country, beyond what is the average teaching for the country and the average teaching for the topic across countries, the more it is especially learned

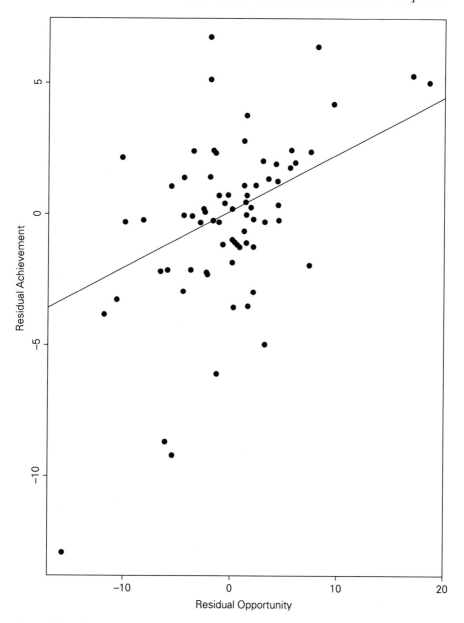

Figure 15.6: Scatterplot of residual achievement by residual opportunity in IAEP World of Differences

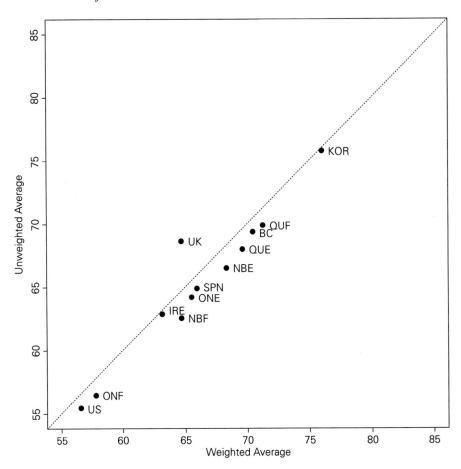

Figure 15.7: Scatterplot of weighted and unweighted average achievement in IAEP World of Differences

in the country, beyond what is the average learning for the country and the average learning for the topic across countries. We interpret this to mean that achievement is determined to some extent by opportunity.

In the IAEP study, the total score comparisons were effectively weighted by the number of items in the subtopics. In Figure 15.7 is shown a scatterplot relating the total mathematics average using that original weighting with another average that gives equal weights to the topics. Since the achievement profiles vary between countries, the country summaries of any composite will depend on the weighting. In this comparison, there is a substantial difference in the rankings of the UK, which is much higher in the equally-weighted scoring than in the original. This is the result of there being a substantial emphasis in the original test on numbers and operations, where performance in the UK is low. However, we need to ask whether the original test is fair for the UK, because that is also the topic with especially low opportunity in the UK!

	Argentina	Colombia	C.R.	D.R.	Venezuela	Thailand	USA
Average achievement	36	41	52	37	40	50	52

Correlations

	Argentina	Colombia	C.R.	D.R.	Venezuela	Thailand	USA
Argentina		.72	.80	.67	.90	.71	.54
Colombia	.72		.83	.88	.83	.59	.61
C.R.	.80	.83		.76	.85	.70	.56
D.R.	.67	.88	.76		.79	.49	.67
Venezuela	.90	.83	.85	.79		.69	.56
Thailand	.71	.59	.70	.49	.69		.63
USA	.54	.61	.56	.67	.56	.63	

Figure 15.8: Average achievement and country correlations of item difficulty for Latin American SIMS pilot

My final example concerns a pilot replication of the Second IEA Mathematics Study Population A (Grade 8) in Latin America, with comparison to SIMS results for Thailand and the USA. The core form (minus one item) from SIMS was given to a small stratified sample in each of six Latin American countries. The average per cent correct by country and the correlations between countries, based on the distribution of item difficulties, is given in Figure 15.8. The averages for the Latin American countries are below those for Thailand and the USA. The item correlations are relatively high within the Latin American region and lower between Latin America countries and either Thailand or the USA. The between-country item correlations are summary indexes of exactly the kind of item by country interactions that we have been examining in the other studies. If the correlations were perfect, there would be no interactions. If the correlations were low, we would know that interactions exist and that comparisons may be biased or inaccurate. From the correlational results obtained, we can estimate that comparisons between Latin American countries are feasible but that for comparisons with North American or Asian, or presumably European countries, profile discrepancies may cause problems.

Conclusions

The implication of the above analysis and demonstrations is that comparisons will be valid and useful for subsets of countries or strata within countries where the achievement and the opportunity profiles are reasonably aligned. Under the random model, profile discrepancies cause unacceptable standard errors that can be reduced only by using very long tests. Under the fixed model, the discrepancies cause systematic bias in the interpretation of differences.

Richard G. Wolfe

Good alignment of achievement and opportunity profiles will probably only occur when the educational and social conditions of the countries or strata are similar.

One consequence of this perspective on international comparisons is that the world may be too large and heterogeneous to serve as Torsten Husén's laboratory. International survey research should perhaps focus on smaller regions (economic, geographical, cultural) where conditions, and achievement and opportunity profiles are similar, and comparisons are interpretable. I am particularly concerned about introducing international achievement surveys in Latin American, which has so far been left out of most of the major international studies. As Latin American begins to participate, it seems very important to promote regionally-based test designs, sample stratifications and analytic comparisons.

References

CRONBACH, L.J., GLESER, G.C., NANDA, H. and RAJARATNAM, N. (1972) *The Dependability of Behavioral Measurements*, New York: Wiley.

HUSÉN, T. (1967) *International Study of Achievement in Mathematics: A Comparison of Twelve Countries*, Stockholm: Almqvist and Wiksell.

LAPOINTE, A., MEAD, N. and PHILLIPS, G. (1989) *A World of Differences: An International Assessment of Mathematics and Science*, Princeton, NJ: Educational Testing Service.

WALKER, D.A. (1962) 'An analysis of the reactions of Scottish teachers and pupils to items in the geography, mathematics and science items', in *Educational Achievements of Thirteen-year-olds in Twelve Countries*, Hamburg: UNESCO Institute for Education.

WOMER, F.B. (1970) *What is National Assessment?* Ann Arbor, MI: National Assessment of Educational Progress.

16 The Rationality and Irrationality of International Comparative Studies

Christine Keitel and Jeremy Kilpatrick

The increasingly widespread use of international comparative studies of school mathematics in the realm of educational policy necessitates a consideration of their characteristics from the point of view of mathematics education. Many of these studies have taken the mathematics curriculum as entirely unproblematic and have assumed that a single test can give comparable measures of curriculum effects across countries. They have also assumed that by supplementing test scores with videotapes of lessons and analyses of textbooks and curriculum materials, a truer picture of national standing in mathematics performance can be obtained. We challenge these assumptions, focusing in particular on the Third International Study of Mathematics and Science and noting some of the problems created when the funding, design and analyses of comparative studies fail to represent fully not only the mathematics education community but also the spectrum of participating countries.

Introduction

International comparative studies have come to dominate educational discourse in many countries when educators, policymakers and politicians consider what is to be done to improve their system of education. The results of these studies are accepted in many places as providing undisputed scientific evidence about the achievement of students in the countries studied as well as indicating how good the curriculum is and how well teachers are teaching.

In this chapter we examine some characteristics of international comparative studies in mathematics. We consider first the problematic nature of curriculum as treated in such studies. Then we focus on the most recent and largest comparative study of its kind, the Third International Mathematics and Science Study, considering questions raised by its greatly increased scale and the consequences. We look in particular at three complementary studies that were designed to allow clearer interpretations of the test data, but that appear to have led instead to some misinterpretation and contradiction. We close with several questions that the researchers in this field seem not to have asked, and some reflections on the taken-for-granted nature of international comparative studies in general.

Investigating Mathematics Curricula

The treatment of school mathematics curricula in international comparative investigations is a story of increased efforts to take aspects of curriculum complexity into account. It is also, however, a story of persistent failure to probe sufficiently below the surface of, and to challenge assumptions about, what is to be understood as curriculum.

International comparative investigations have taken two forms. One type of study seeks to examine how students' mathematical understanding, ability, achievement, progress or (to use a more neutral term) performance differs across educational systems with respect to one curriculum topic — word problems, for example, or whole number addition and subtraction computations. In these studies, the curriculum *per se* is not analysed; instead, the topic is assumed to be present in all systems studied and therefore can be taken as constant and unproblematic.

The second, and more common, form of investigation seeks to assess mathematics achievement or progress (or, more generally, performance) as a whole — although virtually always at selected age or grade levels only. Studies of this second type are inevitably faced with the problem of examining, or at least characterizing, the curricula of the educational systems under consideration.

The most common approach has been to establish some sort of framework for analysing curricula. Performance measures are then developed to fit the framework. Early investigators typically made use of a content-by-process matrix to construct and classify performance items. Recognizing that 'process' variables do not appear to operate across content to yield interpretable differences, and that assigning items to unique cells does violence to what happens in both the assessment and the curriculum, recent investigators (Lapointe, Mead, and Phillips, 1989; Survey of Mathematics and Science Opportunities, 1993, Appendix B) have replaced process by such dimensions as performance expectation and proficiency level, have added dimensions such as perspective to capture noncognitive curriculum goals, and have described performance items using more than one category on each dimension.

A second effort to deal with curriculum complexity has been to distinguish between curriculum as planned and as carried out. A distinction between the intended curriculum (as represented in official documents, textbooks, or both) and the implemented curriculum (typically measured through questionnaires given to teachers) was made in the Second International Mathematics Study, SIMS (Travers and Westbury, 1989). The distinction had already been anticipated in the First International Mathematics Study, FIMS (Husén, 1967) by the use of teachers' ratings of opportunity to learn the content of each test item. Although the terms intended and implemented carry the unfortunate connotation that the only intentions that count are official ones, and that teachers are merely obedient implementers of other people's agendas, the distinction has been useful in helping to separate curriculum plan from curriculum reality.

Unfortunately, as Hans Freudenthal (1975) pointed out some time ago, teachers may end up giving ratings of item difficulty rather than of whether or not students have been taught the content assumed by the item. Moreover, linking 'opportunity to learn' and 'the implemented curriculum' to test performance does not address directly the issue of how much of the curriculum within a system has been learned by students.

When a common set of performance items is given to all students in a cross-system group, an idealized curriculum is thereby defined that serves as a template against which student performance in each system is gauged. Measures of the opportunity to learn or of the implemented curriculum become measures of how well the idealized curriculum has been learned or implemented. Regardless of how expert the group that set up the idealized curriculum by selecting a collection of performance items for the study, it is impossible — as Freudenthal (1975) correctly noted — to construct internationally-equivalent instruments. He pointed out that it would be possible, although quite difficult, to construct instruments that had internationally-comparable relations to the national curricula. He did not spell out how this might be done, but the point remains valid that, by failing to take curriculum as a variable across systems, international studies continue to compare apples with oranges or, in the words of Torsten Husén (1983), are 'comparing the incomparable'.

International comparative investigations have become increasingly sophisticated. In addition to expert judgments of how the mathematics curriculum internationally should be represented, careful analyses are being made of official documents and text materials. Analyses have been made of such variables as the times to be allocated to various topics in different systems, the proportion of systems focusing on a given topic at each grade, how textbook space given to a topic varies across systems, and how textbook organization varies across systems.

Nonetheless, the idealized international curriculum, defined by a common set of performance tasks organized by content topic, remains the standard of measurement. No allowance is made for different aims, issues, history and context across the mathematics curricula of the systems being studied. No one really addresses how well the students in a system are learning the mathematics curriculum that their system has offered them.

The Promise and Perils of Comparisons

As the observations above suggest, international comparative studies using extensive empirical data have been criticized for as long as they have been conducted. Some critics stick to the 'numbers game' and propose other arrangements for the data analysis, other mathematical models, or other representations for the results. More general critiques refer to fundamental problems not adequately tackled by comparisons, such as 'comparing the incomparable', 'many visions, many aims, one test', and 'problems of comparing curriculums across educational systems' (Bracey, 1997a, 1997b; Husén, 1983; Westbury, 1989). It has often been pointed out that studies only test if and how the assessed curriculum matches or fits into the national curriculum, or what is held as such, and that every conclusion beyond that is not justifiable (Bracey, 1996; see also comment by Baker, 1997). In this sense, the best known international comparative studies conducted during the last 30 years by the International Association for the Evaluation of Educational Achievement (IEA) — FIMS and SIMS — have been frequently criticized in that they did not match reality — that is, they did not produce or use 'real' data that would yield insight into what is happening in the classroom and how. The Third International Mathematics and Science Study (TIMSS) was the first of the IEA studies that tried to complement the usual test data that have been the focus of these large empirical studies. In addition to the achievement tests and the questionnaires, three accompanying research studies ambitiously drew upon additional sources of data.

- The Videotape Classroom Study — a study of mathematics lessons at grade 8 in the USA, Japan, and Germany, directed by James Stigler of the University of California at Los Angeles.
- The Survey of Mathematics and Science Opportunities Study — a study of mathematics and science teaching in six countries, directed by William Schmidt of Michigan State University.
- The Curriculum Analysis Study — a study of curricular intentions, directed by William Schmidt of Michigan State University.

All three were large studies conducted parallel to the achievement study of TIMSS. The first (Stigler, Gonzales, Kawanaka, Knoll and Serrano, 1997; US Department of Education, 1997) required the production and processing of 231 videotaped lessons from eighth-grade mathematics classrooms in the USA, Germany, and Japan. The second (Schmidt et al., 1996) necessitated conducting over 120 classroom observations in mathematics and science classrooms in six countries, in an attempt to characterize 'a typical mathematics or science lesson' for 9-year-olds or 13-year-olds in those countries. The third (Schmidt, McKnight, Valverde, Houang and Wiley, 1997) entailed trying to develop an instrument and methodology to analyze curricular guidelines, programs and textbooks from about 60 participating countries. (For a report that applies information from the last two studies to the US context, see Schmidt, McKnight and Raizen, 1997). The three studies demanded that the researchers deal with an ever-increasing amount of 'data' to be gathered, processed and interpreted, an ever-increasing number of people involved in these activities, the application of an ever-larger technical apparatus, and an ever-increasing demand for the funds to conduct the studies. TIMSS was by far the largest and most expensive comparative study ever conducted in mathematics education, and these three studies added to its scope and complexity.

The enormous scale of the study immediately raised certain problems to a new level. The more data, people and financial resources that are required, the more important become questions of the responsibility for and rationality of such an enterprise, and the more the people who are in charge have to be carefully selected and their work regulated. These observations prompt more fundamental considerations about comparative studies and their general value and hazards. We offer three questions about the 'who' in connection with these studies.

Who Directs the Study?

The question of the people directing the study refers to the expertise, competence and specialization of those involved, as well as to their capability and responsibility to keep both an overview and an unbiased orientation, and both a clear distance from and a closeness to the data. They need to develop a common understanding among all concerned with the study.

In the IEA studies, including TIMSS, it is a striking fact that almost all of the people with primary responsibility for conducting the study have been empirical researchers in education, psychometricians or experts in data processing. The problem of the content of mathematics or science education has been dealt with as no more than a technical question. The most monumental and most accurately treated feature of the studies has been the handling of data once they have been collected. Particularly notable has been the fashion in which problems of methodical validity, reliability and quality have been resolved from a purely formal point of view. Questions of content — in all its aspects — have usually been seen as secondary. This orientation is not surprising in light of the expertise these researchers possess and their central concern with methodology. However, the predominance of methodological considerations raises serious problems when one comes to the concrete aspect of mathematical tasks as representing curricula, teacher questionnaires as representing teaching, and results as yielding comparisons of curricula with respect to their cultural or social contexts. Statements about differences and commonalities become problematic, including judgmental statements about achieving and failing or about weak and strong countries.

Who Pays for the Study?

The question of financial support influences whether the goals of the study are politically determined or are research oriented. In other words, what role is played by interest groups like governmental departments, political forces, social organizations or research agencies, and how can various countries influence the concerted activity of the different groups? It also concerns the problem of whether the poor and the rich countries participate equally in collecting, interpreting or evaluating the findings for their own country as well as across countries.

In our western (European–American) culture, international comparisons have no political value if they are not accepted as 'real' research studies. That is, the politicians paying for such a study rely heavily on its being justified, first, through its international character and, second, through the demand that the results be highly valid. This condition explains why the countries who pay most are quite concerned about the quality of the research, and invest not only money but human power as well. The likely consequence is that the studies become dominated by experts from the countries providing financial support, and by those experts' professional understanding and interest. No wonder that the group of people in major positions of leadership in TIMSS were from the rich countries funding the study, with all the consequences of that influence. The research questions, the language and the accompanying studies were selected by the funding agencies, as well as the final goals being determined mainly by those who paid.

On the other hand, politicians have only a limited interest in such studies — for them, their country's relative rank is the most important aspect of the results. They want to succeed in the competition — they want to show off their country's brilliance or efforts to excel in mathematics and science education, or they want to know why the higher ranking countries are higher. This interest is directly connected to economic competition. Some recent critiques of schooling have exaggerated the economic ramification of low achievement in science and mathematics, since a country's economic standing is 'more affected by government trade policies, world financial markets, and corporate flight to low-wage countries than by weak school achievement' (Stedman, 1997:4–5). Nevertheless, the focal point for each country — and in particular for each of the wealthy countries putting the most money into international comparative studies and competing highly in the global economy — is its own rank compared with the countries doing better. That is the primary result. Politicians are rarely interested in merely gaining insight or in just exploring the research possibilities offered by an international comparison. Their perspective is not that of improving mathematics and science education, particularly for those in the poor and low-achieving countries, rather it is that of being compared with those who are the most successful. Their interest is concentrated on the inner aspects of their own country and perhaps in looking for hints that would suggest reasons for the superior performance of the best countries.

This interest becomes especially clear when one looks at the complementary studies undertaken in the context of TIMSS. The TIMSS videotape study of mathematics lessons concentrated on the USA, Japan and Germany. That study, as well as the six-country survey of teaching and the curriculum analysis study, was financed by the US government. All three studies were directed by American researchers, with some small support by experts from each participating country. The American researchers made special efforts to work well with staff members in the cooperating countries, but those staff members contributed only partially to the enterprise by providing the coded data for their country and comment, while the more important data processing and interpreting was done by the American project staff. These observations are not meant as a criticism of the procedure. Clearly, however, locating the funding, management and implementation of an international study in a single participating country creates problems. Weak points of the studies may be overlooked, and issues of possible bias and error may not surface.

Another fundamental and related question is concerned with the scientific reason for the push to obtain results that yield a clear ranking of countries. Does this ranking automatically provide better 'research results' or new insights? Do the studies and their results provide a change in perspective? What does it mean for the German government or US government that Iran's rank or South Africa's rank is so disappointing? Do the rich countries plan to supply some aid to improve this situation? Do the studies uncover a means of, or actually aim at, improving mathematics and science education in the different countries?

Who Controls the Framing and Dissemination of the Results?

Although there is a common myth that 'numbers do not lie', particularly among people who believe strongly in 'objective' empirical studies — and there are many such people in the groups undertaking comparative studies by means of tests and questionnaires — it is now widely accepted that data can be gathered, processed, mathematized and interpreted in a variety of ways, and that these processes can by no means be freed of special interests and intentions. A very important question therefore concerns the way in which results of studies are packaged, distributed, and launched to the public. How can and do researchers deal with 'unwanted' data or with 'unusual' interpretations? Who influences this process, for what reasons and through what means? Is the key power in the hands of the research community conducting the study, or in those of financial supporters such as political agencies? Answers to these questions may vary considerably across the participating countries, because of different research traditions and political constitutions, or because of different 'power games' that may be in operation toward and against other countries.

The high rankings achieved by some countries on the achievement tests in international comparative studies have led some commentators in countries with lower rankings to exaggerate the results, creating a mystique about education in the high-scoring countries. In the USA, for examples, teachers have been urged to return to a curriculum based on 'core knowledge' in mathematics so as to emulate the presumably more effective systems of Asian countries (Hirsch, 1996). In Germany, reports in the press stressed almost weekly after the release of the TIMSS results the contrast between German students, who had mediocre levels of performance on the tests, and Japanese students who — presumably because they had been engaged in the kind of challenging problem solving shown in the TIMSS videotape lessons — scored very high on the tests. By utilizing the public's and politicians' concerns about these reports, a German researcher associated with TIMSS was able to obtain millions of DM, not for improving mathematics classroom practice or mathematics teacher education, but for developing a more sophisticated instrument for measuring students' mathematical performance — at a time when school and university budgets were shrinking dramatically and research funding in all areas was being drastically cut. Germany was not the only country, however, where researchers helped frame the packaging of the TIMSS results for the media and then reaped the benefits when governments responded in alarm by funding further research.

Coming Closer to Classroom Reality

Curriculum Analysis in TIMSS

The TIMSS Curriculum Analysis Study (Schmidt et al., 1997) was the first to undertake the ambitious enterprise of analysing curricular guidelines, programmes and textbooks while simultaneously developing an appropriate and powerful comparative instrument for the analysis. The description of the methodology is impressive, and the complicated procedure for gathering data is admirable. The various graphical presentations of the findings related to the construct of 'opportunities to learn and to teach' and of the corresponding single items like 'major topics' or 'main content', however, are sometimes difficult to follow. Also, the application of constructs like 'performance expectations' (knowing, problem solving, reasoning — just to mention several that may be more easily understood) and '(career) perspectives' is simply confusing. There is no major outcome of the study other than to say that there are 'many visions, many aims', but the study is not connected to any outcome of the main part of TIMSS, the achievement test study. General critiques have been raised from the beginning that addressed the methodology used as well as the underlying assumptions. Here we want to add some additional considerations that should have been thought about more substantially.

The predominant ideology. The ideology behind the curriculum analysis was that through the construct of a 'common curriculum' research design and the use of a 'common English language', for the questions to be answered by the national contributors to the study and for the systematic descriptions to be obtained from them, it would be possible to find distinctive national patterns and practices that could be described and evaluated. How could this procedure possibly catch the flavour of the participating educational systems?

'Pass the test!' is the major imperative underlying comparative research — but how could one deal with different cultures in a single test, and in particular in a test that was supposed to capture different aims across and within educational systems?

The accompanying fictions. One fiction was that guidelines and textbooks (as measures of curricula) 'equally' or universally influence classroom practice, that they represent a major source of teachers' wisdom, and that they dominate the teacher's professional knowledge and actions.

A second fiction was that a focus on countable and measurable aspects of student performance provides important, sufficient and relevant information to be processed. This focus gave rise to constructs like 'opportunity to learn and to teach mathematics', 'performance expectations' and 'career perspectives'. Such artificial constructs may give researchers more space for speculation than for serious interpretation. The language of the coding and the coded data may have so strongly influenced the data that some problems could not be tackled at all. In particular, in the curriculum analysis project, the coded data that served as the basis for all the data processing and the graphical or numerical representations could not be seriously controlled for all countries, nor could the coding procedure itself be checked by the staff in all cases when the data were finally submitted. The researchers' strong predilection for the numbers game — all kinds of correlations and clusters, whose connections did not admit of any easy interpretation and sometimes appeared to be completely meaningless and absurd — did not, however, force the researchers to go back to their data, in particular to the original textbooks and guides, and to examine them carefully. The study depended overwhelmingly on national coding, national experts, the experts' facility in English, and their understanding of the study's purposes, instruments and procedures. The coding was very closely related to the interpretations given to the constructs (often in a foreign language), and the constructs were already likely to have been biased in favour of the developers. Consequently, the curriculum analysis got lost amid the general results of the main TIMSS study. The context studies that should have complemented and supported the empirical study of achievement became irrelevant, and did not help one to interpret the test data. The results of the context studies may even have contradicted the test data.

A third fiction of the curriculum analysis study was that comparison means collaboration, not competition, and connotes equity of the partners. There was 'naturally', however, a strong hierarchy between the large and the small, the 'remote', or the poor countries — and 'of course', most often the (English speaking) research staff was defined by the larger countries, and those people mainly determine what will be taken as the common curriculum as well as the common language.

Classroom Teaching in TIMSS

The TIMSS Videotape Classroom Study (US D of E, 1997) was another way to look at the mathematics classroom as the place where the teaching and learning opportunities are determined. The singular feature of this study was the attempt to get as close as possible to concrete teaching and learning, and to make the concrete situation in the classroom observable later, as well, by anyone viewing the videotapes. Major characteristics of the project were videotapes of 50 mathematics classroom lessons in Japan, 80 in the USA, and 100 (actually 123, with some preceding and succeeding lessons included) in Germany at grade 8 (focusing mainly on algebra and geometry). Special problems and opportunities were provided by the transcripts of all videos (translated into English), by the specially developed coding as a general procedure developed before the analysis, and by the coding constructs, such as the form of interaction, the time taken for individual or group work, the academic level of the content, and the mathematical tasks or problems used in the lesson. The coding process, as well as the detailed examination of content differentiated from pedagogical or methodological recommendations, was open to various interpretations by the psychologists or linguists involved, by participating teachers, by some international consultants or experts (in a given country), by mathematicians and mathematics educators, and so on. The astonishing fact is that the consensus among the various expert groups was the final criterion for coding and interpretation! How might the researchers have dealt in a different way with the necessarily biased views of these diverse groups? Could they not have been taken as resource for discussion and debate about different observations of the scenes? How could the results of contexts — such as pedagogical flow — reflecting cultural conceptions of knowledge and knowing and of appropriate teaching practices be used to interpret data?

A problem not yet clearly checked in the design of the study was the question of the representativeness of the video lessons — the sampling and its relation to major and important circumstances of schooling and opportunities for achievement within a country. The sample of Japanese video lessons has been highly praised by the project director, who has proclaimed it as an example of the typical Japanese problem-solving mathematics classroom. Are all the observers of Japanese education mistaken who offer different descriptions and contradictory vignettes about Japanese school reality (see George, 1995; Goya, 1993; Ito, 1997)? Were the differences in the social contexts between Japan and the other countries respected, such as outside-school learning and private lessons? Having visited elementary and lower-secondary schools without encountering lessons like those in the videotape sample, the first author doubts whether the 50 lessons are typical.

It is known that Japanese researchers have developed prototypical research lessons on videotape for teacher education, that are intended to exemplify certain highly appreciated didactical methods of classroom teaching. The lessons are similar to those on secondary classroom practice from the Open University in the United Kingdom, in which vignettes of investigational approaches are shown. The lessons are by no means meant as typical or especially brilliant — they are just examples of how to conduct such lessons with a focus on independent group work. Many of the Japanese lessons seem to follow a similar plan, although there is less of that focus. Instead, there is a greater focus on a clearly designed development of certain mathematical concepts or insights, independent of students' interests, success or achievement during teaching. There is no motivation or feedback from the teacher on an individual level, and the various ways to arrive at a solution presented at the board are attributed to mathematics only, not as a possibility for different individual approaches and ways to pursue them. Many of the videotapes from the TIMSS study might be like such research lessons, to be shown in teacher inservice training or preservice training courses and carefully planned, prepared and conducted as useful demonstrations of the intended classroom teaching practice supported by officials. The tapes may be useful for observers and preservice teachers without necessarily representing the reality of practice.

How do comparative studies respect the different roles and kinds of autonomy in curricular decision making and design that teachers have in the participating countries? If the teacher's autonomy is very high, as in Germany, his or her curricular decisions may change from one class or group of pupils to another, and may thereby cause a major concern for motivation and involvement on the one hand, and for responsibility or accountability for learning outcomes on the other. If the teacher is the only assessment agency in the school system, the conflict between teaching and assessing may typically occur as a problematic feature to be negotiated at the same time — but it links the teaching and assessing more closely than any test would ever do.

Curricular decisions are not the only features of instruction that differ substantially across countries. Opportunities to learn are also related to the ability of the teacher to motivate students to follow his or her curricular decisions, and to accept or negotiate the content to be learned and the method to be followed. Curricular decisions therefore concern not only the tasks to be designed and done, but discussion, negotiation and broad perspectives on the 'why' and the 'what for' of instruction in addition to the 'how to'. The teacher's ability and propensity to conduct these negotiations and provide these perspectives may be very different from one country to another. Another aspect not yet treated or respected in the studies is national differences among students (and teachers) regarding their beliefs about tests, their positive or negative attitudes toward tests — because they may not ordinarily be required to take tests. Even when the test is the common mode of assessment in a country, the students' willingness to be obedient to tests is different in different countries. German students, for example, are not accustomed to taking tests, nor do they take a test seriously if it is not directly connected to the mark given by the teacher.

How can the in-depth microscopic view provided by the video lessons be compared to any overall impression of reality? How is one to deal with the problem that the various research foci, as well as the follow-up studies, tend to become self-contained, independent and autonomous? Could such a study remain under the control of the research community, or does it easily (and inevitably) become an autonomous concern of politics? Is it at all possible that we might actually get a representative selection of classroom reality? Is it possible to reach a common understanding of what constitutes a cultural flavour of the educational systems as well as of the mathematics classroom?

Christine Keitel and Jeremy Kilpatrick

Putting Performance in Context

Achievement in comparative studies is treated like performance in an academic olympiad. Although only small differences in performance are represented by the ranks, it is not at all clear what the reported averages actually mean. So far, nothing other than superficial interpretations — like 'weak country' or 'failing students' — has been provided, even when these words are attached to the numbers in the middle range. Can averages actually provide a sophisticated interpretation? By playing the numbers game, researchers have shown that it is possible to raise or lower a particular ranking by minor changes in the content foci or the weighting system. Others claim that profile comparisons show many more inequalities within countries, and different 'opportunities to learn' for the students, than an average can provide. They argue that the representativeness of national averages masks underlying variations in regions and in schools. There is not always any guarantee that students have been properly sampled, or that averages have not been dragged down by the conditions of test administration in some developing countries. Reports of performance at the various grades, moreover, dwell on growth in mathematical performance even though neither the tests nor the students are the same across those grades. In addition, changes in a country's rank across grades may be due more to changes in the set of countries participating in the assessment at that grade than to any merits or defects of the curriculum, the teaching or the students.

Concerning contextual and cultural information about the various countries, we know from the accompanying studies that students in Japan, Korea and Singapore have a lot of extra time for studying mathematics in private lessons or in special schools outside the public schools. For Japanese students, mathematics and science are the school subjects they dislike the most but, compared with German students, they spent one third more of their weekly time reworking and preparing mathematics lessons (Schümer, in press), and many of the Japanese students regularly attend afternoon lessons in the *juku* where they are mainly prepared for exams. In 1996, the Japanese government (Moubusho) published a report on the plans for educational policy. This report provides data on the extra learning time taken by students, which show that this time has been dramatically increasing in the last 10 years. In elementary school, 77 per cent of the students, on the average, now take private classes or lessons, and 24 per cent are in private remedial schools of the *juku* type. In the lower secondary school, the averages are now 28 per cent in private classes or lessons, and 60 per cent in the *juku*, with some students participating in both. In the same report, the views of parents and public school teachers on *juku* attendance were analyzed — 60 per cent thought take the *juku* attendance was too excessive, 58 per cent believed that the formation of children's character was adversely affected by excessive competition in entrance examinations, 48 per cent felt that children's health and fitness was adversely affected by long hours of *juku* attendance, 34 per cent saw school education being undervalued because of preoccupation with *juku* studies, 11 per cent saw children disturbed and confused by the differences between school instruction and *juku* instruction, and 15 per cent thought that children showed problem behaviour triggered by *juku* attendance and developed related problems because of excessive competition in *jukus*. More than half of the parents complained that, because of excessive *juku* attendance, children had an inadequate experience of life and outside activities, including play, community activities and family interactions. Almost 45 per cent thought that a child's career path was chosen primarily according to 'standard scores', regardless of the child's aptitudes or wishes, which were generally disregarded. Among the parents surveyed, 38 per cent believed that the extra school system of private classes and *juku* put parents under enormous financial pressure, and only 11 per cent did not see any particular problem in this system (Monbusho, 1996, pp. 33–4). The competition between this second school system of private lessons and *juku* is considered by teachers and parents to be a major obstacle for any reform claims (Ito, 1997).

How can we develop a clear concept of what is an appropriate teaching practice? Is ineffective teaching and learning just a methodological problem? By analysing the videotapes, of course, just what can be seen and then reasonably interpreted counts — methods of analysis are clearly differentiable and therefore preferred. Where, though, can we grasp the meta-cognitive view that the attitudes and beliefs of both teachers and learners, as well as various social factors, determine ineffectiveness? It is easy to determine that US teachers spend more hours in school than teachers in Japan and Germany and that they spent more hours in the classroom instead of preparing lessons (Schmidt et al., 1996:2). Is it then correct to conclude that the American method is 'tell and show' (McKnight et al., 1987:81) while the Japanese use the Socratic method and appropriate hands-on activities (Stigler and Stevenson, 1991:91)? How do countries assure in their own fashion that exemplary 'good' or desired curricular and pedagogical prescriptions might be transformed into reality?

Conclusion

Within each educational system, the mathematics curriculum is an organism that functions at the levels of both rhetoric and reality. The functioning of that organic whole has not been examined on its own terms for each system in any recent large-scale study. Instead, a pseudo-consensus has been imposed (primarily by the English-speaking world) across systems so that curriculum can be taken as a constant rather than a variable, and so that the operation of other variables can be examined. This treatment of the curriculum has had its costs. It is time to begin a deeper and more serious examination of mathematics curricula in different educational systems, so that assessments of what students within these systems know and can do mathematically can be given more productive and more valid interpretations.

TIMSS began with high hopes that it might provide a richer context in which student performance would be captured in detail and would be linked to other information about classroom practice and national curricula. Those hopes have been met in part, but the presumed improvements made in TIMSS over previous comparative studies have been tainted by the dominance of the USA in funding most of the research and directing the data gathering and analysis. The consequence is a study embedded within the research traditions of one country, but too frequently having little or nothing to say to mathematics educators in other countries, particularly with respect to how education might be improved there. Moreover, as the largest and most widely marketed international comparative study in history, TIMSS threatens to poison for some time the waters of educational policy, as politicians and researchers scramble to take advantage of what TIMSS allegedly says about the teaching and learning of mathematics in their country. Unwarranted inferences are made concerning the link between selected views of teaching and fallible indicators of performance so that unsuspecting educators, as well as the public, come to think that the teaching portrayed has produced the performance measured.

International comparative studies are trumpeted in educational journals and in the press as triumphs of rationality. They are cited as though the results they provide go without question. Serious criticisms and expressions of doubt are brushed aside as the carping of ignorant or ill-informed troublemakers. Meanwhile, the built-in irrationality of the studies is swept under the rug. Researchers conducting the studies have too much vested in the outcomes to engage in sufficient reflection about the foundations of their work — how can there be irrationality, when so many serious educators and scientists have worked so hard to produce orderly, scientific results? That rationality and irrationality might coexist in these studies, calling all the well-funded analyses and carefully groomed results into question, occurs to very few. Yet only a cursory examination of the documents produced for these studies shows that for every strength there are flaws. The studies rest on the shakiest of foundations — they assume that the mantel of science can cover all weaknesses in design, incongruous data and errors of interpretation. They not only compare the incomparable, they rationalize the irrational.

Note

1   We use *systems* rather than *countries* or *nations* because countries may be represented in comparative investigations by states, provinces, language groups or even cities (see Westbury, 1989:19).

References

BAKER, D.P. (1997) 'Good news, bad news, and international comparisons: Comment on Bracey', *Educational Researcher*, **26**(4), pp. 16–17.

BRACEY, G.W. (1996) 'International comparisons and the condition of American education', *Educational Researcher*, **25**(1), pp. 5–11.

BRACEY, G.W. (1997a) 'On comparing the incomparable: A response to Baker and Stedman', *Educational Researcher*, **26**(4), pp. 19–26.

BRACEY, G.W. (1997b) 'Many visions, many aims, one test', *Phi Delta Kappan*, **78**(5), pp. 411–12.

FREUDENTHAL, H. (1975) 'Pupils' achievements internationally compared — The IEA', *Educational Studies in Mathematics*, **6**, pp. 127–86.

GEORGE, P. (1995) *The Japanese Secondary School: A Closer Look*, Reston, VA: National Association of Secondary School Principals; Columbus, OH: National Middle Schools Association.

GOYA, S. (1993) 'The secret of Japanese education', *Phi Delta Kappan*, **75**(2), pp. 126–29.

HIRSCH, E.D., JR. (1996) *The Schools We Need and Why We Don't have Them*, New York: Doubleday.

HUSÉN, T. (1967) *International Study of Achievement in Mathematics: A Comparison of Twelve Countries* (Vols. 1 & 2). New York: Wiley.

HUSÉN, T. (1983) 'Are standards in US schools really lagging behind those in other countries?' *Phi Delta Kappan*, **64**, pp. 455–61.

ITO, T. (1997) 'Zwischen "Fassade" und "wirklicher Absicht": Eine Betrachtung über die dritte Erziehungsreform in Japan' [Between 'façade' and 'actual intention': A reflection on the third reform of education in Japan], *Zeitschrift für Pädagogik*, **3**, pp. 449–66.

McKNIGHT, C., CROSSWHITE, F.J., DOSSEY, J.A., KIFER, E., SWAFFORD, J.O., TRAVERS, K.J. and COONEY, T.J. (1987) *The Underachieving Curriculum*, Champaign, IL: Stipes Publishing.

MONBUSHO (MINISTRY OF EDUCATION, SCIENCE, SPORTS AND CULTURE) (1996) *Japanese Government Policies in Education, Science, Sports and Culture*, Tokyo: Author.

LAPOINTE, A., MEAD, N.A. and PHILLIPS, G.W. (1989) *A World of Differences: An International Assessment of Mathematics and Science*, (Report No. 19–CAEP–01), Princeton, NJ: Educational Testing Service.

SCHMIDT, W.H., JORDE, D., COGAN, L.S., BARRIER, E., GONZALO, I., MOSER, U., SHIMIZU, Y., SAWADA, T., VALVERDE, G., McKNIGHT, C., PRAWAT, R., WILEY, D.E., RAIZEN, S., BRITTON, E.D. and WOLFE, R.G. (1996) *Characterizing Pedagogical Flow*, Dordrecht: Kluwer Academic Publishers.

SCHMIDT, W.H., McKNIGHT, C.C. and RAIZEN, S.A. (1997) *A Splintered Vision: An, Investigation of US Science and Mathematics Education*, Dordrecht: Kluwer Academic Publishers.

SCHMIDT, W.H., McKNIGHT, C.C., VALVERDE, G.A., HOUANG, R.T. and WILEY, D.E. (1997) *Many Visions, Many Aims, Vol. 1: A Cross-national Investigation of Curricular Intentions in School Mathematics*, Dordrecht: Kluwer Academic Publishers.

SCHÜMER, G. (in press) 'The TIMSS videotape classroom study', in *Proceedings of the Conference on Mathematics and Elementary Science Education: German, Japanese and US Perspectives* (Dec. 3–5, 1997), Berlin: Japanese-German Center of Berlin.

STEDMAN, L.C. (1997) 'International achievement differences: An assessment of a new perspective', *Educational Researcher*, **26**(4), pp. 4–15.

STIGLER, J.W. and STEVENSON, H.W. (1991) 'How Asian teachers polish each lesson to perfection', *American Educator*, **15**(1), 12–20, pp. 43–7.

STIGLER, J.W., GONZALES, P., KAWANAKA, T., KNOLL, S. and SERRANO, A. (eds) (1997) *The TIMSS Videotape Classroom Study: Methods and Preliminary Findings* (Draft version), Los Angeles, CA: University of California at Los Angeles, Psychology Department.

SURVEY OF SCIENCE AND MATHEMATICS OPPORTUNITIES (1993) *TIMSS: Concepts, Measurements and Analyses (Research Report Series No. 56)*, East Lansing, MI: Michigan State University.

TRAVERS, K.J. and WESTBURY, I. (1989) *The IEA Study of Mathematics, I: Analysis of Mathematics Curricula*, Oxford: Pergamon.

US DEPARTMENT OF EDUCATION, NATIONAL CENTER FOR EDUCATION STATISTICS (1997) 'TIMSS video classroom study' [On-line]. Available: http://nces.ed.gov/timss/video/index.html.

WESTBURY, I. (1989) 'The problems of comparing curriculums across educational systems', in PURVES, A.C. (ed.) *International Comparisons and Educational Reform*, Alexandria, VA: Association for Supervision and Curriculum Development, pp. 17–34.

Notes on Contributors

Albert Beaton is International Study Director of the Third International Mathematics and Science Study (TIMSS). He has served as chair of the Technical Advisory Committee for the IEA, where he consulted on a series of IEA studies, particularly the Reading Literacy Study. He earned both his Master's degree and his PhD in educational measurement and statistics at Harvard University. He is currently a professor in Boston College's Graduate School of Education and director of Boston College's Centre for the Study of Testing, Evaluation, and Educational Policy (CSTEEP).

Jerry P. Becker is professor of mathematics education at Southern Illinois University at Carbondale. At school he has taught at both the elementary and secondary levels. His interests include international mathematics education, problem solving (and cross-cultural research on problem solving), the cognitive development of learners in mathematics and improving practices in teacher education. He received his PhD in mathematics education from Stanford University with Ed Begle, Director of the School Mathematics Study Group.

Christine Brew recently completed her PhD in tertiary biology education at Monash University. She has worked on a number of projects that have continued to highlight gender and socio-economic inequities in secondary and tertiary mathematics education. She currently works at La Trobe University in the Graduate School of Education.

Leland Cogan is a Senior Researcher with the U.S. National Research Center for the Third International Mathematics and Science Study (TIMSS) at Michigan State University. He earned his PhD in educational psychology from Michigan State University. He has collaborated in observation and quantitative studies of educational practices and policy and co-authored several technical reports and articles on TIMSS. Cogan's research interests include parents' and teachers' beliefs, students' learning and motivation, and instructional practices particularly as these relate to the learning of mathematics and the sciences.

Lianghuo Fan recently completed his PhD in mathematics education at the University of Chicago. He was a high school mathematics teacher and a lecturer of mathematics education at a teacher college in China for about 10 years. His current research interests include curriculum development, teacher knowledge, educational policy, and comparative education. He currently works at the National Institute of Education in Singapore as Assistant Professor.

James Hiebert is currently H. Rodney Sharp Professor at University of Delaware. He earned his PhD in curriculum and instruction at the University of Wisconsin. In 1993–1994 he was Visiting Scholar in the Department of Psychology, University of California, Los Angeles, where he participated in the TIMSS video study. He has had seven multi-year grants, over 12 years, from the National Science Foundation and the Department of Education, to investigate the learning and teaching of mathematics in elementary and middle schools.

Geoffrey Howson was the Dean of the Faculty of Mathematical Studies at the University of Southampton until his retirement. He has published numerous papers and books on Mathematics and Mathematics Education, and written several reports, the most recent, for the English Qualifications and Curriculum Authority, being a comparative study of primary school texts drawn from six countries. Amongst the many posts he has held are Secretary of the International Commission on Mathematical Instruction, President of the Mathematical Association and Chairman of the Trustees of the School Mathematics Project. He was consultant to both SIMS and TIMSS and for some years he was a member of the international steering committee of TIMSS.

Ian Huntley earned his PhD in mathematics in 1973. He is presently Director of Continuing Education at the University of Bristol, and was previously Dean of Learning and Teaching at Sheffield Hallam University. His main academic interest is the introduction of Mathematical Modelling into the undergraduate curriculum, and he chairs the Executive Committee of the International Conferences on the Teaching of Mathematical Modelling and Applications.

Gabriele Kaiser graduated in 1978 with a Masters degree as a teacher for mathematics and humanities at the University of Kassel in Germany. She worked as a school teacher and earned her PhD in mathematics education in 1986. Her research interests comprise of the teaching of applications and modelling gender aspects in mathematics education and comparative studies (especially related to England and Germany). She currently works at the University of Hamburg as Professor of mathematics education.

Takako Kawanaka is currently working on her dissertation in developmental psychology at University of California Los Angeles. She was involved in TIMSS video study as a research team member and has conducted an analysis of teacher questioning in Germany, Japan, and the USA using TIMSS data. Her PhD thesis will also be a cross-cultural comparison of instructional practices — comparing and contrasting culture-specific instructional practices, teaching strategies, and student behaviours in order to find out why and how teachers decide the way they teach and how that might affect student learning.

Christine Keitel is Professor for Mathematics Education and current Vice president at the Free University of Berlin, Germany. Her main research areas include studies on the relationship between mathematics and its social practice; modelling in mathematics education; attitudes and belief systems of teachers and students, and the history and current state of mathematics education in European and Non-European countries, in particular in the USA, the former USSR, China, Indonesia, South Africa, and Japan. She has been expert-consultant for TIMSS video study and TIMSS project on curriculum analysis. She is currently member of editorial boards of several journals for curriculum and mathematics education.

Jeremy Kilpatrick is Regents Professor of Mathematics Education at the University of Georgia. He earned his PhD in mathematics education under E.G. Begle at Stanford University. He has taught courses in mathematics education at several European and Latin American universities and has received Fulbright awards for work in New Zealand, Spain, Colombia, and Sweden. He has just completed his second term as Vice President of the International Commission on Mathematical Instruction. His present research interests include mathematics curricula, research in mathematics education, and the history of both.

Gilah C. Leder is a professor in the Graduate School of Education at La Trobe University in Melbourne, Australia. Previous appointments have included teaching in secondary schools, at the Secondary Teachers College (now The University of Melbourne), and at Monash University. Her teaching and research interests embrace gender issues, assessment in mathematics, affective factors that affect mathematics learning, and exceptionality, and she has published extensively in these areas. She serves on various editorial boards and educational and scientific committees, and is immediate past president of the Mathematics Educational Research Group of Australasia.

Eduardo Luna has been a Professor of Mathematics at Barry University, Miami, Florida, since 1989. He received a PhD in Mathematics from The Catholic University of America with a dissertation in Functional Analysis in 1973 and taught at the Pontifical Catholic University in the Dominican Republic until 1989. From 1987 to 1995 he was President of the Inter-American Committee on Mathematics Education, and was a member of the International Commission on Mathematics Instruction from 1991 to 1994.

Curtis McKnight is currently Professor of Mathematics at the University of Oklahoma. Among his research interests are the study of mathematics curricula and international comparisons of mathematics curricula and achievement. He serves as mathematics consultant to the US Research Center for the Third IEA Mathematics and Science Study (TIMSS) and, internationally, has served on its Subject-Matter Advisor Committee, Item-Coding Committee, and worked on development of test items, questionnaires, and document analysis methods. He is a co-author of five books dealing with either SIMS or TIMSS, as well as of numerous contributed chapters and articles.

Ben Nebres earned his PhD in mathematical logic at Stanford University and is currently President of the Ateneo de Manila University, one of the leading Philippine universities. He was one of the founders of the Mathematical Society of the Philippines and the Southeast Asian Mathematical Society. Together with colleagues in these societies he has worked to improve mathematics graduate education and research as well as teacher-training in a network of Philippine high schools. He also holds leadership positions in projects to strengthen science and engineering in a network of universities and schools, and to improve elementary education in the 26 poorest provinces of the country.

David F. Robitaille is professor of mathematics education, Head of the Department of Curriculum Studies at the University of British Columbia, and International Coordinator of TIMSS. He co-edited one of the three major reports of the Second International Mathematics Study (SIMSS) and edited the Third International Mathematics and Science Study (TIMSS) encyclopaedia 'National Contexts for Mathematics and Science Education'.

Thomas A. Romberg earned his PhD in mathematics education at Stanford University. Since 1963 he has been Professor for Mathematics Education at University of Wisconsin, Department of Curriculum and Instruction and is currently also Science Director at National Center for Improving Student Learning and Achievement in Mathematics and Sciences. He has also been Visiting Scholar at University of Tasmania, Australia and Education Director at the National Center for Research in Mathematical Sciences Education.

Glenn Rowley is an Associate Professor in the Faculty of Education at Monash University, Australia. He completed his doctoral work at the University of Toronto in 1975, and since then has worked at La Trobe University and at Monash University. His research and teaching interests have focussed on measurement and assessment, with particular focus on reliability and generalisability, and on research methodology.

Toshio Sawada is a Professor at the Department of Mathematics at Science University of Tokyo and an Honorary Researcher of National Institute for Educational Research (NIER) of Japan. He is a member of International Steering Committee of TIMSS. He has focused his research on international comparative studies in mathematics education and educational statistics. He is also a member of the national organizing committee of the 9th International Congress on Mathematical Education (ICME9), to be held in Tokyo (Japan) in 2000.

William H. Schmidt is currently a professor at Michigan State University. In addition he serves as National Research Coordinator and Executive Director of the US National Center which oversees participation of the United States in the Third International Mathematics and Science Study (TIMSS). He co-authored several chapters analysing results from the Second International Mathematics Study (SIMS) and the Second International Science Study (SISS). Most recently he has co-authored several books on the curriculum analysis for mathematics and science from the Third International Mathematics and Science Study.

Yoshinori Shimizu is an associate professor of mathematics education at Tokyo Gakugei University. He received his Bachelor's degree in mathematics (1984) and Masters degrees in mathematics education (1986, 1988) from the University of Tsukuba. In 1997 he was a visiting scholar at Indiana University at Bloomington. His interests include cross-cultural research on problem solving, the role of metacognition in problem solving, and alternative assessment in mathematics education.

Harold W. Stevenson is Professor of Psychology at the University of Michigan. He has been President of the Society for Research in Child Development, the Division of Developmental Psychology of the American Psychological Association, and the International Society for the Study of Behavioral Development. Since 1979 he and his students and colleagues have been studying the basis for the outstanding performance of East Asian students and the difficulties demonstrated by American students in mathematics. He is coauthor of *The Learning Gap*, a book which summarizes much of this research.

James W. Stigler is currently Professor in Department of Psychology, University of California, Los Angeles and is also Co-Director of Cognitive Science Research Program. He earned his PhD in development psychology at the University of Michigan in 1982. In 1985 he was the first recipient of the William G. Chase Memorial Award for 'Outstanding Research by a Young Scientist in the General Area of Cognitive Psychology,' a prize awarded biannually by Carnegie-Mellon University. In addition, he received the fellowship of several associations, for instance of the Guggenheim Memorial Foundation.

Kenneth J. Travers is currently Professor of Mathematics Education, College of Education at University of Illinois, where he received his PhD in mathematics education in 1965. He was Chairman of the International Mathematics Committee for the Second International Mathematics Study. He received the Max Beberman award for contributions to mathematics education from Illinois Council of Teachers of Mathematics in 1989 and was made AERA Senior Research Fellow at National Center for Education Statistics, Washington, in 1994.

Gilbert A. Valverde obtained his PhD in administrative institutional and policy studies from the University of Chicago. Currently he is Assistant Professor of Educational Administration and Educational Policy at the University at Albany, SUNY. Prior to that, he was Associate Director of the US National Research Center which oversaw participation of the US in the Third International Mathematics and Science Study (TIMSS) and the Survey of Mathematics and Science Opportunities (SMSO). He specialises in the cross-national comparative study of curriculum governance policies, especially policies regarding indicators, evaluation, standards and instructional materials.

Avrum Israel Weinzweig is presently Professor of Mathematics at the University of Illinois at Chicago and has previously served on the faculties of Harvard University, University of California at Berkeley and Northwestern University. He earned his PhD in mathematics from Harvard University. He served two terms as President of The International Commission for the Study and Improvement of the Teaching of Mathematics, the only American in the fifty years of that Commission to be elected to that position. He has been very active in the preparation and enhancement of teachers and has worked extensively with children and teachers in school and classroom settings, particularly in inner city schools.

Richard G. Wolfe is an Associate Professor at the Ontario Institute for Studies in Education of the University of Toronto. He was consultant on methodology to the international mathematics committee for the Second International Mathematics Study (SIMS), prepared the database for the Second International Science Study (SISS), and contributed to the analysis and reporting for both studies. He was the chairman of the sampling and methodology committee for the Third International Mathematics and Science Study (TIMSS) during its initial design stages. He has also worked with a number of national and international assessment projects in Latin America. His specialities are assessment survey design, sampling, and analysis.

Index